FROM FAMILY TO POLICE FORCE

A VOLUME IN THE SERIES

Police/Worlds: Studies in Security, Crime, and Governance
Edited by Kevin Karpiak, Sameena Mulla, William Garriott,
and Ilana Feldman

A list of titles in this series is available at cornellpress.cornell.edu

FROM FAMILY TO POLICE FORCE

*Security and Belonging
on a South Asian Border*

FARHANA IBRAHIM

CORNELL UNIVERSITY PRESS
ITHACA AND LONDON

First published 2021 by Cornell University Press

Library of Congress Cataloging-in-Publication Data

Names: Ibrahim, Farhana, author.
Title: From family to police force : security and belonging on a
    South Asian border / Farhana Ibrahim.
Description: Ithaca [New York] : Cornell University Press, 2021. |
    Series: Police/Worlds: studies in security, crime, and governance |
    Includes bibliographical references and index.
Identifiers: LCCN 2021004129 (print) | LCCN 2021004130 (ebook) |
    ISBN 9781501759536 (hardcover) | ISBN 9781501759543 (paperback) |
    ISBN 9781501759567 (ebook) | ISBN 9781501759550 (pdf)
Subjects: LCSH: Police—Social aspects—India—Kachchh. |
    Law enforcement—Social aspects—India—Kachchh. | Kachchh
    (India)—Social conditions.
Classification: LCC HV8249.K33 I27 2021 (print) | LCC HV8249.K33
    (ebook) | DDC 353.3/6095475—dc23
LC record available at https://lccn.loc.gov/2021004129
LC ebook record available at https://lccn.loc.gov/2021004130

To Mohamed Hosain and Sherbano Khatri,
with boundless gratitude

CONTENTS

Preface

This book draws on close to two decades of ethnographic research in Kutch, Gujarat. During the course of my fieldwork, there were two things in my experience that tended to not be spoken about freely within the family: the first was the devastating earthquake of January 2001, and the second was the fact of "Bengali" women—that is, migrant women from eastern parts of India—as wives. The causes and consequences of these public secrets were differently manifested. Although the presence of "Bengali" women tied into the state's identification of "illegal" migration and "infiltrators" believed to be from Bangladesh, the earthquake was often what would—perhaps *could*—not be narrated, the wounds inflicted by it perhaps not recountable in an interview or even in conversation. It was during the marriage of a much-beloved daughter that some of these tensions played out for me.

In summer 2003, as schools closed for their annual summer vacations, the wedding season kicked off in Kutch. Abdul's younger daughter Rahila was to be married. This was a time of some anxiety for the family; marriages of daughters tend to be emotionally fraught occasions in a patriarchal and patrilocal system. The structure of the marriage itself also dramatizes latent structural tensions between wife givers and wife takers. Further, young brides are sent off to their affinal homes with a certain degree of finality and marriage rituals make much of this rupturing of the natal tie. At the same time, Rahila's marriage was also the first publicly "happy" occasion that Abdul's family was celebrating since the 2001 earthquake, which had brought in its wake much dislocation, physical and emotional. Although money was scarce, for it was not fully clear how much compensatory cash would come through from the state's disaster relief fund to repair their old house, it was also the marriage of a much-loved youngest child.

In January, some months before the wedding, Rahila's mother had begun her preparations in earnest. She traveled to Mumbai (formerly Bombay) by the overnight train, accompanied by female relatives to shop for the event. They stayed a week and returned laden with a full trousseau for the bride and gifts for other family members. Rahila had been engaged over two years, the marriage continually postponed due to the family's multiple displacements, financial anxieties, and the lack of a properly settled "home" following the earthquake. Even though the wedding ceremonies were well attended, in keeping with the families' well-regarded stature in society, it lacked the scale and splendor of her siblings' weddings, which had taken place long before the start of the tumultuous decade following the earthquake. Although nobody in the extended family mentioned this, it became clear to me as I helped prepare for the wedding ceremonies and tried to hang about on the edge of things attempting to make myself useful, that emotionally this event bore the marks of accumulated losses of the past few years.

Rahila's wedding was the first time I saw Abdul's family—impeccably composed through the loss of their home, their savings, and a newborn grandson during the time that I had known them—dissolve into paroxysms of grief that seemed to far exceed the usual laments that accompany a daughter's "giving away" or *vidai*. The marriage became an occasion that dramatized the losses of the earthquake and rendered visible what the family had worked hard to preserve under an exterior mask of perfect composure, even to each other.

During Rahila's wedding ceremonies, this outward calm was ruptured in a fairly dramatic way. One of the events preceding the *nikah* was held at the *jamaatkhana* (community hall). Known as the *mamera*, this involved the bride's uncle (mother's brother, or *mama*) ritually presenting clothes to his sister and niece. He also presents, on this occasion, the veil that the bride will wear continuously over the next two days until her husband unveils her after the *nikah*. The *mamera* is the ritual affirmation of the mother's natal line in an otherwise patriarchal structure that stresses the paternal kinship connection. This relationship stresses the importance of affines within the kin group. At the *jamaatkhana* that morning, the chief subject of the ritual proceedings was the bride's mother, Mehrunissa. At one point during the ritual gift giving, she collapsed and fainted. While I ran to find some water with another member of the family, I recall being surprised later at the relatively restrained manner in which I thought others responded. Someone explained to me in hushed whispers that Mehrunissa had no blood brother (*sago bha*); she was one of six sisters (of whom three were half siblings). She did have a male cousin, who would have normally stood in as her brother on this occasion. However, he along with his entire family (a total of sixteen members counting children and grandchildren) had died during the earthquake, killed under the rubble of their fallen house. Mehrunissa's natal family was thus effectively extinguished with these deaths, as technically sisters do not count in rituals as representatives of their father's line. Her sister was present and had offered to take care of the ritual gift giving, but Mehrunissa had refused.

The wedding festivities were henceforth tinged with more than a shadow of sorrow. Dramatic moments like these constitute more than testimony or ciphers of collective memory; they are also windows into the structures of secrecy, silence, and complicity that families are enfolded in. These moments do not tell us only about how the family becomes a site of intervention for the state (through the management of postdisaster resettlement and compensation, for instance) or of how major political events impact everyday affects within familial relationships, or even of how the family collaborates with the state to police the acceptable boundaries of gender or caste sociality. In this book, I argue that such incidents reveal to us how families are constantly replicating within themselves the struggle between what can and cannot be divulged—to others but also to themselves. Although the presence of a "Bengali" wife within the family may mark the site of a public secrecy that must be maintained vis-à-vis the state, the domestic is also constituted through secrecy, betrayal, and the deployment of "poisonous knowledge" with respect to one another.

Acknowledgments

This book is the outcome of many years of research and thinking about Kutch. It would not have been possible for me to write about this region and its people were it not for their support and love. The faith that strangers and friends alike reposed in me has been a humbling experience. I am grateful to all my friends and acquaintances in Kutch—far too numerous to name individually—without whom this book could never have been written. Mohamed Hosain Khatri and Sherbano Khatri have become my surrogate family in the field. I cannot thank them enough for their unstinting love and affection at all times. Mohamed Hosain has been a long-standing friend and mentor in Kutch. His wife, Sherbano, made sure I was well nourished with delicious meals prepared by her, spoiling and pampering me like a daughter visiting her natal home. Farida became a good friend and confidante, and I will always be grateful to the entire family for opening up their hearts and their home to me.

I must thank Sahana Ghosh and Dolly Kikon who first convinced me that I had enough material to sit down at my computer and just start writing—this was at the Law and Social Science Network (LASSnet) conference in New Delhi in December 2016. Sahana Ghosh was as good as her word when she painstakingly read every single initial chapter draft over the next several months. That writing exchange was both productive and highly enjoyable. The other person who has read every chapter and commented exhaustively when the draft was at a formative stage is my sister, Amrita Ibrahim, to whom I owe more than I can express. Our conversations and discussions on how to teach and research an anthropology of policing over the course of a summer are reflected in every chapter of this book.

My students in the graduate seminar on policing, where I tried out some of the early ideas contained in this book, were the best interlocutors I could have had. Aarushi Punia, Fariya Yesmin, Sanam Khanna, Sneha Sharma, and Shyista Aamir Khan were hardworking and remained engaged despite my overloading them with reading material; their critical perspectives made for rich discussions in every class and also helped me clarify my arguments.

I would also like to acknowledge the support of friends and colleagues during the long months that this book was in the writing and revising phase: Aparna Balachandran, Mahuya Bandyopadhyay, Shohini Ghosh, Radhika Gupta, Ravinder Kaur, Tanuja Kothiyal, Anasuya Mathur, Angelie Multani, and Ambuj Sagar.

Finally, I am lucky to have had the support of a brilliant editorial team at Cornell University Press. Sameena Mulla shepherded the manuscript through review and acceptance with patience and an exemplary professionalism. I am grateful to her and to the other editors of the Police/Worlds series for their vote of confidence in this project. I would also like to thank the anonymous reviewers for their comments and suggestions; the book is most definitely improved as a result.

NOTE ON TRANSLITERATION

Hindi and Kutchi words have been transliterated phonetically. *Ch* is pronounced as in "check." The use of double-lettered consonants indicates that the letter is pronounced with aspiration (e.g., *chh, dhh*).

English words, when used in the original in an otherwise non-English sentence or conversation, are italicized.

FROM FAMILY TO POLICE FORCE

INTRODUCTION

Sometime in 2007, I was traveling back with colleagues to Mumbai, where I was teaching at the time. We were on our way back from Kathmandu via New Delhi. As I passed through immigration and passport control—an unremarkable exercise at the best of times—the official looked at his computer screen for what seemed like an inordinate amount of time. He looked up at me a couple of times, then back to his screen. My colleagues were waiting impatiently on the other side; we had very little time to make our connecting flight. I must have asked if everything was okay; I cannot remember the details. I do remember what he said, though. With the hint of a smile, to just take the edge off, he stated rather than asked, "In 2002–2003, you lived in Bhuj." I nodded, somewhat bewildered at this unexpected conversational turn. He continued, "You lived in Friendship Colony," correctly identifying the neighborhood where I had rented an apartment in a residential complex for the duration of the fieldwork for my PhD dissertation. By now, I was even more bewildered, and he continued, enjoying my reaction. "You lived on the mezzanine floor of Sunlight Terrace." At this point, I asked—maintaining the same tone of careful jocularity that he had used to initiate this conversation—"*Wah* [Wow], does it say all of this on your computer screen?" He responded, "Oh no. You see, I was 'on deputation' to the CBI [Central Bureau of Investigation] that year and I was posted in Bhuj. I lived in the same neighborhood. When I saw you just now, I thought you looked familiar; I used to see you walking home now and then, so I thought I would ask if you were the same person." I recall laughing this off and asking him whether he just had a very good memory or whether his job while "on deputation" was to keep an eye on me, but this marked the end of our exchange; he stamped my passport and waved me through.

This exchange stayed with me and got me thinking about the fieldwork that I had concluded four years previously in Kutch, a district on the border between Pakistan and the western Indian state of Gujarat. Bhuj is the administrative capital of Kutch and the place where I had rented an apartment for my yearlong residence while conducting research for my PhD.[1] Even though many people in the field had warned me about the ubiquity of state surveillance and the possibility of my movements and conversations being monitored by the various state intelligence networks who combed the border region, this was my first "direct" encounter with such "official" surveillance that also disconnected from my fieldwork both spatially and temporally. On the other hand, my notes from that year in the field are filled with what I thought were "suspicious" encounters and regular exhortations to myself not to be paranoid or read too much into everyday interactions with acquaintances in the field even as I was somewhat self-congratulatory about having "escaped" surveillance.

On my next visit to Kutch, I related the incident at the airport in New Delhi to one of my acquaintances, a journalist and editor who also ran a small stationery and office supplies store with a printing press in the old city. He confessed that a mere week after I had moved into my apartment in August 2002, he had received a "friendly" visit from an intelligence official. (The apartment rented by the CBI for its field officers was indeed right behind where I lived, he confirmed.) The official asked about me and what the journalist thought I was doing in Kutch. I was surprised and asked him why he had never mentioned this to me. He replied, "Well, if I had told you, then I would not be doing my job, would I?"

I was puzzled at first and not a little disappointed; perhaps I expected that this kind of information would have been shared with me as a matter of course, particularly by someone I met with so regularly and thought of as a confidant. As I was to learn, however, information was like capital; it had the power to generate enormous dividends. It could be bestowed as a gift or withheld from public circulation. Information was leveraged for other kinds of reciprocal exchanges, material and symbolic. Transparency could not be taken for granted in interpersonal relationships. For me to have expected it was surely naive; after all, as an anthropologist in the field, did I also not manage my persona and encounters in a way that enabled me to most effectively gain access to information from others? Why did I assume that I was the only one collecting information from others without being subjected to a similar exercise in return? The fact is that although I was predisposed to thinking that I would be primarily policed by the state, there were many other forms and sources of policing that I was interpellated in, including those that emanated from my own practices as an anthropologist, and that only became clear to me in hindsight. In this book, the state and its documentary practices are not the only ones disposed to surveillance and the management of information—the credibility of the immigration officials' claims apart, he did not acknowledge his recognition of me on the basis of official records but on an interpersonal exchange at the airport where he claimed familiarity on the basis of living in the same neighborhood.

Anthropology and Forms of Policing beyond the State

Although my interaction with the immigration official suggests that individuals in politically sensitive areas are policed by state agencies—the immigration checkpoint is after all the quintessential site for policing the entry of individuals into state space (Luibhéid 2002; Jeganathan 2004; de Genova 2013)—this book looks beyond the obvious sites, sources, and modes of policing that are usually tied to its institutional elaboration within the context of the state. By "policing" I mean the complex web of discourses and practices that are produced by multiple agents in service of maintaining what is basically a contested social and moral order. In this approach, policing is a form of embodied social practice rather than merely a state institution.[2] It is in this broader sense that we might refer to "moral policing," "caste policing," "community policing," and so on, each of which provides additional texture to the forms of policing that are deployed by the state.[3] Various institutionally organized forms of the police do figure in the chapters that follow, especially in part 1 of the book. However, my intent is to constantly reflect on how modes of practice that are seen as quintessential to institutional forms of policing are also replicated more generally across various social sites that straddle the "public" and the "private," through not only law but also through the family. Domestic order is linked to public order; modes of policing the family, from *within* the family, also have repercussions for how public order and citizenship is perceived in this borderland society.

Even as I make this argument, I am also attentive to the fact that within the institution of police, what counts as "police work" has been significantly expanded.[4] In this western Indian borderland that separates Kutch, a district in the western Indian state of Gujarat, from Sindh, a southern province in Pakistan—a national border between nation-states that cultivate a mutual hostility at the political level—there are civil and border police, the air wing of the armed forces, and paramilitary forces besides various central intelligence agencies that depute officers to the region. A long-standing anthropological engagement with the region has allowed me to observe how policing—as practice—plays out at multiple levels that exceed these institutional sites of order maintenance and also how these distinct institutional forms of policing are experienced differently by residents of this borderland.

This book reflects on the multiple sources and forms of policing that structure everyday interaction on a microscopic scale such as the family, the religious community, and the individual. Thus, I was able to observe how everyday interactions at home or at work among Muslims who lived in this region were continually engaged in policing—and producing—what it meant to live a secure and well-ordered life. A key impetus behind this argument is to suggest first, that relations between state institutions and a borderland public—where mutual cooperation is of essence to the project of national security—go beyond the framework of patronage.[5] I propose the concept of "adjacent sovereignty" to suggest that forms of policing that are elaborated through state institutions in fact derive much of their force through forms of local, even familial, sovereignty that operate in this borderland. Second, through a focus on forms of policing that play out at the level of the family and the religious community, I hope to be able to reclaim some agency for India's Muslim citizen beyond the abjection of "bare life." Produced as the "other" of India's citizenship regime and border management practices, it is clear that the Muslim is more often than not the object of the state's policing regime. I explain this with reference to early debates on policing and the constitution of the police force after Partition in chapter 1. However, one of the questions that also animates this book is, what would it take to envisage the Muslim as a *subject* of policing? How is information and movement deployed within this borderland society by those very actors who are also produced as "terrorists" and "infiltrators" by the state, as they determine their own modes of belonging to the family and the religious community?

Key to my argument is the figure of the "Bengali" Muslim woman, who is marked by the state and allied discourses—such as nongovernmental organizations (NGOs)—as either an "illegal infiltrator" or a trafficked marriage migrant into the region.[6] Muslim families in this borderland society are able to creatively use the presence of the "Bengali" woman to fundamentally transform the nature of sociality that underpins the task of kin making. Everyday life in a borderland society—already saturated with forms of suspicion-imbued sociality—does not always sit well with too much transparency vis-à-vis each other. Consanguineous marriage—where cousins marry each other—is a traditionally preferred marriage arrangement among Muslims in this region. However, the relations that this kind of marriage engenders across the terrain of the social become fragile when affines are too closely related. Much of the work of kinship—as the social practice of *relating* to others (Strathern 2005)—has to do with the transformation of affines (as outsiders) into consanguines (those "of the house"). This is demonstrated for north Indian Hindu society through the practice of gift giving (Vatuk 1975). Giving gifts continuously to affines is one way to smooth over the fundamental fragility of affinal relationships. The work of kinship is thus the continual working through this knotty site of affinity; kin making is a processual task, a constant site of incorporation (Carsten 1997). However, when affines are too closely related by blood, it can rip apart the terrain of the social; the carefully maintained fragility between affines and consanguines threatens to implode across the terrain of the family and the social. How, then, to reintroduce the creative tension of an "outsider" who has to be "incorporated," thereby reintroducing the very logic of kinship?

Although the "Bengali" remains somewhat of a social outsider (what the state refers to as an "infiltrator"), it is precisely her foreignness to the local social context that allows her to become a catalyst for the resumption of an increasingly strained sociality. Arranging marriages with these "outside" women allows Muslim families in Kutch to restore social and familial capital through affinity, something that had become difficult to maintain within traditional forms of consanguineous marriage, where affinity continually collapsed into consanguinity. Marriage with an "outsider"—who nevertheless brings other forms of capital with her—allows for the stability of Muslim marriage in the region albeit through the fundamental transformation of a traditional form of alliance: the consanguineous marriage. This argument is also offered here as a new way in which we can understand marriage migration within India for it moves beyond the restrictive lens of demographic indicators as an explanation for why women migrate for marriage. The literature on marriage migration in India views it primarily as a consequence of uneven sex ratios that lead to fewer girls born in an area, and bases its arguments primarily on the study of north Indian Hindu society.[7] My focus on the Muslim family, in addition to bringing the conceptual lens of policing into the family and marriage, thus also argues that sex ratio or demographic concerns cannot explain all instances of cross-region marriage migration. Kin making and border making—the policing of not only marriage but also of citizenship—is a dialogic process that rests on the work of multiple actors across the domain of the family and the state. Kinship and affinity are fundamentally political values, and this is underscored again in chapter 5 with a discussion on Hindu men from Pakistan who seek to migrate into India through marriage alliances that subvert the traditionally honorable category of marriage among upper caste men. These chapters also allow me to reposit the relationship between the state/law and the family. The family is certainly not a space of interiority, invisibility, or resistance to the state, but neither is it in collusion or alliance with it.

Although South Asian ethnographies on law and kinship are familiar with this relationship, they often fall back into the trope of the manner in which law and the patriarchal family come together to ensure compliance across gender and caste lines. By engaging primarily with the Muslim family, as well as Hindu men who crossed the border from Pakistan in and around 1971, this ethnography argues that policing across the terrain of state, family, and religious community is not always predictable. It is through an ethnographic entanglement with the "imponderabilia of actual life" (Malinowski 2002, 16)—sharing in births, marriages, and deaths, stumbling upon secrets that kept families together but also tore them apart, upholding through my ethnographic practice public secrets that were not spoken of but often shared by the ethnographer and her subjects—that this book arrives at its conclusions about policing practices at a multiscalar level that abound across civil-military and state-society domains, allowing us to rethink these distinctions in the context of anthropologies of policing and security.

Policing and the State

The dispersal of policing "as practice" (Ibrahim 2019) outside of the state institution adds to ethnographic accounts of sovereignty as it is actually performed—that is, its functioning as a "de facto" category instead of "an ontological ground of power and order, expressed in law or in enduring ideas of legitimate rule" (Hansen and Stepputat 2006, 297). In this spirit, anthropologists have revisited this foundational category of political thought to pluralize its meanings and to understand what it actually means to wield sovereign power in a variety of political and cultural contexts. Giorgio Agamben extended Carl Schmitt's notion of sovereign power (as the one who determines the state of exception) to the biopolitical body by formulating the concept of "bare life." The body enters the realm of the political—and sustains it—through its exclusion: its capacity to be killed. Agamben acknowledged Michel Foucault's contribution to the conceptualization of a biopolitics but sought a return to the "juridico-institutional models" of sovereignty that the latter eschewed. Agamben's (1998, 6) project is to examine the "hidden point of intersection between the juridico-institutional and the biopolitical models of power." In other words, "what is the point at which the voluntary servitude of individuals comes into contact with objective power?" (6). The totalizing nature of sovereign power is manifested for Agamben in the space of the camp, which is for him a paradigm for modernity, a "pure, absolute and impassable biopolitical space" (123). This totalizing vision of sovereign power has been criticized by anthropologists who reflect instead on ways in which it might be possible to "disagree with such gloomy, life-denying judgements" (Singh 2015, 44). Sovereign power in practice emerges in rather different light than its idealized projections of transcendence over "bare life." In various accounts, the functioning of sovereign power is "informal," "graduated," "vulnerable," "layered," or "bipolar" (Hansen and Stepputat 2006; Singh 2015; Osuri 2018; Maunaguru 2020) and dependent for its power on the degree to which it is recognized by those whom it has power over (Maunaguru 2020). Even though sovereign power remains bound to the body (whose life and death it exercises power over), the centrality of violence to this relationship is contested. Although some argue that violence is integral to the performance of sovereignty, regardless of whether it is the state that enacts it, thereby constituting an effective challenge to the state's monopoly over violence (Hansen and Stepputat 2006), others argue that violence is not central to the enactment of sovereign power (Singh 2015; Maunaguru 2020). Further, the definition of "life" is also extended to include more broadly considered forms of life: the dead, unborn, spirits, and deities (Singh 2015).

Since I am suggesting here that policing as practice cannot be regarded as the sole preserve of the institution that goes by the name (the police force), it follows, then, that an ethnographic illustration of policing practices also becomes an instance of the dispersal of sovereignty, and an exploration of how sovereignty is grounded in multiple sites across the state-society or civil-military domain. Since the state is not the only agent with a vested interest in the maintenance of social—and moral—order, policing opens up its meaning and becomes about more than crime control or the maintenance of everyday peace. Furthermore, the expansion of policing beyond the state is not just about the privatization of security under forms of neoliberal governmentality alone but also encompasses the domain of the family and kinship, which is equally complicit in producing—and policing—the sociomoral order.

The structure and institution of the state makes it difficult to step outside it in order to disaggregate it; in Pierre Bourdieu's (1994) pithy formulation, how does one think the state and resist being thought by it at the same time? It is the same with policing—the practices of policing are overtaken (even in academic writing) by the police as institutional arm of the state, the vanguard of order maintenance. In modern times, we have fetishized both the state and the police as fundamental sources of law and order (Reiner 2010); this often blinds us to the polyphonous sites that engender the social and moral order, not as a singular normative injunction but as fractious and unstable constructions of what constitutes a well-ordered life.

Anthropological accounts of the police and of law have contributed substantially to opening up the concept of the police, but I suggest that they do not go far enough to think the policing beyond the state. They variously attend to policing beyond state-backed weaponized practices of violence (as in the United States, for instance), focusing instead on the underlying conditions that enable violence and cruelty that constitute "everyday invisible violence"

(Fassin 2013, 137). Further expanding the sociality around police work, police practices have also been imbued with care. Scripted into policing practices even in a highly securitized environment in Gaza, Ilana Feldman (2015, 2) found that "policing was a space of both constraint and possibility, of control and action." Pooja Satyogi (2019, 52) finds in her ethnographic work with the women's cell of the Delhi Police that counseling and mediation allowed for what she terms "restorative practices" of the police. These practices enabled women police officers (who were not required to wear uniform in this unit) to forge forms of sociality with complainants of domestic violence that may have been based more on empathy and care rather than adherence to the letter of the law.[8] Srimati Basu (2015, 193) discovered in her fieldwork in the eastern Indian city of Kolkata (formerly Calcutta) that although the existence of a women's grievance cell indicates "state sensitivity to gendered violence, their tendency to prefer reconciliation and mediation dilutes their mandate of pursuing criminal sanctions." An overall commitment to a patriarchal "familial ideology" (Kapur and Cossman 1996) meant that women police officers rarely sanctioned the filing of a case that may be disruptive of the normative family setup. In effect, Basu (2015, 196) argues that "the only good S498A [the section of the Indian Penal Code under which domestic violence case can be prosecuted] case was one that did not quite become an S498A case," implying that the filing of a legal case was resorted to as a last measure, after all forms of reconciliation were exhausted.

Others locate the police function within a variety of historical, cultural, and institutional contexts that question the assumed universality of the police as it functions in Western democracies (Caldeira 2013; Garriott 2013; Martin 2013; Jauregui 2016). With the reconfiguration of authority in the late capitalist period, it is argued that there is a retreat of the state not just from welfare but also the provision of security and policing (Wacquant 2009; Goldstein 2010; Comaroff and Comaroff 2016). This shift in the relationship between state and police—where the police is no longer the principal punitive and disciplinary arm of the state—corresponds with the changing nature of the state under late capitalism. As Jean Comaroff and John Comaroff (2016, 217) argue, "with their increasing corporate capture, states have ceded to the market control over many of their signature functions, most of all their monopoly of force. As a result, vertical structures of authority are giving way to a lateral montage of partial, overlapping sovereignties, making it even more difficult to separate government from business and business from criminality."

Thus, this body of work argues that policing is no longer the preserve of the state as a vertical model of governance but works through lateral interests and connections. In much of this work, the decoupling of policing from the state either follows from the privatization of security or the ways in which everyday life is reimagined in terms of police power (Garriott 2011) rather than thinking of the ways in which policing can also be articulated as a mode of order maintenance that springs from institutions other than the state and the market.

Ethnographic work on the policing of gender, caste, and family in South Asia has for long been mindful of the constitution of policing as a field of intervention in the family and whose interests it serves. For example, Anupama Rao (2010, 239) alerts us to caste sociality as an agent of policing and "the role of caste in regulating female sexuality and sexual access," which gestures toward the complex relationship between the "state" and the "nonstate" with regard to questions of policing in the broader South Asian context. Pratiksha Baxi's (2006) work on the deployment of law to restrict marital choices of consenting adults in India enables us to ask who in the community stands to benefit from police action and who is at its mercy. She argues that a politics of honor is folded into state law and deployed by the police at the local level, who become instruments of publics constituted through affect rather than the letter of the law. In effect, she argues that there may be an "alliance between the policing practices of the family and the state" (72), a position that bears upon the longer history of work on the state and sexual governance in India. Uma Chakravarti (1996) discusses the sexual surveillance of women in the eighteenth-century Peshwa State (in present-day Maharashtra) that was grounded in a caste-based patriarchal order. The moral policing of kin and community transposed itself seamlessly onto the moral-juridical order of the state, backed by the latter's coercive and legal apparatus. Similarly, Veena Das (1995) discusses the intervention of the state into matters of kinship when it legislated the "recovery" of abducted women during the Partition. In each instance, it is assumed that the state made more stringent forms of punishment that existed within the family. I argue here that the family does not necessarily constitute a space of interiority, site of intervention, or collaboration with the state. When the subject is the Muslim family in a borderland context, already saturated with suspicion and surveillance of various kinds, the theme of alliance between the state and the patriarchal family needs to be revisited.

While I build on these important insights that detail the relationship between law and the family in India, I seek to go a step further and invite a re-evaluation of the relationship between the state and the family. I consider the family not merely an instrument of the state or an ideological state apparatus; nor is it only a field of intervention for the state: a "privileged instrument for the government of the population" (Foucault 2001, 216). Instead, it is a site that allows for a particular conceptualization of the social order as being also a question of moral regulation. The question of a well-ordered population stretches across the fabric of the social, a fabric that is constituted through both state and family, which do not encounter one another as distinct domains (Donzelot 1979). The family and the state relate to each other through the idea of the well-policed society, their tutelary role vis-à-vis individuals and also through their ways of seeing, sorting, and managing individuals and information. Each of the chapters questions the sequence in which policing practices bind the state and family to each other. Rather than a collusion between the state and the family in practices of sexual governance, the book locates within the "interior" domains of the family forms of policing that are evocative of state-led practices of surveillance and information management. The effects of these practices on members of families and communities within an overall borderland context is to heighten the feeling of suspicion and policing and provides a good site to therefore propose an anthropology of policing that is also fundamentally an anthropology of kinship.

To sum up the argument thus far, this ethnography seeks to push the existing anthropological literature on the police by extending the idea of police well beyond its institutional arm and by situating the above debates in the anthropology of policing within a social and historical context that saw the development of policing along routes that are quite distinct from those that are taken as axiomatic in the existing anthropology of police literature. Critiques of the order-maintenance approach to policing caution against the taken-for-granted nature of what we may call "order" and "disorder" as a stable binary. "Disorder" is often produced by the very practices of policing that are designed to contain it (Harcourt 2009), and even the more "rational" forms of neoliberal policing such as carceral punishment are also means to restore a social order that is produced as predominantly "economic, ethnoracial and moral" (Wacquant 2009, 152). In this ethnography, the contours of social order are elastic: legality and morality as defined by the state is continually tested against other sites such as the family or the religious community.

Since there is no singular iteration of the legal, social, or moral order as it plays out among those who live on the border, and yet there are high stakes in the maintenance of order on this political borderland, where the state is unequivocal about the legal, social, and moral order that it perpetuates, the chapters that follow attempt to disaggregate the multiple sites of policing in this everyday borderland context.

Ethnographies of Policing in South Asia

With a couple of notable recent exceptions, the police have rarely been a stand-alone subject for South Asian anthropology. I argue that this should not be read as a critical absence in the literature but be a recognition of the fact that law and policing in this region has always been embedded in other forms of regulation and sociality such as gender, caste, and the family (Chowdhry 2004; Chakravarti 1996; Mody 2008; Rao 2010; Baxi 2014). The dangers of constituting the police as an exceptionally powerful and violent body have been noted through history and ethnography (Chandavarkar 1998; Jauregui 2016). However, ethnographic explorations of policing have often looped back into ethnographies of the state and of law (Das 2004; Mody 2008; Baxi 2014). If the move to reclaim police practice from its contemporary iteration as a particular form of government institution concerned with the fighting of crime alone entails an acknowledgment of its more expansive history as a mode of good governance and the production of a well-ordered society (Garriott 2013), then policing in South Asia is a particularly good site to engage the question of what constitutes policing, both its institutional forms and the question of how state and nonstate actors operate in pursuit of constituting the social and moral order without necessarily adopting neoliberal governmentality as the explanatory route to the fragmentation of authority away from the state.

In South Asia, the state has been central to discussions of conflict and order maintenance, of which the dominant trope is ethnic or communal violence and its containment (e.g., Brass 2011). More recent work on sovereignty (reviewed above) disperses authority away from the state and locates it in other sites and relationships. Recent work on policing in India problematizes the idea of police authority as exceptional, highlighting its deep entrenchment in other forms of local power and authority (Jauregui 2016), touching on the moral ambiguity in police work especially with respect to the deployment of violence (Wahl 2017) and the co-constitutive sociality of citizens and the police (Satyogi 2019). Chandavarkar's (1998) important work on policing in colonial Bombay proposed a focus on everyday police practice rather than institutional or bureaucratic design. "Everyday policing" in nineteenth-century Bombay showed the police forces to be deeply embedded in local power structures and neighborhood processes: they were no monolith; far less did they have a monopoly over violence even in a colonial context. Arnold (1976) discusses the ways in which colonial policing built in significant ways on earlier forms of enforcing order, despite its rhetoric of ushering in the "rule of law" in its colonies. Ethnographies of the state and of the law also indicate that the police do not always constitute themselves outside of social constraints such as caste, gender, or patriarchy (Das 2004; Mody 2008; Baxi 2014; Basu 2015). This ethnographic exploration of policing extends these concerns and provincializes the state by arguing for the ways in which the function of policing may be internal to a range of social and institutional contexts that are nonetheless not necessarily in "collusion" or strategically aligned with the state.

The various ethnographies of policing, law, and kinship referred to here point to an expansion of the field of police work beyond the use of spectacular violence and coercion alone. In South Asia, "coercive violence and police authority are not isomorphic" (Jauregui 2016, 13), and in the South African context, Julia Hornberger (2017) discusses police work in terms of complex forms of reciprocity, exchange, and the management of social obligations with the community. While in India, police functions are known to be exercised by a range of actors inside and outside the formal institution of the police leading to what is perceived as a "delegitimation of police authority" (Jauregui 2013, 646) both within and outside the institution. And yet, there is a deeply ambivalent aspect to the manner in which police authority is recognized especially when it is harnessed by socially marginal or disempowered groups to assert their own legitimacy in society (Hornberger 2017; Khanikar 2018). Those very categories of the urban precariat who are most likely to be at the receiving end of police violence may, in fact, be able to harness the *threat* of violence to their own advantages. Inviting the police into the home to intervene in a marital dispute in a poor urban neighborhood becomes, in this sense, a form of deterrence to political, kin, or gang rivals. The sheer presence of the police and their *potential* to unleash violence becomes a source of empowerment for those who are otherwise on the margins (Khanikar 2018).

Sovereignty and the Moral Order

If police practice is about ways of seeing, the ability to be "equipped with a new field of vision, a new way of perceiving the local landscape" imbued with "suspicion" and "apprehension" (Garriott 2011, 43–44), then a borderland society teaches us that these are attributes that are not necessarily controlled and outsourced by those formally recognized as police, nor restricted to the so-called extrajudicial authority of the strongman, gangster, or political intermediary (Poole 2004; Hansen 2005; Berenschot 2011). Secrecy circulates within the family and community, as "poisonous knowledge" (Das 2007), but the family does not necessarily constitute a space of interiority from the state.

With increasing global concerns around the "policiarization" and "criminalization" of a range of social actions and services such as migration, schooling, immigration, and security, for instance (Fassin 2011; Garriott 2013), we could either say that the boundaries of the police have expanded to encompass the community, training them to think like the police, thereby significantly expanding the scope of what is conventionally understood as police work, or on the other hand, we could acknowledge that the community and the family was always already familiar with forms of surveillance, and produced within its members forms of affect such as insecurity and suspicion that ended up constituting the weft of everyday life as it wove across the domains of its interior life and its public face. Insecurity, suspicion, and surveillance are the very affects and practices that we have also come to regard as constitutive of "police work." Here, it is worthwhile to recall the injunction to treat the "police" not as a preconstituted object but as "a type of sociality that is constituted through practice" (Karpiak 2013, 79). Transparency (and "recognition") is a key attribute of how subjects must appear when they are policed—through forms of biometric and social security data in addition to the more personalized forms of recognition that police employ in their identification of "suspicious" actors. And yet, within the heart of the family, transparency is not taken for granted among its members any more than it is in more "public" or "surveilled" spaces.

Law, Policing, and the Family

If sovereignty is defined as the power over life and death, the family is a primary stakeholder in sovereign power. The family is life generating; it is the primary institution that generates bodies as both biological and social beings. In a compelling shift—though not always a challenge—to the state's sovereign power, the family, certainly in South Asia, has demonstrated that it can also wield spectacular forms of violence against its members and indeed has the power to condemn them to death.[9] This ethnography argues that it is time to bring attention back to the family in the context of broader discussions of sovereignty/policing. Although this connection was never ruptured in the context of South Asia, as will be seen in the ensuing section, the politics of the academy and of knowledge production more generally meant that these discussions did not always make their way into the domain of anthropological theory, remaining provincialized as matters of relevance to South Asian studies. If we agree that sovereignty is fragmented across a range of sites and actors beyond the state that are invested in the maintenance of the social order, then one of the key sites for sovereignty and policing is the family.

The question of how social order was maintained was central to early anthropological accounts of order and control in so-called stateless societies (e.g., Evans-Pritchard and Fortes 1950; Gluckman 1956; Durkheim 2013). In these accounts, what was perceived as the lack of a strong, centralized jural order (in the absence of the modern state) was made up for through a strong kinship or moral order. Max Gluckman's (1956) question for us—where should we look for social order in the absence of the modern state—can be reworked more appropriately for our times to ask—since the concept of the state has itself been historicized and localized—now that state sovereignty has revealed its complex forms of adjustment to other forms of sovereign authority, whether human or divine, what does that do to the problem of social order and who is charged with its maintenance, with or without the use of violence? It is worthwhile again, to recall Gluckman's argument in his essay "Estrangement in the Family." In his view, the long-term stability of tribal society lay in the fact that a man was torn between obligations to his agnatic descent group and his need to enter into matrimonial alliance with a range of others not related to him. Agnatic loyalty (a man's loyalty to his patrilineal kin) conflicted with the need to be able to live amicably with one's neighbors who are—through the logic of marriage—made up of kin from a number of different lineages. Even though the matrimonial tie makes men friendly to other groups, a man and his wife are pulled in opposite directions when it comes to obligations within their own natal families. What this meant for the problem of social order was that individuals were constantly offsetting one set of enmities with other sets of friendships and alliances. What this meant for the study of kinship is that rather than take the nuclear family as a unit of analysis, it is recognized that the spousal unit is actually constituted through a "dispersal of attachments" (Gluckman 1956, 77) rather than through an overattachment to the notion of the nuclear family as a bounded entity made up of spouses and their children. Gluckman went on to clarify that this is a custom-derived estrangement, one that does not have a bearing on the personal affective relations between particular husbands and wives. In effect, affinity or the nature of affines (relationships through marriage) is shot through with ambivalence (Carsten 1997) even as it is crucial to the project of reproducing the family through the production of children. This suggests, as Gluckman (1956, 78) pointed out, "the need to examine family relations in the light of wider social relationships."

Closer to our present times is Marilyn Strathern's assessment of the nature of kinship as a mode of relationality in the context of modern biotechnology. She argues that kinship is certainly about connections between people, but it is equally about their *disconnections*. Even as the Euro-American family was concerned with individualism both in law and in terms of familial ideology, she argues that it is increasingly impossible to draw a boundary around the nuclear family, rendering it more appropriately the "unclear family," a term she borrows from Bob Simpson (Strathern 2005, 22). Biotechnology has enabled the dissolution of the family as we once understood it and has enabled the emergence of new types of "recombinant" families. Recombinant genetics offers ways of thinking about social relationships that allows us to engage with forms of disconnection that enable new ways of relating to each other.

The family and the state, private and public, are not insulated from one another; this is already argued from the perspective of feminist ethnographies and cultural theory (Berlant 1997; Carsten 1997; Brenner 1998; Warner 2002).

In the postcolonial context, what does this mean for the way in which sovereignty is operationalized and of how law straddles the domain of the state and the family? In her study of Partition violence and the state's quest to recover "abducted" women and children in the aftermath of the horrific violence that ensued, Veena Das (2007) argues that the social order of the state is instituted in a very particular form of the sexual order. She suggests that the social contract is not between men "in the state of nature" but between men as "heads of households," thus instituting the nation as a masculine nation. The citizenship of men is predicated on the existence of a "correct" relationship between communities. A woman's citizenship is predicated on her ability to reproduce within the normative group, to provide the nation with "legitimate" children. Thus, Das argues, "a corollary is that a woman's citizenship is an offense not only against the family but also against the sovereignty of the state" (36). The "state re-instates the correct matrimonial dialogue of men" (21) in a bid to maintain the social contract (built, in turn, on a particular form of the sexual contract). We are already in the realm of the law and its negotiation with the family. Baxi (2000) extends this argument and suggests that rape legislation provides the site to unpack the relationship between the state and violence against women. Although rape legislation in India operates in the name of protecting women, Baxi argues that it does not in fact seek the bodily autonomy of *all* women. The law normalizes certain types of violence against women by refusing to name it (rape of lower caste women by upper caste men; marital rape) while it criminalizes only those forms of violence that it deems as pathological (rape of upper caste, married women by "other" men, for instance). The form of retribution sought by the state, "in this case capital punishment, aims at punishing men for having breached the contract between the masculinist state and all men" (Baxi 2000, 1199). The law thus upholds the "familial ideology" of the patriarchal family (Kapur and Cossman 1996).

The political and the domestic are therefore coproduced, even though the nature of the sociality they forge in relation to each other may not always be predeterminable. In her analysis of sexual violence within the family in the United States, Sameena Mulla's (2015) finely rendered ethnography demonstrates that the law enables the suturing together of familial ties that may have come under strain in the aftermath of sexual violence. Far from a breakdown of sociality, the occurrence of sexual violence—when it reaches out to the law—may in fact lead victims to "renegotiate and realign loyalty, care, and intimacy" (Mulla 2015, 174). Sexual violence in this instance does not lead to alienation; rather, through the mechanism of the law and the visibility that it occasions, it may in fact enable new forms of affiliation and care to emerge. On the other hand, Baxi's (2014) ethnography of rape trials in India argues that the law may compromise kinship relations and disrupt sociality. The law does not produce visibility here; instead, Baxi argues that rape trials are the "privileged sites of the production, negotiation, and management of public secrets" (xxiv). The law, she argues, is thus "*the* institutional site that normalizes violence against women" (3, emphasis original). By aligning itself with the patriarchal family, the law delegates the power to name the harm caused by rape to the family or community rather than the individual. Rape is adjudicated not as a crime against the survivor but against the harm caused to society by the act. This is how "the social moves into the legal to birth a public secret—one that severs law from its self-reference" (222).

In this borderland context, the so-called interiority of the family explodes in the face of the policing of citizenship and migration. The regulation of marriage has become a matter of great relevance for border policing as the figure of the "Bengali" bride becomes a site for the determination of potential illegality (as the undocumented "infiltrator" from Bangladesh) even as Hindu men who migrate from Pakistan in search of wives are welcomed as always-already citizens. The juxtaposition of affinity (as a valued social asset that allows for the perpetuation of marriage as an institution among Muslims) with citizenship (for Hindu men who use marriage as a means to political belonging) allows me to explore sociological changes at the level of the family (in terms of new forms of marriage, for instance) in conjunction with broader political contours of belonging to the nation.[10]

Policing, as I approach it in this ethnography, is a form of practice that concerns itself with a quest for social order. Further, the book reminds readers that the social order is also fundamentally a moral order (e.g., Durkheim 2013), the moral coordinates of which are fundamentally elastic. Who belongs and who does not—to the family, religious community, region, or nation—is debated, performatively enacted, and contested at multiple levels. The questions of belonging and boundaries are particularly charged on a postcolonial borderland between nation-states that are politically hostile but share a considerable degree of social and cultural compatibility. Kinship ties and cultural connections persist across this border even at the risk of being criminalized by border security protocols. Even as the conditions of political belonging are set out unambiguously by the nation-state, it is at the level of the social and the everyday that these conditions fall short of unequivocality. As the family, kinship group, religious community, and nation-state confront each other on this border, it becomes clear that there are multiple stakes in different forms of boundaries. How these are maintained and transactions across them are policed in an everyday context is the subject of this book.

Kinship and the Muslim Family

I suggest therefore that this book also be read as a contribution to the anthropological literature on not only forms of policing but also to everyday forms of reckoning kinship and relatedness, especially for the contemporary middle-class Muslim family, a demographic that has received scant attention in ethnographies of marriage and the family in India that have been produced over the past three decades. This remains the case even decades after Imtiaz Ahmad (1972, 172) commented on the "poverty of Indian sociology" in the absence of critical ethnographic work on its Muslims. The only notable contributions to the study of the Muslim family, marriage, and middle-class desires since the 1990s are Osella and Osella (2007) and Osella (2012)—mere drops in the ocean when compared to the richly documented and theorized work on marriage and family among Hindus. Ethnographies on love, aspiration, and middle-class marriage are almost exclusively devoted to Hindus in India (Kalpagam 2005; Fuller and Narasimhan 2008; Abraham 2010; Grover 2011; Clark-Decès 2014; Donner 2016).[11] Muslims in India are written about—including in academic writing—from the point of view of either exclusion/marginality or religiosity, ironically reinscribing through their representation the problem of bordering or marginalization from "mainstream" society (e.g., Gayer and Jaffrelot 2012; Chatterjee 2017; Burker 2018).

The focus here is not only on kinship structure and marriage practices but also on how everyday forms of trust and betrayal, suspicion and favor, aspiration and desire work to police the family order from within as much as from the outside. It reconnects the family to forms of policing—to regard it not just as a site of intervention for the state but also as an active agent of policing it itself. Chapter 4 addresses itself to the question, how do forms of knowledge that are internal to the family structure relationships between affines and consanguines, particularly in the case of cousin marriages that are preferred by Muslims in this field site? The chapters on the family highlight the manner in which familial tensions around marriage—both inter- and intragenerational—and the choice of spouse become charged sites for the policing not just of familial boundaries but also become a potent commentary on the management of interregional migration into Kutch. The family, in this ethnography, is not a site of interiority from the state, nor is it a haven of peace or refuge for individuals. The ethnography turns to the interiority of family life to shed light on how tensions play out within the family, of how "poisonous knowledge" (Das 2007; Mookherjee 2015) is managed and how there is a general agreement about the things that may not be spoken about.[12] These can relate to the everyday management of grief in the aftermath of a cataclysmic event such as the deathly earthquake of 2001 or the fixing up of marriages with women who are deemed to be non-kin, or "Bengali." The "interior" is not what is hidden but what erupts "in the performative techniques actors deploy to make the conflict and violence present on public occasions" (Das 2007, 87). A number of these performances will emerge throughout the book; some of them may be precipitated by the presence of the anthropologist, journalist, or development worker, whereas others may unfold according to their own temporality, the anthropologist feeling like a distinct interloper at times like these. These moments dramatize the tensions that structure the forms of life that relate the interior to the external, the private to the public. There is no pure division of public versus private, state versus family; the terrain of the social is constituted across them, and practices of policing make these terrains visible vis-à-vis each other even as they dramatize the desire to keep them distinct.

Located in a borderland context that is saturated by forms of surveillance and policing across the civil-military and state-society terrains, the following chapters do not describe ways in which the state's technologies of policing are amplified or replicated across society, bringing "nonstate" actors into the domain of policing in some sort of alliance with the state, expanding the state's policing (Andrejevic 2005; Garriott 2011). Instead, they show that practices of policing extend across the larger canvas (the nation-state) and the smaller stage (the family), not because the latter represents "the privileged instrument for the government of the population" (Foucault 2001, 216), but because practices of policing within the family may end up evoking or mirroring those that we have come to associate naturally with the state. This is also not to speculate on which precedes the other but to point toward a field of governance that is constituted by policing practices that does not add up to a coherent whole. What are the contours of the social and the moral order? This is not the product of a prior consensus that is then policed across domains, co-opting the family and the state into policing within a singular moral universe. Instead, the social and moral order are contested and emergent through varied practices of policing.

Sociality and Everyday Suspicion

A central premise of state formation is its control over secrecy (Nugent 2010) and the deployment of fear, the police becoming "trafficke[rs] in dread" (Verdery 2014, 26). Surveillance, secrecy, and fear are indeed central to the state's management of security. Following from the earlier discussion, the chapters argue that discourses of securitization are contested and emergent, sites of strategic maneuvers between different agents rather than mere impositions from the state (Jusionyte 2015). They argue that "a critical, comparative ethnography of security can explore the multiple ways in which security is configured and deployed—not only by states and authorized speakers but by communities, groups, and individuals—in their engagements with other local actors and with arms of the state itself" (Goldstein 2010, 492). Policing can also lead to the production of *insecurity* in society (Ali 2013; Verdery 2014); the transition to a security state may actually produce the insecure subjects that it retroactively seeks to protect. Fear and dread are not the only affects deployed within circuits of policing. Chapters 3 and 4 identify policing practices that are generated within the interior spaces of the family and the community. Interpersonal relations that hinge on mistrust and insecurity may also be enfolded within informational flows that occur across spaces of intimacy, care, and desire that are internal to the family. Rather than a strategic alliance between the state and others (e.g., technology, data, or key informers) to manage a finite body of information, the process of information gathering about each other is a limitless exercise where it is not always possible to detect alliances in any obvious manner. Key stakeholders of information in a region such as the state and its functionaries, police, development experts, tourists, and visiting anthropologists are not necessarily bound together by a central agency that has "offloaded" its task among others. Seen from the state's perspective, Gulbeg, a central character in chapter 1, is an "informer," but when he is situated within his own social context, it appears that he serves as a conduit of information from multiple sources; the police are dependent on him for the success with which they police the border. If the maintenance of everyday peace on the border was a result of its policing, this was in turn defined less in terms of police personnel and materials (weapons and uniforms, for instance) or a monopoly over the legitimate use of violence/coercion, but in terms of the control of *information*, leveraged through various *ways of seeing* that seeped into networks of sociality within the neighborhood and even the heart of the family: the management of information and the deployment of suspicion was central to the way in which communities constituted themselves.

The work of policing the social order—of determining the terms of belonging, of deploying suspicion so that it stuck as a stain onto some people rather than others—goes well beyond the work of "the police" in this book. It is certainly true that although it is the Muslim who is uniformly the object of suspicion by both the state and society, it was not always so. Chapter 1 discusses how suspicion could be deployed among Muslims to carve out boundaries *within* a group that the state produced as homogenous. In this case, suspicion came to structure forms of sociality among Muslims based on what was known—and just as often suspected or speculated on—about which religious sect (*maslak*) they belonged to. An important conclusion of this ethnography is that even though border management practices in India have consistently defined the Muslim as the suspicious "other" from the beginning (Jayal 2013), suspicion also circulates *within* the Muslim family and community, thus tearing apart the notion of a homogenous group that is bound together in an intimacy produced as a consequence of being policed by the state. Added to this, a key contribution made by the book is that it identifies the Muslim as *internal* to policing practices and not just as their target. To this extent, it is an attempt to disaggregate the way in which we may understand the relationships forged between the postcolonial state and those who are constituted as specific targets of its policing. India's borderland regime is structured quite explicitly around the question of policing Muslim migration. Muslims constitute disproportionate numbers of those who are unlawfully detained and harassed and those who are the victims of police violence (Sethi 2014). Even though Muslims may increasingly constitute disproportionately small percentages of the police forces in India, a key contribution of this book is to locate a broader range of practices in which Muslims on this borderland engage in policing within or without the institutional structure of policing.

A Note on Method

Although my fieldwork covered a substantial cross section of rural society in north and northwestern Kutch and middle classes in Bhuj, in this ethnography I find myself returning to the people whom I have come to know quite well over the years. Of these, more were Muslims than Hindus. This was a biographical constraint pertaining to how I was read by my interlocutors. Given the suspicion that characterizes intercommunal relations in Gujarat more generally, and especially during the years of my fieldwork, I could not have hoped for—even had I desired it—a more representative demographic cross section. The fieldwork that this ethnography draws from was conducted over periods of varying intensity that ranged from August 2002 to March 2017. My longest research visit was thirteen months, the shortest six days. During these visits, and increasingly over the years as fieldwork time became more and more precious, it was the time spent with a few people whom I returned to over the years that produced the interpersonal relationships that are by definition impossible to achieve with a large demographic sample. These relationships are ones that produced most of the insights presented here. Ethnography is dialogic, and to the extent that "relationability" is dependent on the identities of both the ethnographer and her subjects, only a few spaces make themselves available for research (Navaro-Yashin 2012, xii).

Over these years, the nature of my relationships transformed from fleeting encounters to something more durable and changed the nature of access I had to people. When I moved back to India from the United States after my PhD, I was within easier access of "the field." As I continued to write about people who no longer saw me as an anthropologist interloper but as a friend or member of the family, it remained harder to see them as "informants" or "research subjects" alone. I increasingly pondered the question, what does it mean to become a part of another's family (Gold et al. 2014), when the boundary between anthropologist and research assistant (and their family) has broken down? Mohamed Hosain started out as my language teacher in 2001 and then moved to becoming a research assistant in 2002 when I began dissertation fieldwork. He and his wife, Sherbano, took me in as a member of their family, a relationship that deepened after our formal relationship as researcher–research assistant "officially" ended after my PhD. I was present at their children's weddings and have known all their grand-children since they were infants. The youngest generation in the family has simply accepted my presence in their lives as a matter of course. To them, I am either *phuphi* (father's sister) or *masi* (mother's sister). I have known the grandchildren—Saqiba, Zobiya, and Zaid—from the time they were born; they have grown to become my special little friends in the field, surrounding me with the most ardent and heartfelt love and affection. They have brought me joy and hours of entertainment and over the years have become frequent companions on journeys around Kutch.

My status as a daughter of the house, which quickly superseded my pre-carious status as visiting anthropologist as soon as my PhD was complete, was confirmed to me when one time, my usual gifts for the family were ac-cepted rather more reluctantly than good taste dictates. This time, I was chastised quite severely for bringing gifts of clothing for all the women in the house. Finally, Sherbano articulated what was bothering her: it was not at all the "done" thing to accept gifts from a *niyani* (a daughter and her mar-ital home, who are affines to her parents). Daughters are only given gifts *to*; one cannot accept gifts *from* them in this cultural universe. Once the kin-ship muddle was sorted out, this was how it was to stay. In future, whenever she traveled to her favorite shopping destinations—for instance, to Karachi or to Mumbai—she would buy pieces of cloth for her daughters, and inevi-tably on my next visit, no matter how many months later this occurred, she would pull something out for me. "I have three daughters," she said on one occasion as she gave me her gift: "Nasreen, Farzana [her daughters], . . . and you." In her inimitable style, once she pronounced this, there was no argu-ing with her. I just became a part of the family. When visiting others as part of my various research agendas, she or her daughter-in-law began to ac-company me even as her husband, my original "research assistant," started taking more of a back seat. As far as they saw it, now that my "official" research—that is, for a PhD degree—was over, my subsequent trips were altogether more social. As my visits to others began to be conducted in a more familiar—even familial—mold, the nature of my interactions also altered subtly. This period of research also coincided with greater linguistic facility on my part, and I could more easily take part in conversations in Kutchi with women, something I would have been far less confident of when I first began research in the area. This made me less fiercely dependent on Mohamed Hosain's presence for interviews. As the contours of my own belonging in the field shifted with time, I was able to become gradually more aware of the dynamics of other forms of belonging: of the shifting scales along which marriage between "insiders" and "outsiders" was evaluated by different agents, and of the transactions made by the "Bengali" wife or the "Pakistani" husband to belong within families along this national border. My location in the field and the forms of sociality that I became imbricated in as time wore on had a direct bearing not only on the forms of familial interaction that I was able to observe and participate in but also on the questions that I was able to ask and indeed the social contexts that produced—and often dramatized— issues relating to secrecy, intimacy, and kinship. This interpersonal context is central to my ability to argue here that the family is a site of policing not only in the external sense of its collusion or alliance with the state (the mainstay of South Asian ethnographies of law and the family) but also in the sense of how it structures its inner workings—how consanguineous marriages begin to give way to cross-region marriages, not as a consequence of demographic compulsions such as a declining sex ratio as is argued by much of the literature on cross-region marriage in India but as a consequence of what it means to maintain the familial and social order.

I conducted fieldwork primarily in two languages, Hindi and Kutchi. Most men and younger, educated women were conversant in Hindi and spoke to me in it. My interactions with officials of all stripes and in institutional contexts of the NGO were all in Hindi. Kutchi is a spoken language that does not have a script of its own. The written language—and of official business in the state— is Gujarati. Although I am conversant in it, its proximity to Hindi meant that most people used Hindi when they spoke to me. Women more generally— including Sherbano and her cohort—and especially rural women in Banni spoke only in Kutchi. The exception were "Bengali" women who, because they were from "outside," tended to speak more fluent Hindi than local women.

I have identified broad areas (such as *taluka* subdivisions) within Kutch but used pseudonyms for all village names except Bhuj, Madhapar, and Dhordo and for all the people who feature in this book with the exception of Mohamed Hosain and Sherbano in Bhuj and those who have been written about in the public domain—that is, Gulbeg and his family (Miyan

Hussain, Phupli, and Sofiya) in Dhordo, and Virubai and Hirubai in Madhapar, or those who are public figures, such as Ram Singh Sodha.[13] This is with their consent.

Structure of the Book

The book is divided into two sections. Part 1 (chapters 1 and 2) delineates the landscapes of policing on this border. The variegated landscape of peacekeeping on a hostile political border is made up of distinct types of uniformed police and military personnel, in addition to official and unofficial intelligence networks. Part 2 (chapters 3–5) examines contours of policing that evoke more conventionally understood practices of state policing but are forged outside of them. Each of these chapters will depict how policing is about the social order, but there is no shared consensus about its social and moral coordinates. These chapters focus on how the family, the anthropologist, and the NGO may all be part of a universe of policing that often uses similar techniques—the use of surveillance, techniques of tracking information, the deployment of fear and suspicion, the lack of trust—even though they do not work toward a common end. The nature of the social order opens up along a moral spectrum rather than narrows down under the gaze of the state or its security discourse.

Chapter 1 redefines border policing in terms of networks of sociality rather than as a preconstituted institution or arm of state. It opens with debates on police reorganization that took place along this border in the years immediately following decolonization. These debates give us a critical perspective on what the state considered to be the essential attributes of professional policing: the cultivation of social distance, and attributes such as suspicion and the deployment of fear for effective crime fighting. Once these debates set the context for how institutional policing was envisioned, the chapter opens up the question of policing beyond its institutional or professional forms alone. It identifies practices of policing—such as the use of suspicion, fear, and the management of information—as attributes that circulate beyond the formal confines of the police as an arm of the state alone: they can be located within families and communities. The chapter uses the figure of Gulbeg, a charismatic resident on the border, to think more broadly about forms of sovereignty that I term *adjacent* rather than *nested* within the state, and of modes of policing during times of peace. Gulbeg had an affective relationship with the military that thrived on a shared masculine ethos of friendship, camaraderie, and adventure. His hunting and shooting expeditions across the desert, accompanied by senior police and army officers, complicate the idea that surveillance and information flows were deployed by the state and reveal instead how they were managed and negotiated across the so-called civil-military terrain with officers of the state dependent on Gulbeg rather than the other way around.

Chapter 2 disaggregates the multiple faces of uniformed peacekeeping/ law enforcing that people encounter in an everyday context in Bhuj, examining the ethnographic nuance of the term *militarywala* (military man) as it is threaded into everyday conversations and encounters within an overall context of an everyday militarization that is nonetheless *not* evocative of war or occupation but is seen as a basic constituent of peacetime. The chapter emphasizes that the work of policing is not just about ways of seeing and the deployment of information but also a form of labor, often performed under conditions of great physical duress. In this chapter, a shared experience of wartime labor allows for a very particular kind of civil-military intimacy to develop between the armed forces, who are seen as laboring to protect the country's territorial borders, and Patidar women, who also share an ethic of hard work through laboring on the land. Through the shared experience of laboring under exceptionally trying circumstances that pushed their levels of bodily and emotional endurance to a degree not encountered before, Hindu peasant women who worked on rebuilding a bombed runway during the 1971 war remind us that the work of policing is a physically and emotionally demanding one. Even as they are enshrined into the nation as its core members, valorized as the nation's mothers, they resist this narrative of belonging. Instead, they insist on the embodied, raw, and physical attributes of the labor they performed and the emotional quality of courage—*himmat*— that they forged through the tutelage of military men.

Much of the time, police work on this border consists of the detection of the "illegal infiltrator." Chapter 3 describes how the migrant woman from the east is, on the one hand, the subject of policing by the state and border security forces for she indexes the fear of the "illegal Bangladeshi migrant"; on the other hand, the designation by ordinary people of a host of migrant women as "Bengali" points to the difficulty of asserting in any "accurate" way, who is the target of censure and by whom. When a woman designated as "Bengali" marries into a family on the border, she—and her affinal family—work to manage her appearance and disappearance across interactions. The chapter describes the work they have to do to "belong" locally but resists casting the family as a place of refuge from the heightened visibility of the state. It argues instead that the possibility of exposure runs through every interaction, inside or outside the family. The idea of the "safe" space is recalibrated throughout as "Bengali" women move in and out of focus through multiply-mediated interactions and encounters as sometimes competing demands for visibility (for the police and border patrol, for NGO-led development work, or for the anthropologist) are managed. The family-NGO-state-anthropologist network pushes people to dissimulate differently, even as they are required to make themselves transparent—albeit in different ways—to each of these institutions and people.

Chapter 4 continues with forms of policing that may be continuous across the domains of the state and family even though they may operate within different moral universes. Notwithstanding forms of bureaucratic rationality that are believed to structure practices of governmentality of which policing is a key component, the police rely on ways of seeing that often rely on intuitive assessments of who is inside or outside the law. Similarly, in the family, an imbalance in the flow of information, suspicion, and trust may threaten to destabilize the traditional order. Even as the "Bengali" wife is seen as a threatening outsider to the state, she may be a desired wife or daughter-in-law within the family, her lack of familiarity being her biggest appeal. Traditional consanguineous marriages may at times jeopardize the delicate balance of information management: when cousins know too much, how do they maintain the balance of trust within the family? Information can be deployed within the family: here, the key fault lines are not necessarily between kin and nonkin or between "wife givers" and "wife takers," the key categories through which much of South Asian kinship has been understood, but through the management of generational cohorts and the use of lateral surveillance therein. The availability of the "Bengali" wife who is an "outsider" allows the family to circumvent the crisis of intimate knowledge attendant on marrying within the family while also saving face by not marrying a different (possibly lesser) local Muslim caste.

Chapters 3 and 4 also refute the currently dominant view that such long-distance marriage migrants represent a sociologically new form of marriage that is an instance of socially sanctioned nonendogamous, intercaste marriage among Hindus (Kaur 2012; Mishra 2013). Dealing with contemporary Indian Muslim marriage, family, and kinship—on which there is a huge gap in the existing literature on South Asia—these chapters suggest the need to situate what is regarded as a relatively "new" form of marriage practice within the local "field" of marriage, in this case consanguineous marriages. They examine how practices of policing that are attached to the detection of the "long-distance" bride by the state (which may be replicated by the anthropologist) may also exist within the order of the family. Different types of marriage and the forms of social practice that they engender (trust or its absence, surveillance, threats of detection, exposure) exist on a continuum rather than as opposites of each other.

Chapter 5 turns to migrant Hindu men from the west who—no less than the Bengali women from the east—have to work to belong locally. Although the men in this chapter are no strangers to the state (i.e., they are Hindu rather than Muslim), who welcomes them into the fold of the nation as always-already citizens. The police and local administration abet their border crossings regardless of their formal legality, often granting permission for entry and residence that are at odds with explicit official orders they have received. Even though, as "Hindus," these Pakistani men are welcomed into citizenship by a state eager to manage its border demographics, they do not always meet with a similarly effusive reception among the family for whom they remain strangers, regardless of being connected as kin through the maternal line. Despite state patronage, within social networks, the stigma of being "from Pakistan" or the corrosion of trust through suspicion of their being "traitors" (*desh drohi*), informers (*sources*), or "*double agents*" makes it much more difficult for these border crossers to be seamlessly accepted within the family or the wider society. Once again, the work of belonging involves a reconfiguration of traditional marriage patterns and the place of "honor" in reckoning political lineage.

To sum up, the book argues that family, marriage, and forms of reckoning kin involve modalities of policing that are not necessarily discontinuous from those that we are used to associating with the state, even though they do not necessarily spring from the same source and may not agree over the shared outcome of the moral and social order. Multiple forms of policing are not categorized as forms of regulation that are "state" or "nonstate"; this distinction is not a primary focus for the ethnography. Thus, I see this book not as an anthropology of the state but of policing practices. Threaded through the chapters are reminders that forms of identification used by the state—that often the social scientist is complicit in using—do not always tell us how political belonging at the level of the nation-state is translated into the microprocesses of everyday life: through negotiation, adjustment, compromise, and adaptation.

PART I

Landscapes of Policing

Chapter 1

Policing Everyday Life on a Border

In December 2015, the Indian Intelligence Bureau (IB) organized its annual conference on policing.[1] The occasion brought together directors general (DGs) and inspectors general (IGs) of police from across the country to Dhordo, a village in the Rann of Kutch, which runs along the India-Pakistan border and is situated in the western Indian state of Gujarat. The conference was an annual gathering to review internal security and police organizational matters. Usually held in the capital New Delhi, the newly elected prime minister and leader of the Hindu nationalist Bharatiya Janata Party (BJP), Narendra Modi, decided to shift the conference's location to more field-oriented sites. The first two conferences after he assumed office were thus organized in places that had a close proximity to national borders: in 2014, the northeastern city of Guwahati was chosen for "increasing the morale" of police forces serving in the politically and militarily sensitive northeast.[2] The following year, it was convened in the Rann of Kutch, on India's western border. Here, a vast tented space was erected on the salt-encrusted desert that stretches from Kutch into Sindh, called the white Rann after a successful advertising campaign emblazoned it onto the tourist map of the region. The prime minister was in attendance on all three days of the conference, a fact noted as exceptional in the extensive media coverage accorded to an event that seemed to draw more comment for its spectacular staging than its agenda. Local and national newspapers splashed images of the prime minister and home minister taking a walk in the Rann, doing yoga with conference participants, riding a camel safari, and watching the sun set over a pink-hued horizon, "adding," as one newspaper reported, "a touch of glamour and spirituality to an otherwise straitjacketed event" (Jha 2015). These officially released images were of the same genre and quality as photos on tourism brochures for the annual festival in the Rann—the *Rann Utsav* (Scroll .in 2020). Against this picturesque and strategic backdrop, the prime minister emphasized the importance of "sensitive" policing, reiterating that "sensitivity has to be vital element of policing. Police forces should establish strong links with local community and connect with people [*sic*]" (Jha 2015).

On the ground, preparations for this star-studded event had begun well in advance in a village just off the conference venue, some of whose residents already felt a deeply emotional connection with the prime minister. A month before the conference, Miyan Husain's home in the village of Dhordo was abuzz with activity; he was the chief liaison with the local administration and was overseeing a number of the preparations. Juggling two mobile phones as he fielded a stream of calls, he looked piercingly at me as he entered the room I was sharing with his sister Phupli and their niece Sofiya. We had been catching up on local news since my last visit. Looking at me intently as he tried to place me, he murmured, "I don't forget people" (*main logon ko nahin bhoolta*) but asked to be excused for his memory lapse this time due to his state of preoccupation. "You have a big event coming up," I said. "A very big [*bahut bada*] program," he concurred. Four hundred tents had to be erected to accommodate the "VIP visitors," and coordination was required with the IB to put in place an impregnable air-to-ground security blanket. Local dancers had to be vetted and trained to put up a cultural show for the prime minister. Above all, he was "one of them"—a fellow Gujarati, one-time chief minister of the state, and, as Miyan Husain and his family saw it, someone with whom they not only had a "direct line" of communication but also a deeply personal connection. Modi came to visit them in 2001, and since then, according to Husain, he has been more than responsive to every overture made by them.[3] In fact, the "development" of the Rann as a tourist destination is attributed by him to Modi's receptiveness to their ideas. "He went out of his way to put this little remote village squarely on India's map," even holding a special session of the state's legislative assembly there to highlight the symbolic importance of the site to the state, and now, by making it a venue for the annual police conference, he was cementing its place in the annals of the nation-state. Sofiya had said to me earlier, *hamare gaon ki dua se woh Dilli pahuche* (the collective blessings from our village sent him to Delhi [i.e., enabled his victory as prime minister]).[4] Miyan Husain's family in particular saw themselves as interpellated within the state's performance of sovereign power on this borderland. For a family of Muslim pastoralists on India's border with Pakistan, one might argue that they were always-already enmeshed within the discursive and military production of security by India in its borderlands. With every passing decade from the initial period of decolonization, India's citizenship and security regime has defined itself more and more clearly against the figure of the Muslim.

The Muslim is thus central to the Indian imagination of national security and citizenship even if only as the negative "other" that has to be purged in order to produce the "authentic" (by definition Hindu) citizen.[5] Although this has been true of successive elected governments, this research was conducted during a decade and a half that witnessed the singular and hegemonic ascent of the Hindu nationalist BJP to power in Gujarat (where the BJP has governed continuously since 2002) and subsequently at the center (2014 onward). The general elections of 2014 marked the nationalization of what came to be known as the Gujarat model authored by the then–chief minister and subsequently prime minister Narendra Modi. Although the "Gujarat model" was used by the BJP to advertise its so-called model of economic development in Gujarat, critics have used it to address the spread throughout India of a model of governance that has reduced minorities to second-class citizens, grounded in extrajudicial killings and the systematic disbanding of democratic institutions such as the legislature, courts, and media, leading to a concentration of power in the executive to levels unprecedented outside of the Emergency during 1975 (Newsclick 2019). The new prime minister also had a controversial track record as the chief minister of Gujarat, a state that had witnessed large-scale state-abetted violence against Muslims in 2002 and is regarded as the laboratory of Hindu nationalist politics (Spodek 2010). For borderland Muslims, alienation from and attachment to the state are both legitimately felt affective modes of relating by its citizens that do not preclude each other.[6] I read this not as a paradox or as a situational response but as part of an overall affective mode of relating with the state as an equal rather than as a subject of patronage alone. Subjection, desire, and surrender are all modes of engagement that states and citizens invoke with each other (Ali 2019). Although I often discussed the relationship of Muslims to the BJP in Gujarat during the 2000s, I never elicited a direct condemnation of the state from Miyan Husain. All he said was *"politics to kuchh aur cheez hai"* (politics is something else altogether). There is perhaps a recognition here that to be political entails potential contradictions in the determination of the social.

Miyan Husain was anxious that all preparations for the conference remained on track. Despite the burden of this significant responsibility, he seemed unfazed. "VIP" guests were no strangers to this village, and Miyan Husain's family was well equipped to handle them. Ever since my acquaintance with his sister Phupli and niece Sofiya from the early 2000s, I had become used to hearing of Dhordo referred to as "India's last village," their geostrategic location woven into the tourist-friendly narrative they produced for visiting guests. The Rann is a saline desert that does not support agricultural production. Habitation is sparse; village settlements consist of agnatically related Muslim pastoral communities living on a currently precarious grassland ecosystem known as Banni. Animal breeding and milk production is still the mainstay of Banni's *maldharis* (animal herders), all of whom are Muslim. The predominantly Muslim demographic profile of this border region has ensured that Banni remained highly visible within policy discussions on how best to police the border; significantly, one of the questions that occupied early postcolonial border management debates was how to generate "trust" within predominantly Muslim border residents in the aftermath of India's partition: these regions were now bordering Pakistan, an ostensible homeland for the Muslims of undivided India. Dhordo is the last of these pastoral settlements in Banni, located just before the international border. Like the rest of Banni, home to once-renowned pastures, Dhordo was also famous for its ghee (clarified butter), hand churned from thick milk collected from the distinctive horned buffaloes bred by the *maldharis* in Banni and across the border in Sindh. The opening up of the Rann as a tourist destination through the annual festival of the Rann organized by the Gujarat state tourism department with increasing success throughout the 2000s brought cinema stars, industrialists, and hordes of tourists primarily from other parts of Gujarat who are keen to participate in a kitschy mix of desert safari and border tourism (Nair 2016). Dhordo's location on the "nation's edge" is keenly reinforced by the state administration and its military-security apparatus, which uses the village as an important site for the performance of sovereignty in its borderlands, more spectacularly so in recent years.

Thus singled out for a conference organized by the IB on behalf of the Ministry of Home Affairs (MHA) to discuss matters pertaining to police, intelligence, and security reforms, not only was Dhordo's strategic and symbolic importance underscored, but it was also not the first time that this border had been the site for a discussion on policing. Although the theme of the 2015 conference was how to bring the police closer to the common people, the question of policing the borderlands was a strongly debated one within the state bureaucracy in the early years following decolonization and Partition. A key strand in this debate hinged on the issue of police professionalization and the extent to which it should be distant and professional or more closely connected with the local civilian population. In the following section, I present an overview of this debate as a way to begin to set out the ways in which we tend to think about "the police" as an institution of state and then "policing" as a more general form of social control. I then shift away from the statist optic of police as an agent of violent mob control or crime fighting to thinking more broadly of policing during times of peace. This also attempts to redefine borderland policing in terms of networks of sociality across a series of sites rather than as a preconstituted institution or arm of state.

Policing the Border, 1947–1949

Subsequent to the announcement of a formal partition of British India, new contours of border management were put in place in India. These were neither uniformly nor seamlessly iterated across newly constituted borderlands. In Kutch, two distinct views on border management emerged within the state department. Although one viewed border security in terms of the local custodianship of border residents, the other favored professionalization of border control by investing in men and materials from elsewhere, thus ensuring, it was believed, their impartiality vis-à-vis the local population.

S. R. Chaudhri, IG of police (Delhi and Ajmer-Merwara), was in favor of the former view. Barely a few months after the partition was announced in

1947, he toured the state of Kutch and submitted a set of recommendations on police reorganization for the newly constituted border region. He was quite categorical, noting that there was no need for the commission of a separate border police force. In his report on the reorganization of Kutch police dated February 2, 1949, he emphasized that the Rann was a useful geographical deterrent for "any raider from Pakistan area to visit any of the villages in Kutch State near the border *for purposes of loot only.*" Elaborating his belief that cross-border raids in the region would only be with a criminal intent, he added, "I was also told that the people on both sides of the border are *interrelated and are mostly Muslims*; so there can be *very little communal motive* behind a raid. There have been a few incidents near the border, but they related mostly to *the satisfaction of private grudges* against each other by the men from the other side. . . . It would not, therefore, be necessary to have a special police force for the purpose of protecting the border only" (emphases added).[7] Chaudhri proposed that existing police stations at border outposts were sufficient to tackle smuggling activities through known routes. In his reckoning, a community that was threaded through with ties of kinship—and by this he assumed relations of trust—at the local level would essentially police itself, protecting itself against (external) criminal threat. There would be no major cross-border incidents of the type that would threaten national security, Chaudhri reckoned. With a high degree of assumed social order and internal regulation—because all residents were mostly Muslims and interrelated due to consanguineous marriages—there was no need for external policing through the state in this view.

On the other hand, the commissioner of police in Kutch, H. R. Thakkar, had different ideas on police reorganization. Some months earlier, in a letter dated November 10, 1948, Thakkar had written to the chief commissioner, the highest administrative officer in Kutch, broaching the subject of police reorganization.[8] He was shocked during his inspection of the Bhuj police headquarters and city police station. The constables were shabbily turned out, he wrote; they "hardly appeared to have any rudimentary knowledge of drill." The social composition of the force was also a cause for concern. He observed, "A majority of the men are illiterate and Muslims," urging a firm overhaul in standards of recruitment. "Kutch," he added, "is more vulnerable to Pakistan activities, and therefore a strong, well-trained armed strength and intelligent L.I.B. [Local Intelligence Bureau] are fundamentally needed."[9] This letter contained a detailed proposal for the reconstitution of Kutch's police force, touching on almost all aspects of organization—dress, recruitment, training, housing, salary, mounted constabulary, and intelligence; it made a strong argument for the institution of village police, deeply embedded in local social networks. In contrast to the visiting IG of police's assessment, the police commissioner in Kutch was of the firm view that the border required specific attention from the security point of view. He wrote, "The Northern Boundary of Kutch faces Pakistan and intensified police patrolling is essential on this border." Acknowledging the increased vulnerability of Kutch to what he cryptically referred to as "Pakistan activities [*sic*]," he felt that "a strong mounted patrol on the border line is all the more necessary for security purposes."

These were the two views on border security and the proposed division of responsibility between civilian populations and the military-police complex in the maintenance of national security. The first point of view—held by Chaudhri—was that the absence of violence along this border in the wake of the partition—unlike in Punjab—was encouraging; cross-border kinship ties between Muslims in Kutch and Sindh would, in his view, continue to serve as a strong deterrent for violence. In other words, there was no need for an external provision of border security because it was assumed that the local community was a harmonious one owing to their being related to each other. The second view—represented by Commissioner of Police Thakkar's insistent letters to the chief commissioner of Kutch—argued that national security was far too important to be left to local residents, all the more so if they were Muslims on the border with Pakistan, therefore with suspect national loyalties. Thakkar proposed a plan for the professionalization of the police force in Kutch, noting that at the time, such was the pitiful condition of so-called policemen that there were certain border outposts where there was practically no distinction to be made between policemen and local villagers. He underscored the fact that existing "policemen" had "no arms, no uniforms, no sanads . . . nothing with them to show that they are policemen."[10] They had no training and were unaware of police duties. "They are," stated the disgruntled police commissioner, "simply local people told that they are policemen to check smuggling, etc. They draw their pay and work according to their own sweet-will [*sic*] with practically no supervision or check."[11] Thus, professionalization and an upgrade of police infrastructure in the borderlands was of utmost priority from the point of view of national security.

These two early views on policing the border may be taken to be the general framework within which the state understood border policing in the immediate aftermath of Partition—the role of the police force in the containment of violence, the necessity for professionalization, modernization of its materials, and its strict demarcation from the local population. Eventually, the second model, professionalization, predominated. In this ethnographic study of border policing, I focus on a key question that this debate does not address—who or what is the police? Although the state is focused on the significance of guns and uniforms and the overall context of violence (or its absence) in the constitution of effective policing, the sections that follow indicate that policing is perhaps more effectively constituted through networks of sociality that devolve on the control and flow of information during times of "peace," not all of which are confined to the institution of the police as an arm of state alone but on social networks that circulate more ubiquitously in this borderland society. These networks of sociality undermine a strict distinction between state and society, police and policed, and (especially in this context) underscore the position of the borderland Muslim as the subject *as well as* agent of suspicion.

Civil-Military Interactions

As we saw in the case of Miyan Husain and his family, there are complicated ways in which the lives of border dwellers intersect with those who are officially charged with border maintenance. In other words, it is difficult to constitute the authority of the civil police or the military independently of the more locally embedded forms of sovereignty that exist adjacent rather than supra- or subordinate to them. Policing emerges as a collaborative enterprise that brings state officials—those in and out of uniform—into various kinds of mutually reinforcing relationships with those who are technically "outside" the military-police apparatus and indeed who may belong to those very categories that are regarded with a more or less permanent suspicion— as Muslims are on this border. Suspicion and surveillance are forms of practice that are just as often deployed by the state in its management of populations as they are used the other way around or laterally between groups of people. The sovereign power of the state, when it encounters its counterpart in Banni, must learn to coexist with it in some form of arrangement; its aspiration to totalizing power must be set aside.[12]

Miyan Husain, who was busily arranging for the police conference when I visited him in 2015, was heir to a sovereign power that did not derive from the state. Recall that his niece Sofiya indicated to me that it was the prayers (*dua*) of their village that cemented the political fortunes of the prime minister, as he was able to graduate from head of a provincial government to the highest elected position in the land. The implication is that the sovereign power of the state is here dependent on the prayers and goodwill of Gulbeg's sovereignty. Gulbeg, colloquially referred to as *sarhad na santri*—guardian of the border—was the de facto sovereign of all of Banni's pastoral populations, cutting across their own *jati* and agnatic ties.[13] As a charismatic figure, his de facto "control" over Banni's *maldharis* was rarely questioned in public, even if there were privately expressed reservations about his means and motivations. Gulbeg's family has always held the *sarpanch* (headman) position for the group of villages that came under its jurisdiction. "We never have elections," said one of his relatives who prefers to remain unnamed. "A meeting is held in the *otlo* [the public guest-receiving room] and the headman is decided. While Gulbeg was alive, he made the decisions. The year the position was reserved for a woman candidate, his daughter Phupli became *sarpanch*." During the time of my field visits, the position was occupied by Miyan Husain. Gulbeg is recalled as someone who made his own rules and defied opposition from among his kinsmen and kinswomen. Whether he was their friend or enemy, Gulbeg was no doubt a force to reckon with. Betrothed in his youth to his first cousin in the village (his mother's sister's daughter), legend has it that he fell in love with a woman from a neighboring settlement. He "abducted" her and brought her home (*uthha kar shadi kar li*, literally "picked her up and married her"), a known form of marriage in earlier times. The abduction and marriage were an open declaration of hostility by Gulbeg on his neighbors whose honor and pride were deeply insulted. They lodged a "case" against Gulbeg with their learned relatives, and an Islamic scholar—a man from the same community as the warring parties but from a neutral village—came to adjudicate. The bride was shielded behind a curtain and asked her views on the matter; she relayed her consent to being Gulbeg's wife. The "case" was resolved; the social feud continued for two generations during which no marriages were conducted between the warring villages. Eventually, even these ties were restored. However, it was not just the *maldharis* and their women over whom Gulbeg's authority extended. It was suggested in Bhuj, the district headquarters, that not a single file moved in the district collector's office without Gulbeg's assent.[14] When I visited Dhordo for the first time in 2002, Gulbeg had passed on, but he still lived on larger than life by way of the influence he clearly wielded in the corridors of power. As the one-time leader or chief (*agewan*) of Banni's *maldharis*, he was a liaison between Banni and the state, a mantle that has passed now to his son, Miyan Husain. Middle-class residents of Bhuj called him a "smuggler" and "informer," part of the "public secret" of law enforcement on the border that allowed state officials to patronize him, but this does not credit him as a sovereign power in his own right. As I argue here, Gulbeg's sovereign power did not accrue from his proximity to the state; indeed, it often appeared as though the state derived legitimacy through its proximity with Gulbeg. His family recalled that he worked for the state in an *honorary* capacity, commanding the armed forces in the India-Pakistan war of 1971 but not taking a salary for it. Gulbeg clearly did not see himself as merged within the military-security or policing apparatus of the state, but I would suggest that he is not entirely a "semiautonomous" zone of local sovereign power that remains uncolonized by the state (Hansen and Stepputat 2005).

The figure of Gulbeg allows us to formulate what the concept of an *adjacent sovereignty* might look like, the terms of which may be clarified through the following examples. Gulbeg's sovereignty is not quite the exception or margin within state law, as documented, for instance, by Deborah Poole (2004) in the figure of the Peruvian *gamonal* or the strongman in other parts of India (Hansen 2005). In many ways, the figure of the *gamonal* is evocative of Gulbeg: "A highly personalized form of local power whose authority is grounded in nearly equal measure in his control of local economic resources, political access to the state, willingness to use violence, and the symbolic capital provided by his association with such important icons of masculinity as livestock, horses, and a regional bohemian aesthetic" (Poole 2004, 43). Yet, Poole's rendition of the *gamonal* is a figure who is a representative of *both* the state—as "magistrate, police officer, and jailer" (44)—and "extrajudicial, and even criminal power that the state purportedly seeks to displace through law, citizenship, and public administration" (43–44). The *gamonal* represents that form of primitive control that the state has not entirely suppressed, that lies within it. Gulbeg, on the other hand, is *not* a representative of the state, but he is essential to the state's claim to sovereignty in its borderlands.

In adjacent forms of sovereignty, the state does not garner for itself a priority of form. In other words, it is not evident from Gulbeg's example that it is the state that provides a model of practice, such as writing, that other forms of sovereign power emulate or mimic.[15] Even as the state was doubtless keeping a close watch on Gulbeg, even deploying his assets—both material and symbolic—within the larger *maldhari* network in Banni as it sought to garner their "trust," it was clear that he kept an eye back on the state and its allies as he meticulously documented every discussion and visit to him by tourists, police and security officers, and other officials. Records of visiting officials from the police, army, and the local administration are maintained in diaries and visitor's books that run into volumes. They are kept locked in a steel wardrobe, the key in Miyan Husain's safe custody. The visual archive is easier to access: photographs are carefully pasted into albums or framed and adorned on the walls of the main entrance to Dhordo, in the *mehman khano* (room for receiving guests). In almost all these photographs, except for the most recent additions to the collection, when Miyan Husain assumes center stage, Gulbeg is in focus. He cuts a charismatic picture: posing sometimes in the jeep he bought at a military auction and then refurbished, posing other times with a rifle, a dramatic figure in the midst of the Rann; in yet other photographs, he is flanked by one or another official from the police or army. There are photographs of visiting officials in and out of uniform dining at his home with their families and one black-and-white photograph where Gulbeg is pictured attending a meeting with state dignitaries, including the prime minister, in Bhuj in the aftermath of the 1971 war with Pakistan.

The photographs also speak eloquently of a masculine affinity between Gulbeg and his guests as they went riding into the Rann on horseback, binoculars and guns in hand, on joint hunting (*shikar*) excursions, the "rituals of virility" that often mark the relationship of informers with officials (Glaeser 2011, 288). Here, however, the symbolic markers of sovereign police and military power in the borderlands—weapons, uniforms, and vehicles—bleed into each other. When officials visit Gulbeg and are photographed with him, with a few exceptions, they are not wearing uniform. The forms of interaction between Gulbeg and his guests make it clear that it is Gulbeg as host who scripts the interaction. The guests, regardless of their rank or status in the military-bureaucratic apparatus, for the greater part leave their uniforms and insignias of status behind, dining with their families, ostensibly as mere guests, in civil clothing. In the wide expanse of this desert, it is Gulbeg who is king. He knows every nook and cranny of the lay of the land, where camels can safely cross the border avoiding the sticky wetland sections of the Rann (*daldal*). This knowledge is honed through generations of living a pastoral life and updated through his frequent sojourns across Banni. His jeep— having once been a military jeep—is also indistinguishable in these parts from stately signs of authority, even though he has personalized it to suit his own needs. The members of the military-bureaucratic elite come from New Delhi and belong to different parts of the country; they must familiarize themselves with this terrain in order to effectively police it.

Gulbeg dined his visitors sumptuously at his home. The written entries in a series of visitor's books unanimously bear testimony to Gulbeg's hospitality, what those who remember him today refer to as an unstinting and generous *mehman nawazi* (hospitality). In these books, which contain valuable insights into the sociology, ecology, and politics of Banni during Gulbeg's lifetime, visiting experts in the fields of wildlife, fodder development, animal husbandry, dairy development, and tourism all commented on his finely honed knowledge of the area and also his hospitality. Gulbeg's generosity was received warmly by guests, who were nevertheless reminded of the strategic importance of his location. In 1975, a flight lieutenant of the Indian Air Force stationed at Bhuj visited Dhordo and wrote of his visit: "It's better to stay with people of [*sic*] such a large heart. They would come forward to help at any time and no matter what difficult situation they are in."[16]

It is in this spirit that Gulbeg was visited so continuously by a stream of guests. Although his charisma was doubtless part of the connections he made seemingly so effortlessly with a succession of officers posted to the region, they were aware of what Gulbeg had to offer the military-security complex of the state in return. Indeed, it was Gulbeg who oriented each successive set of officers to the local issues and suggestions for how to develop the area in a way that would be of mutual benefit to both the *maldharis*—in terms of the ecological governance of Banni and its human and animal population— and the state's security concerns. In this respect, he inverted the role of the "expert," imparting his own expertise to the technocrats of the state, who needed Gulbeg's guidance to navigate the terrain. A regular stream of dairy development officers visited from other parts of India and came away impressed by Gulbeg's knowledge about bovine breeds and the finer aspects of milk production. Dairy development was seen not only as a form of revenue generation but also as a form of surveillance and to cultivate loyal border subjects, integrated into the mainstream of the national economy.

Securitization, Surveillance, and Development

Documents in the state's archives indicate a growing mistrust of Muslims in India from the 1950s and discuss the imperatives of earning their "trust," a corollary of securing their loyalty.[17] In more contemporary times, the development of tourism is an important component of the Border Area Development Program (BADP) in Kutch, just as the development of industries in the Rann is also a part of the overall project of surveillance through development.[18] Notwithstanding the fact that work and labor were seen as central to controlling and pacifying the border, from the perspective of Dhordo's residents, all the development projects in the Rann—tourism and industry—are rescripted as miracles and prophecies set in motion through Gulbeg's charisma and foresight rather than an imposition from the state administration. Bromine mining in the Rann is a source of income for many in Dhordo as they are employed as managers in the single factory complex a stone's throw from the village.

The industrial plant is almost at the border and painted with military camouflage colors. Although technical staff come from outside, local people (mainly from Dhordo, a source of some resentment in other villages) are employed in small managerial capacities and as contract labor. Setting up the plant involved collaborating with the central government and the army, which controls this section of the Rann. The manager stressed that employment of locals has paid dividends, as earlier "there was a lot of cross-border activity which has gone down." Similarly, women's work of embroidering textiles at home was pitched by nongovernmental organizations (NGOs) as an important service to the nation. "We work in so many villages, most of them border ones," asserted a senior manager of a large organization that has been working with women in Dhordo for decades. He continued, "We need this, otherwise Kutch will become another Kashmir," a reference to Islamic militancy and the movement for Kashmiri independence.

In Dhordo, on the other hand, the rationale for the industry is reconfigured around the person of Gulbeg. His son Miyan Husain recounts the story: "As far back as 1979, my father said to the *sarkar* [government], 'Next year, you won't find us in Dhordo anymore.' He was right; the saltwater [*kharo pani*] from the Rann was steadily encroaching onto the village settlement. That's when he persuaded the *sarkar* to build a bund and to test the water. They found it was full of mineral deposits. This was how the idea came about to manufacture bromine in the Rann; it was basically my father's idea." Similarly, the idea of promoting the Rann with cultural festivals and tourism is attributed by his descendants to Gulbeg himself. On February 29, 1992, an entry in Gulbeg's visitor's book notes that a delegation of thirty-one members of the Gandhidham Chamber of Commerce and Industry visited Dhordo as part of an itinerary to the neighboring locations of Khawda and Karo Dungar (the famous "black hill" of Kutch) on the occasion of the "First Rann Festival of Kutch" and commended the work of the state and central governments' "step to bring Kutch on the map of tourism for the foreigners and local inhabitants of India who has [*sic*] a poor opinion about Kutch."[19] Miyan Husain talks of how, in a bid to continue his father's legacy in Banni, he has succeeded in getting the state to provide a national highway, a secondary school, electricity connections, an ATM, and even a helicopter joyride for the children of his village—all through constant negotiation with the state. Although these bring "development" to the village, they are couched in the language of mutual benefit for both sides. *"Baccha rota nahin to ma doodh bhi nahin deti"* (even a mother does not give a child milk unless he cries for it) is Miyan Husain's pithy justification for his constant demands on the state. In this case, the state is only too eager to provide because it enables them to share in the sovereign power of Gulbeg and his family.

Yet these additions to everyday life—the gift of "development"—on a border village are not applauded by everyone. What happens to the seat of sovereign power in Banni, Gulbeg's home, when it is overexposed to public gaze? Phupli's (Gulbeg's daughter) open distaste for the constant stream of visitors who flock to Dhordo as a result of the new tourist promotion brochures comes up often in her conversations. Not only was Gulbeg's *control* unchallenged, but there were also the "God-given" (*Allah-diney*) bounties of the land. "Banni was like a mother's womb [*ma ka pet*]; our children could roam free in the Rann; that's how secure it was. Now we have to be careful of whom we let into our houses; it's not the same at all," she emphasizes. Phupli was groomed by Gulbeg to receive the unending stream of "VIP guests," making sure everyone was comfortable when guests came and stayed the night, which was usual in the days when it took the better part of a day to drive from Bhuj to Dhordo. She made lasting friendships with many of the women and became for some "the face of Kutch" (Shah 2013, 14). Phupli gives us a sense today of how to manage the degree to which one may wish to make oneself transparent to a world that is pressing in more and more forcefully, allowing a careful calibration of the relationship between the physical margin (emphasized when Dhordo is referred to as the "nation's *last* village") and its centrality to Banni's sovereignty. She clarifies that because of her father, they were always networked into circuits of sociality with the policing function of the state. Yet, surveillance was at least a two-way affair, if not more dispersed as I have suggested, with Gulbeg's keeping an eye on the administration as sustained as the other way around. In present times, the neoliberal state has packaged every available piece of land into a tourist extravaganza. Border tourism is a useful way to generate revenue as well as to keep an eye on sensitive subjects. However, Phupli is not so happy with the addition of new forms of surveillance and the feeling that she is now expected to be transparent as fish in a bowl (being in a zoo is how she put it).

"So much has changed and nothing has changed," she sighed on a hot summer morning, lowering herself onto a bright patchwork quilt on the floor on which I was sitting with a cup of steaming tea. "Wait, I will send for another cup for you; this tea is so hot you will scald your mouth," she announced. In seconds, one of the young women huddled in the kitchen is summoned with a clean white cup, daintily patterned with pink roses sitting on a matching saucer. I am directed to pour half of the piping hot brew from the full cup into it. Phupli is well respected as an elder aunt and grandmother; she enjoys the status her fame and renown has brought her, and today she can exercise some degree of *control* over the younger women of her extended family.[20] She was also Gulbeg's favorite child, always with him when he received his "VIP guests," and this allowed her to cultivate her own status and following. She is still striking looking with a tall strapping physique. "I am strong," she told me one time with a twinkle in her eyes. "I gave birth to twelve children of whom nine lived. Nowadays, girls are like waifs [*doobli-patli*]; they don't eat, and they are unable to bear the loads we did in our day." Nonetheless, she has taken many young girls from other villages in Banni under her wing, training them in the technique of *bharat* (embroidery) that once earned her so many accolades. Now she has *retired*, her own term for this new phase of her professional life when she sits back and watches the winds of change wash up at her village. Phupli learned how to interact with visitors at her father's knee; there is a practiced ease to the manner in which she plays hostess. However, she has been quick to remind me that she has no interest in meeting the random assortment of people who land up at their doorstep nowadays. On another occasion when she and I sat together in the calm hum of the mid-morning, everybody busy at work, she expressed sudden anger with the constant attention they received. *"Aakho Hindustan tooti pyo ai"* (the entire country has burst in upon us), she exclaimed dramatically throwing up her hands, her black head covering sliding to the floor, eyes flashing in indignation. "The *rann utsav* has brought all sorts of people; some are good and some are bad. I only come out to meet old acquaintances of my father's and other old-timers. I am not interested in displaying myself like an animal in a zoo [*chidiyaghar*]!"

The day we discussed change, turning back to my cup of tea she had remarked, "Look" (*dekho*), gesturing to the now-empty cups of tea next to me; I had admired the delicate design on the cup. "People are often surprised to see Chinese [foreign] things here; I say, what's new? We have always had foreign goods in our village. It was because of my father and the links he had with the outside. There was constant coming-and-going—*aana-jaana.*" Returning to her opening comment, she reiterated, "Yes, things have changed, too. Earlier, we did not always have two meals a day; if there was *rotla* [bread] in the morning, then perhaps there was none in the evening. If there was plenty for the night, then there may not have been a meal for the next morning. Now we have plenty to eat, and that is no small thing. But there are other things to be wary of as well . . . too many people, too much unrestricted coming and going. Not like when *Baba* [Father] was alive. . . ." she trails off, emphasizing not for the first time the one quality of Gulbeg that is most often recalled today—*"control."* The presence of "Chinese" or foreign goods from a time before roads, satellite television, and mobile phones becomes, for Phupli, a measure of modernity and connection with the "outside" even as visitors who have traveled on a long and arduous journey to this seemingly forgotten border outpost are "surprised" to see things that, to them, are evocative of the more cosmopolitan spaces they have come from.[21]

As reiterated by Phupli, *control* is also about retaining some element of agency in how to engage with others, determining constantly who is to be let in and when, rather than the present time when hordes of tourists threaten to challenge her carefully maintained sense of home and the world, inside and outside, testing her family's hospitality to the extreme. *Control* allows for a strategic management between watching and being watched. Although Gulbeg observed the observers, crafting his own narrative, the sudden explosion of tourism, its democratization, as it were, for the new hordes, not the carefully handpicked elite of the officer cadre or foreign visitors interested in learning about textiles, but the vast masses from across the country, fills Phupli with distaste. She does not want to be rendered transparent (like animals in a zoo); thus, she returns to the idea of *control*, which allows her to maintain these boundaries between the work of observing and being observed. Gulbeg's famed hospitality incorporates a relationship between hosts and guests that is a complex mix of pragmatism and virtue; as Magnus Marsden (2012) reminds us, hospitality may be tinged with ambiguity, even hostility.

On his part, Gulbeg maintained meticulous records of official visits to him that were nevertheless often made in a playful, "personal" vein—including wives and children, out of uniform, even to go on hunting or shooting trips. His visitor's book recorded everyone, regardless of what brought them to his home. Miyan Husain was persuaded to share some of his father's papers with me, although I have no doubt that I have only scratched the surface of this fascinating archive constituted by books, photographs, and stacks of paperwork: letters, visitor's books and personal diaries, together providing an invaluable record of Banni and its *maldharis*, as well as a very material archive that has kept an assiduous, even intimate, track of the state and its functionaries, ironically by a largely nonliterate population. Although it is clear that Gulbeg was a valuable resource to the administration, whether we call him an informer, or a coproducer of borderland security (as is implied in his appellation *sarhad na santri*), Gulbeg kept an eye on the administration, too. His personal diary records sundry details of his day-to-day life in an amateur Gujarati script: of marriages attended, cricket scores, lyrics of Hindi film songs, and routine household expenditure on staples such as wheat, rice, and sugar. It also records a trip made by bus into Bhuj where he met with the district collector. This entry, made on April 27, 1963, mentions his traveling by bus to Bhuj to see the collector and records his dinner with the police commissioner in the official state guesthouse, an honor usually reserved for official guests. The following day at 9:00 a.m., Gulbeg had an appointment with the collector. These notations indicate that Gulbeg was received as an equal, on par with the most senior government functionary. This is what suggests that the nature of his sovereign power was adjacent to, rather than nested or graded within, state sovereignty.

Gulbeg had an affective relationship with the military that thrived on a shared masculine ethos of friendship, camaraderie, and adventure. His hunting and shooting expeditions across the wide expanses of the Rann of Kutch, accompanied by senior police and army officers, could be read as a way in which to anchor the local deployment of state power in his person: the person who was also—as a Muslim man on the border—the recipient of the state's surveillance. On the other hand, I contend that the relationship is a more complicated one where the direction of control and suspicion are not always easy to detect. Surveillance and information flows are not a one-way deployment from the state or the military alone but are managed and negotiated across the so-called civil-military terrain whose contours are therefore only murkily distinguishable (Lutz 2001). The relationship between Gulbeg and his officer acquaintances may have more than a passing shade of similarity with the relationship we, as anthropologists, cultivate with our research subjects. The latter have at their disposal information that is valuable for the anthropologist, just as Gulbeg no doubt had for his contacts in the police and security infrastructure of the state; the question is, how is this information trafficked and negotiated by them to yield social capital vis-à-vis each other but also relative to other networks of sociality? It is not enough to read the figure of Gulbeg as an informant to the state; the category of informer maintains intact a network of patronage that infuses the state with a primary form of power that it bestows on those it needs to cultivate for its own purposes. Instead, what if Gulbeg has the space to decide how to use his sovereign power, where he is located in a field of information management and surveillance that also allows him to leverage his own family's status relative not only to the state but also vis-à-vis other Muslims in Banni? This also allows one to decenter the trope of patronage in the way in which state-society relations are frequently understood in South Asia.[22]

Policing, Subjectivity, and Intimacy

Although police deployment and militarization are often justified by states as means of securing their own sovereign power and for the production and maintenance of security, they are often central to the way in which order-disorder and security-insecurity are experienced as forms of everyday life by those in the vicinity of policing. Police and military presence may be experienced as reassuring, as is the case with the retired Hindu schoolteacher we will meet in chapter 2, who reposed faith in the sound of daily military air drills, but it may also compound a sense of insecurity and suspicion among peers, especially in the context of a borderland society already saturated with the deployment of various kinds of intelligence agents, producing what Nosheen Ali (2019) has described in the context of northern Pakistan as "suspicious subjects." She underscores that suspicion is not an innate pathology of people but a direct consequence of their subject formation within the context of militarization. Suspicion, she argues, is "integral to the emotional structure of state power" (Ali 2019, 9). The question here is, does this kind of subject formation enable intimacy within subjects so designated, or is it in the very nature of suspicion that it is inimical to intimacy for it precludes trust? Those who are subjected to policing do not necessarily create community just because they are policed by the same agents. In a nutshell, my argument is this: we know that Muslims occupy a particular place in India's citizenship and security regime. The existence of Muslim-majority Pakistan, carved out of British India on the eve of Independence, ostensibly as a homeland for India's Muslims (nevertheless one that many of India's Muslims chose *not* to relocate to) is the stick that Indian Muslims (and other dissenters) are beaten with every time their "patriotism" is found lacking. If, following Giorgio Agamben, Muslims are the "bare life" against which a totalizing sovereign state produces itself, we need to ask what forms of life does it facilitate among those who are thus produced? Does the fact that Muslims on the borderland are the expendable *Homo sacer* of India's democracy lead to the annihilation of life, or in fact, does it actually allow for other forms of life to flourish? I suggest that even though they are read by the state as "Muslims," therefore "bare life," this appellation does not necessarily produce intimacy or coherence within the Muslims of this borderland. But this does not mean a denial of life either; forms of policing by the state do not lead only to collaboration or resistance to the state. How do borderland Muslims respond to surveillance by the state? Well, they engage in surveillance of their own. In fact, the Muslim citizen on the border is part of a variety of policing practices that s/he deploys vis-à-vis the state but equally vis-à-vis *each other*, breaking apart the coherence of the catch-all category of "Muslim." "The Muslim" as a demographic category that is produced and disseminated

by the state and its agencies in fact ceases in that moment to exist. This also
allows me to reclaim for the Muslim citizen of India's borderlands some
measure of agency as s/he is part of his/her own sovereign forms of policing
that take place within the family or the *maslak* and are not always and only
directed with or against the state.

Forms of policing that are embodied in agencies of state, such as the police, army, paramilitary forces, and intelligence services, mirror forms of policing as they play out in the domain of the family and networks of kin and
community. I do not speculate on which is logically prior to the latter but
instead gesture to connections between the two realms to broaden the scope
of what we understand policing to be—that is, to delink its associations as a
form of state action alone.

Although one view in the state department—as shown through excerpts
from some of the debates in the 1940s—believed that a common religious
identity would be a deterrent to violent social disorder in the aftermath of
Partition—assuming therefore that all Muslims would find intimacy with
each other in a homogenous religiously defined identity—I found during my
stay in Kutch that this was far from the case. In fact, the very identifier "*Mussalman*" (Muslim) was hotly debated in Banni. The Muslim male was, without a doubt, the subject of a heightened suspicion by non-Muslims and the
Indian state during the entire duration of this research. This will be illustrated in subsequent chapters. This did not produce intimacy within those
thus produced. Relationships between borderland Muslims were often structured by a deep suspicion, even hostility. This came through most starkly
with respect to *maslak* (sect) affiliation. In chapter 3, Hasham introspects on
what it means to be called a Muslim: "We think growing a beard makes us
Mussalman," he says, concluding that they are not really Muslims at all because
they do not follow what is generally recognized as good Islamic practice
"from the heart" and do not follow Koranic injunction strictly. This is a sharp
contrast to the state's view of its border populations, whose identities are read
primarily—as archival documents indicate—as a homogenous category of
Muslims. Whether this homogeneity was seen as a positive factor promoting social order (Chaudhri writing, "people on both sides of the border are
interrelated and are mostly Muslims; so there can be very little communal
motive behind a raid") or a deterrent to national security (Thakkar's concern that "a majority of the men are illiterate and Muslims"), it did not account for the multiple ways in which these border populations negotiated

their identities vis-à-vis each other, notwithstanding their being lumped together as one category by the state, development agencies, or even the anthropologist.

In the early 2000s, when I had first begun my fieldwork in Kutch, Muslims in Gujarat were scarred and disillusioned with the state. The pogrom against Muslims had taken place in February and March 2002, and the aftermaths were felt over the course of the decade and beyond. In 2002–2003, many Muslims—particularly in the cities of central and southern Gujarat and its commercial and cultural hubs such as Ahmedabad and Vadodara—still lived in refugee camps. Hundreds had been burned or hacked to death, women raped and maimed (Ghassem-Fachandi 2012). Although Kutch had not witnessed this kind of violence firsthand, people were keenly attuned to the events farther east. Muslim men in the border villages that formed my fieldsite, who were my earliest informants (I was able to access women only much later), often spoke to me of the "war" (*jung*) against Muslims that they felt was unleashed by the state. Some of them admitted that they could be candid with me because I was "one of them." This assumed proximity—of religious affiliation, even though I was vastly separated from them in terms of class—which was something that enabled me to be "trustworthy" even though they knew very little about me when I first entered their lives. I remained keenly aware of this dynamic. It was not uncommon for me to be "warned" about the ways in which the state and its intelligence networks operated. An older Muslim man, for instance, said to me on my very first meeting with him as a PhD researcher when I told him my name, "So you are a Muslim. Then I will be direct with you [*ek cheez bolta hoon, apke mooh par*]. Often when we sit and talk among ourselves, these things come up for discussion and I will share them with you. When you go to border villages, there will be an IB [Intelligence Bureau] man following you just as there is with us. You will do a study on the Jatts [a Muslim group in Kutch], and they will do a study on you," he warned me. Yet, this acknowledged targeting by the state did not produce a shared sense of community among them in any de facto way, and this is important for it allows us to acknowledge that the tracks along which trust and suspicion flow are not always predetermined.

Although I was taken into confidence by most Muslims I met—even if only for the sake of appearance—who nevertheless paid scant attention to the details of my biography or practice of religion, I found that there was much discord and suspicion among Muslims in Kutch. Much of this had to do with *maslak* or sect affiliation between those who adhered to the (in this context) reformist Ahl-e-Hadis and the more traditional Ahl-e-Sunnat wal Jama'at. I have discussed this in detail in earlier writing (Ibrahim 2009; also see Simpson 2008). Nizam was the one person I got to know in the field who made no secret of his suspicion vis-à-vis me. Our encounters always left me slightly uneasy, often trapped, and with the distinct impression that he was testing me with trick questions, trying to trip me up in one or another way. I always got the feeling that I did not quite pass his tests. I first met him during the summer of 2001, on a brief preliminary visit to the field. He was the *maulana* (religious teacher) at the madrassa in the village of Sonapar, which became a key research site for me the following year. I remembered him as a shy young man, sharply turned out in a crisp white kurta pajama, a stark contrast to the squalid surroundings. My fieldnotes for the day recorded this meeting along with the observation that the NGO group that had accompanied me on this visit had spoken highly of his efforts to educate the children of the area. A year later, I was back to begin my dissertation fieldwork in the village and asked after him. There was what I felt was a somewhat long pause after which I was told that he had been dismissed from his job and was probably back in his home village in Banni. Surprised, I pressed for more information on why he had been dismissed but was only told that he had not been found to be "suitable" (*barabar nahin laga*). "Did you have some work with him?" I was asked. Intuitively, sensing an undercurrent, I found myself responding vaguely: "Well, no, not really. Now that he's left, perhaps I will not need to look him up after all."

My second meeting with Nizam was many months after this. I had set out with Mohamed Hosain to look him up in the village that we had been told he was from. He was now teaching at the madrassa there and he lived next to it, a few kilometers away from the main village settlement. I could not recognize him as the man I had met a couple of years ago. At first, he said we had not met before, but on some prompting, he said he remembered our meeting. I tell him I am interested in the state of education, or the lack of it, in Sonapar, and as a former *maulana*, what did he think? I say by way of an icebreaker that I had discussed this with others of the community in Bhuj, and he gave me a couple of anecdotes that described the state of affairs as he saw them in Sonapar. Much of their illiteracy, he felt, was a result of their "un-Islamic" ways. As a follower of the Ahl-e-Hadis *maslak*, he had tried to stop them from visiting the tombs of saints. I thought this was likely a cause of friction that led to his eventual dismissal. Before leaving, I asked if I could photograph him. He did not respond to say either yes or no. When I took out my camera, he declined politely: "Perhaps some other time." On the way back to Bhuj, I mentioned to Mohamed Hosain, my research assistant, that Nizam had struck me as far shiftier than when I had first met him in Sonapar. I thought part of this was his discomfort at being tracked down—as he was seeing us off, he had asked me, "What exactly did you say to people in Bhuj?" I assured him that I had not said anything about him, just a general conversation about the state of education among Muslims. I could not shake off the slightly suspicious vibe that I felt from him, but I did not want to be overly paranoid about this. When I asked him why he left Sonapar given that he was clearly doing good work there, he said he wanted to return home after the earthquake. Mohamed Hosain did not share my discomfort with the interaction; his explanation for Nizam's altered demeanor was far more prosaic. "In Sonapar, he lived with people all around him. Look at the loneliness here in Banni: the harsh terrain, only animals around you. How do people pass their time here? One would lose one's mind," he added, shaking his head.

Even though we had exchanged phone numbers, I was surprised to receive a call from Nizam some weeks after this meeting. He happened to be in Bhuj, he said, and wanted to meet me. Mohamed Hosain was not free, so I invited Nizam over to my apartment for tea. I made us a cup of tea each, and we settled down on a cotton rug on the floor, facing each other. His first question to me, without preamble was, "Which *maslak* do you belong to?" As I tried to dodge the question as best I could, he proceeded to make a number of insider jokes about *maslak* practices that I did not catch. As I became increasingly uncomfortable, wishing Mohamed Hosain had been around to help steer the conversation, I tried to indicate that we were on the same side as far as *maslaks* were concerned. Whether or not he believed me, after this I found Nizam more forthcoming. He talked about his childhood and upbringing. Spontaneously, he brought up a number of topics that I had wondered about but had not been sure how to broach. He told me that he was invited to teach at the madrassa in Sonapar. He had not wanted to at first, but then he agreed to go. "Everyone there used to go to *dargahs*, they used to all indulge in *shirk* [non-Muslim ways—that is, they were not Ahl-e-Hadis]." He said it was his hard work for the two and a half years that he taught at the madrassa that "converted" them to "the right path" (*sahi rasta*) and they became Ahl-e-Hadis. In his telling, elderly women looked around them surreptitiously to see if he was in sight and try to sneak off to the *dargah*, such was the fear he inspired. Soon, all of these *jahil* (un-Islamic) activities stopped. He ensured that the mosque was completely filled up.[23] Then he went on, and I was surprised to hear him say, "I felt really bad the other day when you came to visit me that I was not more forthcoming. After you left, I realized what an important thing you had said, that along with religious education, people also need secular education in order to progress. I feel grateful for you to have come and made me see this fact. I am a teacher and I ought to take more responsibility to this effect."

I was quite taken aback by Nizam's volte-face, as it were. From this point onward, he became very interested in my research, calling me regularly for updates, wanting to drop by my apartment if he happened to be in Bhuj. He arranged for me to meet his father who was a poet and was interested in the history of his people. Despite Nizam's keen interest and cooperative attitude, I could never quite shake off either my early suspicions or my guilt at having earned his trust by letting him believe I was a believer in a particular *maslak* when it was a nonissue for me. I was never quite certain that I knew why he was being as helpful as he was. He always seemed to know whom I had gone to meet and of events where I had been spotted by (he claimed) someone he knew. On one occasion, an older woman in Sonapar told me that he had indicated that I might approach her ("You know the young man [*chokro*] who used to be the *maulana* at our village? He had come to the house and told us that you would be coming round"), even though he had said to me that after his dismissal, he never set foot in Sonapar. On another occasion, Nizam was concerned that because he had not heard from me in a while, I might have been "brainwashed" by others and therefore no longer interested in his father's version of their history. He was at pains to stress that others would mislead me and that he and his father should be my sole informants. But if I was conscious of being potentially manipulated by Nizam for his own purposes, it is no less true that I also policed our interactions to conform to a certain public persona that I had crafted for myself as an anthropologist in a polarized society.

Although I was usually accepted as one of them by Muslims in Kutch, my class position and the fact that I was clearly a woman from an urban metropolis allowed me a certain facility with members of all religions and castes.

I had a number of Hindu acquaintances and informants, some of whom became friends during the course of my research. My class position allowed me the ability to rent an apartment as a single woman in a middle-class Hindu housing society in a neighborhood that had only one Muslim family in residence (they were in fact the ones who found me the apartment I rented). Mohamed Hosain and his family had never set foot in this neighborhood until they came to visit me, even though they had lived in Bhuj their entire lives. I was keenly aware of my class status and other privileges that allowed me to make choices that were not available to others—women or Muslims. This privilege was certainly key to my access to Muslims as well as (to some extent) Hindus during the course of this research and allowed me to transcend to a certain extent the ghettoization that Muslims tend to face in Gujarat. The first time Nizam brought his father to see me brought home to me the precarity of my position and of what I had to do in order to maintain the public persona of "neutrality" that I had assumed. In my fieldnotes, I had written: "The doorbell rang; I opened the door and beheld Nizam's father for the very first time. I saw them today, standing outside my apartment, as the other Hindu middle-class residents of [the neighborhood] would see them: a young Muslim *maulana* in a white kurta pajama [loose trousers with a long shirt] with an older man; the latter is wearing the traditional *lungi* [lower-body wrap] typical of Banni, a bright *ajrakh* [hand–block print technique typical of Banni and Sindh] turban on his head. He had a henna-dyed beard and kohl-rimmed eyes. He carried a long pole on his shoulder, at the end of which was slung a cloth bundle. Textbook representations of the Muslim: one a scholar, the other a *maldhari* [pastoralist]. *And I knew that I could not continue with them visiting my home*, would perhaps have to arrange another venue" (emphasis added).

As they left that day, I saw Sonal—a Hindu friend who will make an appearance in chapters 3 and 4—walking toward my apartment with her mother. Sonal worked with the NGO through whom I first met Nizam in the summer of 2001. I introduced them and asked whether she recognized Nizam from a few years ago, but she did not. Quite inexplicably—for there could be a number of reasons why Sonal and Nizam may not have interacted with each other—I became uncomfortable, with thoughts racing through my head: Is Nizam really the person he says he is? I could not recognize him when I saw him either, but then, I had first seen him two and a half years ago; is that why? He seems a little unsure around me. Why does he keep calling me? What is his stake in my research?

On subsequent occasions, I always tried to manage my interactions with Nizam so that we could meet at Mohamed Hosain's home. Although Nizam resisted at first, he eventually complied, and over the years, his father became a frequent visitor to Mohamed Hosain's home when he transited through Bhuj on his errands even when I was not in town. Mohamed Hosain's young grandchildren always delighted in his stately presence and came to call him *chhay vara kaka* (the buttermilk-drinking uncle) as he steadfastly refused to drink tea, asking for the traditional *maldhari* staple buttermilk instead.

Policing as Sociality

There are thus various sites and forms of surveillance in the field; it often appears that everybody is keeping an eye on every other. Who is keeping watch? And who is at the receiving end of surveillance? It is clear that the state is no longer the only purveyor of a coherent form of surveillance but is one site of information production and management. Contrary to what we might expect from a Muslim man living on a politically sensitive borderland in a state that barely disguises its Islamophobia, Nizam seemed concerned not by forms of policing and surveillance that emanated from the state but by how other Muslims—those of rival *maslaks*—viewed him and what forms of interaction I forged with them. He was deeply concerned about how he appeared to me. In other words, he wished to remain in control of the narrative as it was being related to the anthropologist, much of which was related to the forms of management of *maslak* affiliation—how the Muslims of Banni presented themselves to me. Who qualified to be identified as a Muslim and who did not, from Nizam's perspective, was a far more finely nuanced discussion based on their *maslak* affiliation. The state, on the other hand, had a far starker assertion of "Muslims" as a hold-all category, something that he did not want the researcher to adopt uncritically.

Yet, in an overall environment of uncertainty and fluidity, of borderland connections and passages, where nothing is always quite what it seems, it is not entirely clear who is keeping track of whom. Interpersonal relationships between friends, neighbors—and certainly the anthropologist—were structured by secrecy. Information was as often given as it was withheld. A new phone or electronic diary that its owner refused to share with others, even a length of cloth or obviously foreign-looking piece of crockery, when its owner refused to divulge where s/he got it from, became cause for the circulation of rumor and suspicion: "Did it come illegally across the border?" Is the new "shy" bride in so-and-so's house who refuses to speak actually a Bengali speaker, smuggled from across the eastern border with Bangladesh? These questions are just as easily asked by the police on their regular morning and evening patrols in border villages as by friends, relatives, and neighbors. Since most of Banni's residents are Muslims, in the 2000s and beyond, there is a new language of global terror to express distrust and fear of the Muslim male that structures the state's policing. This is, in turn, contrasted with the ideal transparency that good citizens must have to the state. In present times, this is expressed in the move to make mandatory the biometric identity card for all citizens, in contravention of its initial stance on its voluntarism (Dreze 2017). In less technologically savvy times, it was alleged that the IB "knew everybody by name in Banni" and managed to keep track of all their activities. "The police roam about here every evening," whispered one of my informants, circling her finger all around indicating the expanse of Banni. "Be careful of who you visit." However, as I have indicated above, exposure to the state as "Muslims" did not produce intimacy or coherence within a group. There were multiple ways in which those policed—by the state—also police themselves and maintain their own sets of boundaries that are meaningful to their lives. This could be boundaries between different *maslak* adherents or between rural and urban Muslims. Social interactions with "others"—that is, with police intelligence and other agents of law enforcement but equally with visiting tourists and anthropologists—also become an important set of social networks and entanglements—of hosts and guests, of circuits of commodity circulation and exchange that reiterate a more textured understanding of surveillance and secrecy. How to negotiate the "public secret" or the agreement to know what *not* to know constitute the enactment of social relationships that are negotiated and performed among and across groups that include the police and state officials, kin groups, and the anthropologist. How transparent people want to be and to whom is actively negotiated in everyday interactions. Information was currency; as the intrepid ethnographer who was trying desperately hard to be at the top of her game, trying to be everywhere all at once, I found that on a number of occasions, people commented on my ability to compile information from a number of sources. Mehreen, whom we will meet in chapter 3, commented on one occasion to her kinswomen in my presence, "Look how smart she is; she knows things that even we don't know about our own village!" This is once again a pertinent reminder of the ways in which the tools of anthropological research and of the state may end up willy-nilly mirroring each other and being the arbiter of information is one way of establishing one's position. Gulbeg kept assiduous track of events and information. The police as an institution of state is not alone in the ability to collate and use information to its advantage.

Conclusion

This chapter has argued that an ethnographic study of security, surveillance, and policing should heed the various stakeholders of securitization, dislodging a state-centric view. Police and military personnel are without doubt in possession of impunity with respect to the perpetration of violence against civilians; this book does not undermine this fact. But there are many other loci of sovereign impunity as well, both in the so-called public and private domains. In this book, I seek to turn the ethnographic lens away from the spectacular moments of police violence to the production of peace. A key argument presented by this case study of borderland policing is that there is no clear-cut separation between those who are agents of law enforcement and those who are at the receiving end of policing, especially in "peacetime." Networks of secrecy, surveillance, friendship, and trust in the above examples are produced through a series of dialogic relationships between state police, borderland residents, and other actors not conventionally taken to be a part of the security apparatus—for example, tourists, air force lieutenants, dairy development officers, and the anthropologist. When the debates on policing of the late 1940s are read together with borderland encounters in the present, they prompt us to critically interrogate our object of analysis to ask who or what is the police and where can we locate policing *practices* more generally? Moving beyond the police as a preconstituted subject and violence as one of the primary frameworks within which ethnographies of policing are situated, the chapter suggests that policing is perhaps more productively conceived of as a set of relationships that weave together multiple forms of the management of information. Finally, it seeks to disaggregate the manner in which to read the relationship forged between the postcolonial state and those who are constituted as specific targets of its policing. India's borderland regime is structured quite explicitly around the question of policing Muslim migration, a theme that is explored in subsequent chapters. Muslims constitute disproportionate numbers of those eliminated through extrajudicial killings, "disappeared," or detained on frequently unproven charges that are enabled through fast-track legislation justified in the name of counterterror operations (Sethi 2014). It may seem paradoxical, then, to encounter their enthusiastic support for the state—especially when it is led by a stridently Hindu nationalist party—by borderland Muslims such as Miyan Husain and his daughter Sofiya, son and granddaughter of Gulbeg. It is not just a hard-nosed pragmatism or instinct for survival that creates these relationships. I have suggested in this chapter that these relationships are forged as two sides of policing in practice, the negotiated settlement between forms of what I have referred to as adjacent sovereignty. The state and its institutions are interpellated with other institutions such as the family and the community as they deploy strategies of policing such as surveillance, suspicion, and control to negotiate and police various boundaries between the inside and the outside. State and nonstate models of policing are no longer distinct and discontinuous but operate within a more inclusive fabric of sociality. If Gulbeg and now Miyan Husain are intermediaries between the community and the state, they still do not speak on behalf of a homogenously constituted community. As Nizam's example indicated, Muslims are just as often engaged in policing their boundaries vis-à-vis each other as they are with the state or the anthropologist. Questions of access—whether Phupli would agree to meet visitors who dropped in unannounced to her home, whether Miyan Husain would give me access to Gulbeg's diaries and visitor's books—were all constantly negotiated and managed across a complex field of activity that should be understood as constituting policing on this borderland.

Chapter 2

Militarism and Everyday Peace

Gender, Labor, and Policing across "Civil-Military" Terrains

The previous chapter argued that we need to take seriously the distinction between the police force as an institution and policing as a form of social action. Policing practices, it suggested, are far more generally dispersed across the terrain of the social and are not only concentrated in the formal state institution that in fact may rely on, or mirror, forms of sovereignty that are anchored in the family or the community. This chapter focuses on how the work of policing, even in its institutional form, is not just about ways of seeing, the strategic deployment of information, or the heroic celebration of masculine work. Instead, I argue that work of policing is also primarily a form of labor, often performed under conditions of great physical and infrastructural duress. In the popular imagination in India, the police are often denigrated as corrupt and ineffective, but the military is extolled as a superhero. Both attributions eclipse the fact that policing also entails often difficult forms of labor. This chapter argues that forms of sovereign power that are embodied in the military are nevertheless rendered vulnerable when we take into account the laboring body that is stretched both physiologically and psychologically in the course of their work. In this chapter, a shared experience of wartime labor allows for a very particular kind of civil-military intimacy to develop between the armed forces, who labor to protect the country's territorial borders, and Patidar women, who subscribe to a collective ethic of hard work through everyday forms of manual labor.[1] Through the shared experience of laboring under exceptionally trying circumstances that pushed their levels of bodily and emotional endurance to a degree not encountered before, Patidar women who worked on rebuilding a bombed runway during the 1971 war with Pakistan remind us that the work of policing is a physically and emotionally demanding one.

Their experience draws attention to the gendered labor of policing *not* because women are enlisted in military work for their so-called maternal or caregiving capacities but because their experience of wartime labor allows us to understand the ambivalent affects—fear, freedom from familial constraints, and exhilaration—entailed in working for the military. These affects are actively produced as a *consequence* of women's enlisting for the military during an extraordinary wartime moment and do not exist solely in the more generic forms of civilian pride in the military that exists in the mode of spectatorship rather than participation. They are ambivalent about recent political moves to appropriate their efforts as heroic mothers of the nation; instead, they insist on the embodied, raw, physical attributes of their labor that is rendered not as extraordinary heroism but as everyday courage and strength—*himmat*—that is forged through close interaction with and under the tutelage of the military. This episode, as recounted by two Patidar women, Viru and Hiru, allows me to gender the concept of sovereignty and to reflect on its limits—a vulnerability that is experienced through the body, that resists masculinist tropes of sovereignty as infallible and totalizing (Osuri 2018). This chapter brings together the everyday and the extraordinary in a single analytical framework to understand civil-military relations. The militarization of a civilian population is not a state of exception, experienced only during wartime or commemorated through public, political memorials; instead, it is an integral aspect of peacetime and is one of the conditions that shape civilians' experiences of peace.

Since the location of this ethnography is a national borderland, it is saturated with all kinds of civil and military policing practices. This allows me to underscore that the way in which this book—even when it refers to the police as institutional arm of the state—expands the definition of police to include not just the civil police but also various types of paramilitary forces (such as the Border Security Force [BSF]) and the armed forces (army and air force). The anthropology of war and militarization has pointed to the gradual redefinition of the domains of the strictly "civil" and the "military," with armies becoming more involved in "civilian" tasks such as welfare, education, and development (Bhan 2013). Armies have become more reliant on nonmilitary personnel and services, which is also another way of saying that civilian life is becoming more militarized, so that the distinction between the two domains becomes blurred (Lutz 2001, 220). One of the classic distinctions between civil police and the armed forces—where the former has charge of internal order, the latter of external territorial defense—has been erased in present times. The militarization of everyday life in postcolonial, democratic contexts such as India is manifested in "the privileging of the military in domestic *and* foreign policy, where it connotes a progressive increase in the military capacity of the state, *and* the use of domestic [military] force by the state to secure the acquiescence of social groups" (Kazi 2009, 23–24). Civil political control of the army in democratically elected popular governments makes untenable the distinction between civil and military regimes (Kazi 2009). On the other side, expanding jurisdictions of national police forces in Europe and the United States along with the easing of institutional checks and balances on their power, especially in the context of post-9/11 antiterror legislations, has also erased some of the classic distinctions between internal and external policing through the police and the army, respectively (Fassin 2013, 216–217; Samimian-Darsah and Stalcup 2017).

This chapter begins by disaggregating the multiple faces of uniformed peacekeeping/law enforcing that people encounter in an everyday context in Bhuj, the *taluka* subdivision where this ethnography is based. Bhuj houses the district police headquarters for Kutch Police, a body that is under the jurisdiction of the elected state government. They take care of law and order, traffic, and crime and are organized across various *thana* or beat jurisdictions. In addition, they also deal with the registration of foreigners and the issue of tourist permits to visit "restricted areas." They maintain citizenship and visa records of family members who visit from Pakistan and women who have married Indian citizens in Kutch, and in this, Kutch Police constitute an interface with the Ministry of Home Affairs (MHA) in New Delhi. In collaboration with the various intelligence services, the civil police (as opposed to the "military") also handle the detention of "illegal infiltrators" and investigation of "trafficking" cases, discussed in chapter 3. This wing of the police force recruits locally, and these policemen are far more socially embedded in the everyday contexts of life in Bhuj than the military, which thrives on a social distance from the local. Therefore, the civil police force is also less deified as an institution.

Bhuj is also an important base for the Indian Air Force (IAF), a wing of the Indian Armed Forces, and the BSF, a centrally constituted paramilitary body in charge of border patrol. Thus, the landscape of security and policing in a borderland such as this is fairly variegated and complex. The next sections track the experience of these quite distinct agents of institutional policing for the citizen, examining the ethnographic nuance of the term *militarywala* (military man) as it is threaded into everyday conversations and encounters within an overall context of everyday militarization that is nonetheless *not* evocative of war or occupation but is seen as a basic constituent of peacetime. The presence of absence of militarization is not necessarily an indicator of wartime or peacetime as mutually exclusive temporalities. Militarization of a borderland is also experienced and normalized as an integral part of "peacetime."

Everyday Militarism: The Sights and Sounds of Peace

Living in Bhuj, I was acutely conscious of its militarization in everyday registers, yet it is not an area under formal occupation or war. Its occupation by the military is a sign of everyday peace, a potent reminder to citizens of their location along a national border with an "enemy" country a stone's throw away. "Civil-military" interactions, however we may define the content of either category, have a routine and everyday quality to them here. The term *military* was invariably used in English across conversations that took place variously in Kutchi, Gujarati, or Hindi. A range of actions and affects were attributed to the *militarywala* ranging from aggression and hubris, to care and fraternal concern. The "military" is present ubiquitously in the everyday: they own lands and buildings, cars, and jeeps and are an unmistakable part of the physical and social landscape.[2] They patronize shops in the market and rent houses and workshops, all providing a reliable source of income for locals. Although military presence in Bhuj certainly does contribute to the local economy, primarily through the recruitment of cooks and drivers, this does not contribute in any significant way to the "political economy of feelings" (Ali 2019) with respect to it.[3] The military infrastructure in Bhuj is marked by a *social distance* from the local population, in continuation from colonial practice. Army, air force, and border security officials sent to the region are always recruited from elsewhere. They do not speak the local language and tend to live as much as possible in residential enclaves (the "cantonment"), or barracks if they are young men posted out in their battalions. Among senior officers, their children go to separate schools and their wives socialize in segregated clubs that are all a part of cantonment life. They are discouraged from mingling with the local population as far as possible. The structure of awe and deference and disinclination to critique that is felt by the locals toward the military is less because they are an avenue of employment than the fact that the military is presented to the civilian population in the mode of a spectatorship that encourages hero worship and national pride, as will be seen below.

The "military" has also left an unmistakable stamp on the sonic landscape of the city. On countless occasions, I sat with friends on their front porch steps talking into the night as aircraft of the IAF practiced their routine drills, dramatically blazing trails of orange fire darting across the night sky. The deafening roar of military aircraft often punctuates conversation during the day and becomes a way of marking time; people could easily distinguish between these and the (relatively) softer sounds of civilian aircraft arriving and departing. They seemed accustomed to the ear-splitting sounds of the military jets that although they had normalized themselves in the everyday, yet evoked a shared experience of the necessity of aggression for the production of an everyday peace. They distinguished these from the sounds of civilian aircraft arriving and departing. In the middle of interviews, people would pause and point upward: "It's [the flight] left for [or arrived from] Mumbai," followed by some comment on whether it was late. Military aircraft were just accepted as a matter of course, even though the sonic disruption (and discomfort) was significantly higher. Young children would continue playing outdoors even as they dramatically covered their ears for effect. Mohamed Hosain's young granddaughter had never quite gotten over the sounds of fighter jets that punctuated her life quite literally from the day she was born. As a toddler, she would squeeze her eyes shut tightly, cover her ears, and snuggle into her mother's arms each time a jet flew past. Growing older, she refused to enter a movie theater because of her lasting fear of loud, reverberating sounds, even as her twin sister reveled in the thrill of an outing and taunted her sister for being a "crybaby." People were accustomed to these ear-splitting sounds that had nevertheless normalized themselves in the everyday; yet they generated various different affects that nevertheless shared a common evocation of war. Some people attributed their first sense of the terrifying earthquake on a cold winter morning in January 2001 to a military attack by Pakistan. Many middle-aged residents of Bhuj recalled the bombs that had fallen in the sub-urbs of Bhuj during the 1971 war; for them, the sounds of the earthquake were bodily assimilated first as a declaration of war by the "enemy" country just across the border. For others, these were also the reassuring sounds of peacetime. The regular air drills reminded some middle-class Hindu resi-dents of Bhuj of what they saw as a performance of India's superior military strength. "Don't you think they can hear these sounds on the other side?" asked a retired schoolteacher as we sat sipping tea in his living room through the roar of the aircraft engines whose impact rattled the windowpanes as we spoke. *"Achha hai* [it is a good thing]," he commented approvingly. "Let them [Pakistan] know that we have an alert and well-trained force that is always ready to respond [*jawab dene ke liye taiyar hai*]."

The "military" may also be regarded with suspicion and annoyance. Bhuj is an important border station for the IAF; a couple of civil passenger flights operate during an hour or so every morning and afternoon out of a terminal that shares a runway with the military airport. This airport is a significant node in civilian-military interaction in the region. The terminal is simply built, perhaps in deference to the fact that it is projected primarily as a mili-tary installation or perhaps because it hosts only a handful of flights to Mum-bai. There are extra security checks in place for passengers, and as with other "sensitive" and military spaces, photography is prohibited. On a pillar in the single room that serves as the departure lounge is a blue-and-white sign in the devanagari script: *"Hindi hain hum; watan hai Hindustan hamara"* (We are Indians; Hindustan is our homeland). These words are from Mo-hammad Iqbal's famous Urdu poem "Sare jahan se achha . . . Hindustan ha-mara" (Better than the entire universe . . . is our Hindustan). Ironically, Iqbal was Pakistan's poet laureate, and his poetic creation has been bypassed in contemporary India's own nationalist self-perception, which tends to favor songs with a more Hindu nationalist imagery, for instance "Vande mataram"

(Praise to the motherland). Nevertheless, these words are a reminder that national identity and belonging are not to be taken for granted, especially in a border area next to a military air base.

In another example of how the military was always perceived as being socially external to Kutch, people I met or traveled with frequently complained about the "ego clash" between the air force and civil airport authorities. It was common practice for passenger aircraft to have to wait for anywhere between five and twenty minutes on the runway awaiting air traffic control clearance while IAF aircraft completed their drill. Many of us were frustrated by these delays, which frequently entailed missed onward connections. "They [the IAF] set aside an hour in the morning and an hour in the afternoon for one single flight [on occasion, two] to land and to take off. These are scheduled hours; why must they do their military routine at exactly the same time? This is for show [*dikhava*], nothing else," muttered aggrieved fellow passengers.

This sentiment was echoed by many others in Bhuj when they passed BSF trucks filled to the brim with uniformed soldiers on their way to and from their stations at border checkpoints. These trucks often stopped for tea at Bhirandiyara, a popular halt en route from Bhuj to Banni or the northern border checkpoint at Khawda. Young men were particularly irked by what they perceived as the high-handedness of the armed soldiers, none of whom spoke the local language; instances of road rage were common as they pressed down on the accelerator or drove in the middle of the road to prevent the BSF vehicle overtaking them. Driving in these contexts made possible the emergence of particular types of social and political subjectivities in encounter with specific others (see Bishara 2015). The suspicion seemed to be mutual as I discovered on the single occasion that I was invited to spend an evening at the air force officers' mess in Bhuj. Over dinner, young air force officers displayed what struck me as a deep paranoia of civilian populations. Cautioning me against mingling too much with the "locals," I was warned that many nongovernmental organizations (NGOs) were in fact front organizations for more "sinister" activities ranging from smuggling to terror and providing covert support even to the CIA! Yet garnering support from local civilian populations in border security was also a concern that was uppermost in the minds of visiting officers of the IAF as indicated, for instance, in the visitor's book entry made by an officer on his visit to Gulbeg's home in Banni discussed in chapter 1. The mutual suspicion that was routinely performed by either side does not discount other faces of civil-military interaction and intimacies.

"The Border Man"

Military Masculinities

Just as the soundscape of the city is integrally bound up with an unmistakably military presence in the city, there are other ways, both visual and affective, in which the region's peacetime militarization is signaled. If the sound of IAF planes registered their presence across the skies in a magisterial fashion, the BSF *jawan* (soldier, literally [male] youth) was a regular presence in Bhuj and villages across the Rann. Uniformed BSF cadres were visible on the streets, in public teahouses and at bazaars, or in transit to and from their border posts in large trucks owned by the BSF. Policing the border is acknowledged to be a man's work: it involves hard labor under adverse conditions. Unlike senior IAF officers posted on duty with their families, the BSF *jawan* was sent to "man" the borders, far away from his family and home region. They did not speak the local language and were posted as part of a battalion from one border to another, living in all-male barracks. Posters and hoardings extol the BSF's contribution to border protection, depicting them as masculine superheroes, an act that erases the mundane labor involved, including hours of boredom on solitary border outposts.

Unlike beat policing—tasked to the civil police—which is not invoked as a particularly heroic or laudable task, and in general policemen are often castigated by ordinary citizens as lazy, corrupt, and deskbound, the BSF is part of a state-managed narrative that extols its manliness and bravery at the borders. Posters and hoardings to showcase the BSF are set up in border areas during the annual tourist festival of the Rann. During this four-month-long festival, the dry, barren surroundings are suddenly transformed by the periodic appearance of huge hoardings and posters in addition to the more routine signage that is the more general characteristic of border infrastructure in India. The everyday immersion of the military in Kutch in the routine sonic and visual ways described above contrasts with the spectacular presentation of the BSF soldier or the "border man" as superhero in these posters, usually packaged for tourists who will visit from other parts of the country. Images of male soldiers of the BSF in physically challenging terrain and combat situations are accompanied by militant-nationalist slogans such as BSF war cry: *"Bharat mata ki jai"* (Glory to Mother India); *"Har jawan, desh ki shaan"* (Every soldier, the nation's pride); *"Iss desh ki [sic] shahid ko koi chhoo nahi sakta, jis desh ki nigahewan hain seema suraksha bal ki aankhe"* (Nobody can touch that country's martyrs, whose guardians are the eyes of the BSF); *"The more you sweat in peace, the less you bleed in war"*; *"Guards of frontiers of India: The border man"*; *"Hum seema ke prahari hain hum seena taan khade; hum bharat ke gaurav ki bankar pehchan khade"* (We are the guardians of the border, we stand at attention; we stand as the symbols of India's pride).

Although these hoardings and slogans invoke the BSF through hypermasculine affects that conjoin the "border man" to experiences of patriotism and pride in the state institutions of policing, they end up subordinating the everyday work of border patrol to the spectacular optics of policing as masculine work. Unlike sections of India's eastern border with Bangladesh—also patrolled by the BSF—which are far more actively negotiated in daily comings and goings for visits to kin, markets, and jobs (Cons 2013; Ghosh 2017; van Schendel 2001), making the daily routine of the border officials quite packed with activity, a typical day for the border guard at the Kutch border is solitary and quiet. The endless landscape of desert and sky is unbroken except by the solitary movement of a fellow BSF jeep or the wanderings of a *maldhari* out in search of his herd. The periodic activity of tourists is welcomed by BSF *jawans* posted at the border. Those lucky tourists who are able to get permission through personal contacts in the army to "spectate" in otherwise restricted areas such as "India Bridge" beyond Khawda in northern Kutch are welcomed by the soldiers on duty who candidly admit that they literally can go out of their minds in the absence of human company day after day in these desert expanses. Even though the Kutch-Pakistan border is officially a "closed" border—that is, there is no legally sanctioned crossing point or road that connects the desert across the two countries[4]—one of the tasks of the border patrol officers is to search for "footprints," the tangible, physical sign of cross-border activity. When such footprints (and camel hoofprints) are found and identified, they are assessed for their direction and intensity. Deep and heavy camel prints, for instance, lead to an unmistakable conviction that they are heavily laden with "arms" or "lethal material." These reports make their way into the local newspapers and provide much by way of conjecture to the ongoing saga of cross-border infiltration and "terror." On one visit to the border outpost in Lakhpat, as soon as I had left the village settlement behind, a young patrolman caught up asking officiously who I was and why I had bothered to come so far just to wander about; in those days, it was well off the regular tourist circuit. Besides, it was technically off limits, a "restricted zone." "Where does the restricted zone begin?" I asked. "Right where you stand," was his prompt response. We were perched on a rocky outcrop, just outside the sturdy fort walls. The rocks gave way to a beach-like zone that is partly seabed, partly Rann. "You can't step down; that is restricted area," says the young patrolman, agitated. He looked to me like he must just be out of school. This sandy bed is where trackers comb the ground for the appearance of "footprints" twice a day, searching desperately for evidence of cross-border activity to fragment the searing monotony of another endless day on the salt expanses. Success on this score is far less spectacular than the reports that are regularly churned out for local consumption by the media. For the most part, these border patrol guards are waiting for the day when they will be transferred to a more hospitable part of the country, somewhere they are more familiar with the language and local customs, where they are not assigned to futile weeks and months of combing the Rann for elusive "infiltrators" or tracking circuitous escape routes.

Gender and Labor across the "Civil-Military" Terrain

When posters and slogans invoke the BSF *jawan* as superhero and war as a spectacle for tourist consumption (e.g., Lutz 2001), they depict the military as a masculine force that uses its heroic powers to protect the nation's borders.[5] This is very much in line with the normative and gendered view of war and military protection that is carried out in the name of civilians, especially women and children (see Yuval-Davis 2013). Yet, as I have suggested above, representing the achievements of the "border man" in spectacular mode does not do justice to the everyday and mundane forms of labor that are entailed in the work of policing. The solitude and the boredom of a day on the border post is not captured in these more heroic renditions. In this section, I present a case of civil-military intimacy that although forged during a spectacular moment—during the 1971 war with Pakistan—nevertheless provides an extremely textured sense of the everyday labor of policing by men—and women. The women who form the subjects of a close intimacy with military men do not deify or sexualize this relationship. Instead, it is presented as a fraternal bond that is forged through physical labor performed together, literally on the battlefield. The rest of this chapter uses the example of women's wartime mobilization in 1971 to discuss the consequences of the time when a number of women from a village close to Bhuj went from being contract construction workers to labor donors for the air force. Even as these ordinary women from a peasant caste labored during wartime, repairing a bombed airstrip in record time, they focus on the everyday work ethic and strength of the military rather than its spectacular dimensions alone. In this, they also resist the retrospective appropriation of their own labor into hypernationalist narratives of heroism and war, seeking to ground their experiences instead in the everyday rather than the extraordinary.

"Runway" Heroines and the Commemoration of War in Nationalist Times

In August 2015, a "war memorial" was inaugurated a few kilometers east of Bhuj, in front of the main entrance to the village of Madhapar. The union defense minister flew in from New Delhi and presided over its unveiling. The desirability of a memorial had long been acknowledged in newspaper editorials and conversations among local intelligentsia; in these circles, there was a frequently expressed desire and need to publicly commemorate the contributions made by the border district of Kutch to postcolonial border defense and security, underlining the "sacrifices" made by its people in the process. The year 2015 was a significant date for the inauguration of the memorial. Although the year marked the fiftieth anniversary of the 1965 war with Pakistan, the memorial was not, in fact, dedicated to that war. In 2014, a Hindu nationalist government had just been elected into office in New Delhi. In the months and years following this, violence between Hindus and minorities such as Muslims, Christians, and Dalits (formerly "low"-caste people) increased substantially. Already in 2015, the government had been criticized for a growing climate of "intolerance" in the wake of the first of what would turn out to be numerous public lynchings of Muslim men charged with the transportation of cows or the consumption of beef, accused by the lynch mob of hurting Hindu sentiments (Burke 2015; Kumar 2017). By early 2016, the government's preferred means of tackling dissent was to call its opponents "antinational" and to encourage them to "go to Pakistan."[6] It is in this context of an aggressive Hindu nationalist politics and a sharpened attack on Pakistan that the politics of this memorial must be located.

The war memorial in Kutch was dedicated to *viranganas*, "brave women," who had participated in the war with Pakistan in 1971. This event brought into the public eye the three hundred Patidar women from Madhapar village, who had gathered together to repair an airstrip bombed during the 1971 war.[7] This was an interesting theme to have structured a memorial to war. As a district on India's western border with Pakistan, residents of Kutch have not been immune to either of the two wars fought between the two countries in 1965 and then in 1971. The memorial enjoys high visibility, located along the main eastern highway, and is called the *virangana smarak* (memorial to brave women) dedicated per its inscription to the "bravehearts of 1971." In the form of a roadside installation, it is a tableau with eight sculpted figurines, six of which are sari-clad women. They are engaged in the construction of an airstrip under a canopy of three model IAF aircraft.

In choosing the 1971 war as the inspiration for the memorial and further by dedicating it not to territorial conquest or victories but instead to the memory of laboring women, the invocation of the *virangana* by the defense minister pushed the memorialization of war and its nationalist appropriation outside the strictly "military" into the realm of the domestic and the maternal. The most well-known contemporary attribution of the *virangana* is in Bangladesh, where the term *birangona* was used to designate Bengali women raped by the West Pakistani army during the Liberation War of Bangladesh, the very same war that started out as a civil war within Pakistan before India intervened in support of Bangladesh, thus becoming a combatant in the 1971 war and commemorated in Kutch by the *virangana* memorial. Unlike the forced sexual labor that the *birangona* was called on to perform during the war, which subsequently entitled her to the status of a freedom fighter, the Kutch *virangana* is ostensibly memorialized for the physical labor she performed during wartime, but the political appropriation of the *viranganas* made them into a symbol of Hindu nationalist pride by invoking them as mothers of the nation.

The official ceremony marking the unveiling of the memorial on August 27, 2015, constituted an important political and media spectacle in

Kutch. Union ministers for Defense and Human Resource Development (HRD) came in from New Delhi.[8] The latter minister—who in an earlier professional avatar was a hugely popular television actress and had played the role of a Gujarati housewife in one of Indian television's longest-running soap operas—came dressed in a traditional red Gujarati tie-dye sari. Keeping her company were some of the *viranganas* themselves, dressed in white saris with tricolored borders symbolizing the Indian flag. Front-page news coverage of the event bore the caption, "*Aavi mataon chhe tyan sudhi desh no bal banko nahi thay*" (As long as there are such mothers, nobody can touch the country; literally, cannot push a hair out of place).[9] The defense minister invoked the *viranganas* to pay tribute to Kutch, declaring that the region was the epitome of *deshbhakti* (patriotism) and *narishakti* (women's power), whereas the HRD minister in her speech said that the memorial would now serve to inspire the rest of the country. The former also promised that a tank and jet actually used in wars with Pakistan during 1965 and 1971 would eventually be added to the memorial, an indication of the contemporary political significance of the memorial.

The mother and the heroic woman or *virangana* are of course not new tropes in nationalist imaginaries. Women have been integral to the way in which the nation's body has been imagined: safeguarded both as the female body that must be protected against dishonor by the "outsider," as well as the cartographic body. In India, this latter position is best exemplified in the iconic representation of the nation as *Bharat Mata* or Mother India. Pointing out that nationalisms are not only the products of a so-called liberal public sphere, Tanika Sarkar (2001) has argued that family and conjugality were important sites for the imagination of an anticolonial cultural nationalism in India. The questions of women's chastity, morality, and domesticity became central to the formulation of Hindu nationalism from the nineteenth century onward. Charu Gupta (2001) argues that the nineteenth-century Hindi literary public sphere, constituted by advertisements, pamphlets, and other literature, helped consolidate and reconstitute conservative sexual moralities around the question of Hindu women and domesticity. The consolidation of a conservative morality around Hindu women enabled the construction of a Hindu nation with its iconic representation in *Bharat Mata*; she was simultaneously an agent of militant activism as well as a victim of the lascivious gaze of the Muslim man, against whom she must be protected. It was through the circulation of stories related to the abduction of Hindu women by Muslim men that Gupta (2001, 222) argued that "Hindu publicists used the figure of the victimized and the abducted Hindu woman to promote an identity agenda, emphasizing fear of a common 'enemy.'" The figure of the *virangana* is a departure from the characterization of the woman as mother in that it layers the maternal image with that of a fighter. Kathryn Hansen (1988, WS-26) proposes the *virangana* model as one that is an "alternative female paradigm" to the bipolar narrative of wife or mother (goddess), "combining direct assumption of power with exemplary virtue." Lindsey Harlan (1992) discusses the *virangana* as ancestral heroine and role model for Rajput women; here, women's heroism lies not in mothering alone but in disregarding traditional conventions of gendered segregation and going outside the home to fight. Symbols of mothering also stretch to incorporate struggle and militancy, as Julie Peteet (1991, 107) argues in the context of the Palestinian resistance movement where such reworked symbolism became an important conduit for the politicization and mobilization of women. In the Palestinian intifada, she argues that women were able to reconstitute the meaning of motherhood so that it came to provide the contours of political activism for some women. "Reproductive and caring labor have acquired new public and militant meanings," she argued (Peteet 1997, 107). Tarini Bedi (2008) suggests the optic of "adjustment" to conjure a female subject whose emancipatory prowess does not necessarily lie in any consistent or overt subversion of the "domestic." As she points out in her study of Shiv Sena women in Mumbai city, the domains of kinship and politics are mutually intertwined, the one not necessarily in contradiction of the other.

The concluding sections of this chapter discuss how the *viranganas* themselves resist this heroic appropriation into a nationalist imaginary, choosing instead to focus on the work of military policing as everyday courage and labor and not just the subject of an extraordinary event like war. The memorial became an important public acknowledgment of the political symbolism of war and national security in this borderland at a time when a new right-wing Hindu nationalist government elected into office the year before in 2014, was seeking cultural-nationalist legitimacy across India. However, in the ensuing commemorations, there appeared to be significant dissonances between the significance accorded by the *viranganas* themselves to the nature of the wartime labor undertaken by them and the manner in which they felt the memorial had been appropriated politically by the state. Although the state invoked them as brave mothers of the nation, the *viranganas* I interviewed sought to relate their wartime participation in far more ambiguous terms. Their memories of participation in the war do not sum up neatly as the "brave woman," "fearless mother," or "nurturer" of the nation; in their narratives, the *viranganas* are fairly candid about their memories of a raw, painful, yet exhilarating time when they were consumed by doubt and fear and had to face the wrath and opposition of their families and the constant barb of being a "bad mother" whose service to the "military" was premised on an abandonment of their biological children. Love for the nation was not a predefined, preexisting state of being but something that was forged through the act of laboring at a bombed-out construction site, through the very physical and visceral experience of fear, exhilaration, and independence for women who found themselves in open contravention of their family's—especially husband's—wishes for the first time in their lives. The military-bureaucratic personnel became, in these narratives, their fictive kin who recognized them as their "sisters," but the relationship that they describe has overtones of a relationship whose contours were far more ambiguous especially for young married women who worked in close physical proximity with men in uniform during an adrenaline-charged time. Unmindful of their families' words of caution, these women compromised their physical safety and reputations as good wives and mothers to go out to work with the military men every day. Their narratives do not seamlessly map onto the official *"virangana"* story, which is a retrospective rationalization, in their view, for narrow political ends. The "true" meaning of *deshbhakti*, or service and selfless sacrifice, according to these women, was taught to them by the military. In the memories of some of the *viranganas* I interviewed, the category of the "military" is clearly the air force, but during wartime, this category stretched to accommodate an arm of the civil administration (such as the district collector). They make a strong distinction between their understandings of the "military" and the elected political machinery of the present, to which they attributed greed and self-aggrandizement at the cost of their labor.

Women and Wartime Labor in 1971

In December 1971, India was at war with Pakistan, a consequence of its intervention in the latter's civil war, fought for the independence of Bangladesh, formerly East Pakistan. The western border became, for a short duration, one of the theaters of war. I will return to the implications of military action on this border for the migration of Hindus from Tharparkar, Sindh, to Kutch during this period in chapter 5. Indian and Pakistani forces attacked each other and the Pakistani Air Force bombed sites in Bhuj, Okha, and Barmer (Rajasthan). Airfields, ports, and railway tracks or stations were frequent targets.[10] The Bhuj air base was a strategic and vulnerable target, situated as it was just across the border. Bombing in Bhuj began on December 3; air raid sirens were sounded six times between midnight and the early hours of the morning on December 8. Between December 3 and 9, it was estimated that a total of 136 bombs fell, 64 of them on the night of December 8 and 9 alone, "reducing the runway to a rubble [*sic*]."[11] In the ensuing panic, the town of Bhuj saw an exodus of citizens trying to seek shelter in safer areas. The district collector at the time, N. Gopalaswami, "hopped onto a motorcycle, announcing on a megaphone that people should not panic, but the exodus wouldn't stop."[12] Depleted thus of its human resources, there was no labor available to undertake the task of rebuilding the runway. Building contractors who worked under contract for the air force refused to take on what they perceived as too dangerous a project. It was at this crucial juncture that, according to a news story in the *Times of India*, the *sarpanch* (headman) of Madhapar village offered the services of the women of his village: *Behnon ko le aaun?* (Should I enlist the ladies?)[13]

To understand this somewhat unusual offer, we need to understand the socioeconomic and family structure of Madhapar and its residents. The economy of this village, dominated by Patidars, was driven by remittances from overseas even in the 1970s. Men worked abroad and sent money home to their families, visiting them once every couple of years or so. Village households were constituted by elderly parents, their young daughters-in-law and children. These young mothers—most of them in their early twenties—worked as daily wage labor. Wing Commander Karnik recalls that even in 1971, the village boasted the distinction of having a refrigerator in every household and many car owners, including brands such as Mercedes.[14] It is characteristic of Patidar villages even today that early economic prosperity has not dulled their relationship to manual labor. It was not uncommon during the tenure of my fieldwork to see Patidar women working with their hands in construction and other manual tasks even if they were reasonably well-off in the local context. It is this overall economic and familial structure of the village that may help us understand the circumstances under which large numbers of young women from

Madhapar went out to work on the airstrip, rebuilding it in a record four days.[15] The dedicated and fearless labor of these women was invoked as a "glittering example of patriotism and selflessness."[16] Their stance was compared by the then–prime minister Indira Gandhi to the heroism of the legendary queen who fought against the British, Rani Laxmibai of Jhansi, and most recently, the installation of the roadside memorial invoked them as brave mothers to the nation.[17]

However, as I argue here, the *viranganas'* (also known in Madhapar as the "airport ladies"—*airport vara behnon*) recruitment into wartime activity was not necessarily a commitment driven by any overarching political or nationalist ideology. The women I interviewed talked about their work for the air force as a decision taken for them by the headman of the village in consultation with a contractor. Thus, they were not driven by nationalist sentiments to "volunteer" for this work; they were dispatched to work on the airstrip much as they were rounded up for any other construction-related work by contractors. This was simply what they did for a living and this was the way in which they got work, according to Viru, one of my *"virangana"* interviewees. Both Viru's and Hiru's narratives indicate that the role of motivating them with nationalist sentiment and the implications of the work they were doing for the nation (*desh nu kam*) was played by the "military" (expanded to include the air force and the district collector of the time). It was the "military" rather than the family that deserved credit, in their opinion, for their heroism and *himmat* (courage, strength) that they were able to develop under trying circumstances. Even though the "military" encouraged them (and later gave them due respect—this was an important source of acknowledgment for them), the biological/affinal family tried to prevent them from taking up this "unmotherly" role and abandoning their children. The *viranganas'* participation in the task of rebuilding the airstrip, an activity that required their presence on the battlefield, open to the risk of attack, was significantly premised on a critical *absence* of male kin, this role taken over by the "military." The contemporary elected state government in charge of the *taluka* and panchayat offices was derided by them as selfish; the politics of the *virangana* memorial was something they viewed as none other than political corruption. Finally, they brought to their work for the military qualities that were not offshoots of their domestic labor such as caregiving or cooking (e.g., Hewamanne 2013) but significantly in contravention of these qualities. They were reminded on a daily basis by their mothers-in-law of their duty to their infant children as they set out to work every morning. Their fathers-in-law reminded them of their commitment to be dutiful daughters-in-law (*vau*) in the absence of their husbands who toiled in distant lands to earn for the family.

"MILITARY WORK, NOT MOTHERS' WORK!"

Viru's and Hiru's responses to their memorialization through the *virangana smarak* in Madhapar enable a complex reading of the relationship between civil and military domains forged in an everyday register of hard work, dedication, and bodily discipline. Military men are rendered in this narrative as brotherly figures who stick by the Patidar women in their physical labor, inculcating in them a military ethic of bodily discipline, strength, and courage that is forged through highly grounded actions of work rather than as a transcendent masculine heroism. Their conversations on the subject ranged across a variety of themes, including the organization of the family with absentee husbands at its heart, the "unshackling" from patriarchal obligations that this enabled (albeit not without struggle), and the manner in which they were almost accidental recruits into the task of rebuilding the runway.

Yet the motivation and discipline they required for work performed under enormous tension and pressure were attributes that they did not put down to any innate feminine or motherly quality—such as patience, fortitude, or sacrifice—but firmly handed over to the "military" men who stayed with them as they worked, who constantly encouraged them: "It was just work, work, work, all the while we were at the site; no talking, no time to eat. The military men kept urging us on to work and work without stopping. They said, *'Jaldi ho jayega, desh ka kam hai'* [It will finish quickly; it is work for the country]; what will happen if Pakistan drops another bomb? What will you do? Just keep working. And so, we did." And finally, they refer also to the effects of nation-building through the very tactile and physical bond that they developed with military infrastructure during wartime, the impact of the bombs on their eardrums, the hot water that scalded their tongues as they drank to quench their thirst, and the absence of machines that made their task all the more strenuous. Every day, they had misgivings: "Every evening when we returned home, we said to each other, 'This is truly dangerous work; let's not return tomorrow.' But then, every morning we found ourselves back at the site, drawn by the voices of the military men who stayed by our sides as we worked, who were repeating constantly in our ears, 'This is for the *desh* [country]; it is *desh nu kam* [work for the country].'"

These affects—a sense of connection to the military forged through a shared recognition of what it means to be physically and viscerally involved in the gritty task of policing the borders of the nation, ensuring that its citizens could "sleep in peace at night" (*chain ki neend*), formed the core of the intimacies that developed between these women and the air force. This affective relationship to the military is a far cry from the superhero type of hyperbole that marks the state's commemoration of both the BSF—through the posters it commissions—and the *viranganas* who are marked as sacrificial mothers; the latter is received by a deep ambivalence: "What did we know of the nation or even of motherhood?" commented the women who were now mothers to adult children. Hiru was twenty-two years old in 1971. Her husband, like Viru's, worked in Nairobi. "In those days, there were no mobile phones to keep in touch. We communicated via airmail with our husbands. My husband wrote to me forbidding me from embarking on this work," Hiru explained. "By the time the letter reached me, we had finished!" she declared triumphantly. Begoña Aretxaga (1997) argues that because women's political practice has an interstitial character, it allows for greater social and feminist transformation. These Patidar women were housewives whose work outside the house on construction sites was subordinate to patriarchal authority of their parents-in-law in the absence of their husbands who worked overseas. Even their decision to enter the war was not framed as an agentive choice (it was the contractor who sent them to the airstrip). Yet the sense of independence they developed appears to have continued into the present. My first meeting with Viru was marked by the serendipitous nature of many fieldwork encounters: I was taken to her home by a mutual acquaintance who knew of my interest in the "*airport vara beheno.*" I arrived, thus unannounced at Viru's home at that time of the mid-morning when most homes are temporarily calm and quiet, the kitchen taking a very brief respite in the aftermath of breakfast preparation and consumption and before women settled down to the serious task of lunch preparation.

In this brief lull, markets are visited for fresh produce or vegetables haggled over and bought from a passing vendor; neighbors might drop by for a quick chat or consultation. Viru had just made a cup of tea for her husband who was reclining with the newspaper, enjoying the comforts of a retired life. She welcomed us in, without missing a beat poured us all another round

of tea and then introduced her husband who nevertheless did not seem in-
terested in local history. Viru indicated that he was hard of hearing and that
I should not be offended. The discussion that followed was led entirely by
Viru and, once Viru summoned Hiru on the phone, by both women.

Viru began by recounting the context for me. "He [pointing to her hus-
band] was in Nairobi at the time. Look [*dekho*], we are Patels; most of our
menfolk worked abroad anyway. He used to come home to visit every couple
of years. I was about twenty-five to twenty-six years old at the time. I looked
after my *saas-sasur* [parents-in-law] and children, two sons and a daughter.
In those days, we had no *kheti* [agricultural work]. So all the women were
like that; we used to work in *majduri* [manual labor]. The contractor used to
subcontract the work to agents, and they used to gather women—as many
as they could find—and give us work. This was how we used to get work."
Both Viru and Hiru denied any active nationalist sentiment that drove them
to work for the military. They were used to working as daily wage earners
in various construction projects, but war was a different matter altogether.
Hiru continued, "Eighteen bombs were thrown by Pakistan: four of them
fell on the airport runway, some fell on the Khari Nadi road in Bhuj, near
the airport, some fell on a field in Mirzapar killing a cow and a calf. The
runway needed urgent repair. The contractor for the air force refused the
work, saying, 'It will take three/four months at the very least; we'll see how
it goes [*dekhten hain*].' The people of Mirzapar village were approached for
help, but they refused. Collector Gopalaswami, along with the military people
[*militarywala*] approached the panchayat [village council] in Madhapar. Our
sarpanch [headman] at the time, Jadhavji Shivji Hirani, agreed to help the
military. All of us formed a group and went to work; there must have been
about three hundred of us." Viru added, "There were some men in the group,
too, but mostly it was women who went to work."

They described the frenetic pace of the work as well as the tense atmosphere that surrounded them both at home, with their terrified mothers-in-
law holding the fort, and at the airport. "The family was totally against the
idea; my mother-in-law begged me not to go," emphasized Viru. Hiru added,
"I was only twenty-two years old. . . . We used to leave the house at 7:00 a.m.
and returned home at 7:00 p.m. The children were left at home with our
mothers-in-law to look after. My *sasuma* [mother-in-law] beseeched me to re-
consider. 'If a bomb falls and kills you, who will be mother to your children?'
she would say to me with tears in her eyes." They were constantly made aware

of their husbands' absence at home and the fact that had they been around, they would have prevented them from going out to work because they were abandoning their children. "We did it for the military . . . and for Gopalaswami [the district collector]. . . . He had tears in his eyes when we finally completed the work; he said we were like his sisters. Did we not owe them our loyalty and our hard work?" Viru asked.

Every evening, they vowed to not return the next morning, and yet the morning found them once again at the site of the runway, working harder than they ever had. The men from the military stood by them, telling them what the war meant and how they should protect themselves at the site. Most of all, the men motivated them to work harder and faster so that their work for the nation (*desh nu kam*) could be accomplished without delay. Viru explained, "The runway had these three big craters [*gadhha*] where the bombs had fallen; we repaired only those, not the damage done to the sides." Then Hiru held up her fingers and said, "In four days, we made the runway, can you imagine? . . . The military people told us, 'When you hear the siren, it means a bomb will fall.' So when we heard the siren, we'd duck into the twenty-five-foot-long trenches along the sides."

The theme of bodily discipline and motivation to work—a military ethic that they owe to their brief apprenticeship with them—recurs across their narratives; this was at the behest of the military who urged them to work without stopping: "We had no time even to take a food break. We used to pack our food from home in the morning and bring it with us. The Swaminarayan temple in Bhuj contributed food every day: they sent *sukhdi* [a semolina-based sweet] and fruit for each of the four days we worked.[18] But there was no time to even stop to eat; they [the military supervisors] did not let us stop. We just took our *kholis* [here, Viru demonstrated by holding the end of her sari out to make a small pouch], dropped the food into it, and in this way, we kept working and eating, working and eating, not stopping, not stopping."

Working on the runway also led to a very visceral and literal bodily contact with the materials and effects of war along with the military men. "The sound of bombs—it was really ear-splitting; you felt as though your eardrums [*kan ka parda*] would just burst!" And further, "all the work was manual; there were no machines at all in those days! There was a horse-drawn cart [*ghoda gadi*], and even drinking water came in large canisters; it was so hot, it burned our mouths! The contractor provided all the implements we needed—cement mixer, *pavda*, *ghamela*, etc. When we put the *reti* [sand] on the road, the chemical stung our eyes so badly with its fumes; still, we worked and worked, worked without a break." When air-raid sirens sounded, they climbed into trenches to protect themselves from bombs and then found that the trenches "were covered with *desi bawal*. It was so thorny that our faces and arms got badly scratched and bloody. . . . We just kept praying silently to ourselves *ram . . . ram . . .* and we remained safe; nothing happened at all."

At the end of the entire ordeal, they returned home safe and sound. They were shaken and had a whole new set of experiences to assimilate. Viru summed up the experience in the following words: "Saraswati mata gave us *budhhi* [intelligence], Bharat mata gave us *shakti* [strength], and Ram gave us *raksha* [protected us]."[19] Hiru was more forthcoming. Dressed in a sky-blue sari with silver sparkles all over, she strode into Viru's living room, a sheaf of papers under her arm, which contained a record of all the women who had worked on the runway, their names and photographs attached. More confident and articulate than Viru, I discovered that she was also very angry about the new *virangana* memorial. "After the runway work was completed, the collector came to meet us. He had tears in his eyes when we refused to accept payment for our services because for us this was our service to the country and the nation [*desh nu kam; rashtra nu kam*]. He said, 'You all are my sisters.' We assured him that we would happily step forward again if needed."

Wartime Mobilization and Civil-Military Contestations

The above narratives contest the view that women's recruitment into discourses of nationalism, war, and militarism are primarily forged within the idiom of nurture and sacrifice, as represented in the figure of the mother. Viru and Hiru strongly contest the political appropriation of their wartime labor in service of the nation as sacrificial mothers alone. For them, consciousness of and love for the nation (*desh*; *deshbhakti*) was inculcated by the military, forged through the physical labor they provided for the military during wartime. In turn, they seek to make a distinction between the military-bureaucratic complex and the elected political government; they hold the latter responsible for capitalizing on the *viranganas* for political gains, using the trope of motherhood and sacrifice in order to do so.

In thinking more broadly about discourses of securitization and women, Viru's and Hiru's narratives show us how so-called ordinary women can become integrally a part of military apparatus during war but in a role that challenges their contribution in terms of giving birth to and nurturing the male soldier alone.[20] How did "regular housewives" become involved in the development of the military infrastructure during wartime, and how do they regard their role as "*viranganas*," the designation accorded to them by the state through the inauguration of a war memorial honoring them? As seen above, their narratives resist any easy assimilation into a broad or homogenous "nationalist" discourse; in offering their physical labor for the nation during wartime, they were not driven by love or sacrifice for the abstract nation, nor were they performing quintessential acts of mothering such as nurturing or caregiving to soldiers fighting on the battlefront. The figure of the *virangana* was, as they saw it, an ambivalent figure and a work in progress, actively produced by the military, aided through the very tactile, visceral, and back-breaking work of building wartime infrastructure. Further, the role they attribute to the military commends them for their everyday heroism rather than only superheroic feats.

This Is Now India's Memorial: What of the Virangana Sisters?

Although the *viranganas* refused payment for their work, the air force felicitated them on "Air Force Day" (October 8, 2014), when a cash award was handed over to the headman by a representative of the Air Force Wives Welfare Association (Regional).[21] This grant was used to construct a second story above the village panchayat's main office in Madhapar. Called the Virangana Bhuwan (mansion), it was dedicated to the spirit of their work. They also received a commemorative plaque from the air force, now placed in the village high school. Although Viru and Hiru were full of praise for the district collector and the IAF in the manner in which they motivated them to undertake this difficult and dangerous task, they expressed anger and disappointment over the politics of the memorial inaugurated in 2015. Vehemently denouncing the memorial, Hiru cried out, "Have you seen it? It says *Jai Jawan, Jai Kisan; yeh to Bharat ka ho gaya, virangana behenon ka kya?* (This has made it India's memorial, what of the *virangana* sisters?)."[22] She continued, "Where is the *kisan* [farmer] in this? We put in the labor and we undertook the risk. We did it for the military. Now these local politicians put their names ahead of ours. At the inauguration ceremony of the *virangana smarak*, elderly women, some of them with walking sticks, were made to sit on the floor, while this woman [she named one of the district-level politicians whom she alleged was central to the hijacking of the memorial for its political gains] who was not even born in 1971, sat up on the stage! I wanted to ask her, 'Did you take a photo of what was happening while you were in your mother's womb? You have no idea of what happened at the time and you are taking away all the credit!'"

Both women reiterated that even though the collector of the time and the military had given them a lot of respect and courtesy, the local political parties and village administrative machinery (panchayat, taluka panchayat) had only insulted them (*apman kiya*). The memorial, which in effect was dedicated—as they saw it—to some abstract nationalist principle, was the last straw. "*Hamne lohi pani ek kar diya aur sab kuch airport ko de diya, aur ab yeh hamara apman karte hain*" (We have combined blood and sweat and given our all to the airport and now they insult us). When I asked them what they would like, Hiru said, "We never wanted money; our only demand is that our names should be listed publicly on the memorial so that when we are gone, our children have something to remember us by. Some '*Jai Kisan*' doesn't work for us [*koi Jai Kisan se kam nahin chalega*]. I have a memento [that was given by the IAF at the felicitation ceremony] that they [the headman and local politicians] wanted to take away and install in the panchayat office. I dared them by saying, 'First you go and show that you have the courage [*himmat*] to do this work and then you can keep all the mementos you like.' These people are just making money out of our hard work [*hamare nam pe paisa kha rahein hain*]. . . . They call us brave mothers, but this is military work, not mother's work!"

Himmat—courage and strength—are qualities of mind and body that they absorbed from the military, borrowing from their work ethic. This was the military ethic that was infused into them through the men in uniform who steadfastly stood by their side throughout that dangerous time unlike those who are now trying to appropriate their experiences for political mileage—some of whom were not even born at that time. For these *viranganas*, it is the military who understands the value of their work and courage and has rewarded them appropriately. In return, they applaud the military for what they see constitute the true elements of national pride: hard work and endurance under pressure, rather than empty political slogans alone. They resist the claims made on their bodies by the nation in service of its Hindu nationalist aspirations that seeks to anchor security in women as mothers. Their comments are a strong indictment of the 2015 memorial and the manner in which, they argue, the political machinery of the state has stakes in the memorial that are quite distinct from the "military" and civil administration of the time as it honed their courage (*himmat*) and instilled in them the contours of patriotism.

Conclusion

This chapter suggests that despite its projection in a heroic or spectacular (and very masculine) mode, the work of policing also constitutes hard physical labor and requires qualities of mind that are not innate but forged in connection with the materiality of the work that is done. Women who constituted military labor during wartime remind us of these qualities that they too partook of in their close interactions with the military. This chapter tells us that interactions between women and the state's military-security apparatus are not always coercive, but they are also not always forged within a gendered idiom of sexuality, care, domesticity, or mothering alone. It is crucial to be mindful of the social composition of those who are able or invited to merge their interests with the military. For example, Nira Yuval-Davis (2013) urges us to be conscious of the specific ways in which racial or ethnic minorities may be deployed or excluded by the military. The migrant "Bengali" and Muslim women discussed in chapters 3 and 4 are far more likely to be constituted as objects of policing than the Hindu *viranganas* of this chapter. Although hailed as brave mothers and heroines of war through the trope of the *virangana* as in the instance of the unveiling of a memorial to their wartime contribution, the *viranganas* do not see their contribution to the nation only in being a good mother and nurturer of male soldiers but also in the gritty task of building the nation's infrastructure. The *virangana* inhabits the nation viscerally as she inhales the fumes of shrapnel in the aftermath of shelling, feels the reverberation of the bombs that the enemy nation drops and scalds her hands as she rebuilds what is destroyed by the enemy during wartime. In doing so, she is also paying homage to the military man who shares these experiences with her and distinguishes him from the civil political establishment that seeks political mileage from war. Being a good patriotic woman is premised here not on staying at home as virtuous woman or even as the militant mother but on transcending the limits of home, in defiance of the family and abandoning her children. In doing so, she forges a visceral connection with the nation as her body bears scars for the war and she labors under the gaze of uniformed officers. The "state" itself is further disaggregated into constituencies such as the military and the civil administration, not all of which are necessarily evaluated in a similar manner.

PART II

Policing and the Family

Chapter 3

Policing Muslim Marriage

The Specter of the "Bengali" Wife

It was a chilly January afternoon in Sonapar, a predominantly Muslim village southwest of Bhuj. Mohamed Hosain and I had finished with our interviews for the day and were waiting for a bus to return to town. A passerby informed us that the 4:30 p.m. bus had been discontinued; there were no more buses scheduled for the day. A biting wind had picked up, and the bus shelter began to fill with men lighting up their *bidis* (hand-rolled cigarettes), as they wrapped their woolen shawls tightly about them, their talk turning to politics and the recently concluded elections to the state assembly. Just as we were about to go off in search of some other means of transport, a young woman approached us, speaking in perfect Hindi. I turned around in surprise. It was unusual to find a Hindi-speaking woman in the area; moreover, one who had the courage to walk into a public space on the street dominated by men, as she had just done, was practically unknown in my experience in the area.

I had just spent the better part of the day interviewing women of all ages in the village, our conversations held in a mix of Gujarati and Kutchi; I would

have been happy to have had someone to speak with in a language I considered myself to be more fluent in. She introduced herself as Razia, from Udai-
pur, in the neighboring state of Rajasthan. She was relatively new to the
village, having moved after her marriage four months previously. "Why didn't
you join our meeting?" I asked her, but Razia simply shrugged off the question. Suddenly, a flicker of recognition dawned: I had caught a glimpse of
her on a visit the previous week. The women I was meeting with at the time
were dismissive of her and told me that she could not have anything relevant
to add to our discussion. Although not fully convinced about this explanation at the time, I had let it slide and had more or less forgotten about it. Now,
at the bus stop, Razia wanted to know who we were and what brought us to
the village. I asked if she was the only person from Rajasthan in the area,
thinking that perhaps she could introduce me to others, but she shrugged
and said she did not know. The following week, I was back in the village
again. This time, I was with the outreach team of a local nongovernmental
organization (NGO) that worked with rural women artisans. I asked Sonal,
who took classes in health education with them, whether she knew anything
about Razia. "Oh, yes!" she exclaimed in the small room packed with women.
"The girl from *Kalkatta*—I have never heard her open her mouth. I have
tried and tried to get her to participate in our sessions, but she won't budge
from her house."[1] Looking meaningfully at the other women, she said, "You
must encourage her to go out and about and to overcome her shyness. Otherwise, how will she ever settle down into her *sasural* [affinal home]?" The
women looked on in silence, and we began the day's session as though Sonal
had not spoken at all.

   On our drive back to Bhuj that day, I asked Sonal why she had referred
to her as "the girl from Kalkatta" when I had been told distinctly that she
was from Rajasthan by Razia herself when she came up to me at the bus stop.
Furthermore, none of the women addressed by Sonal that morning had made
any effort to correct her "mistake" in referring to Razia as from Kolkata
rather than Rajasthan. And finally, Razia certainly did not seem to be a shy
and reclusive person as our encounter at the bus stop had already demonstrated. So what exactly was going on? Sonal turned to me and offered an
explanation: Razia was *actually* one of the many "Bengali brides" who had
been "bought" (*kharid ke*) from Kolkata by her husband who had traveled to
Bengal to bring her back. However, the family was afraid of her presence
being detected as an "illegal immigrant" by the police, so they tried to cover

up her being from the eastern region of Bengal, claiming instead that she was from a western state, Rajasthan. Since she spoke Hindi, a language spoken in Rajasthan, this was a good enough cover for now. Soon, Sonal reflected, she would be able to blend in once she had learned the local language and customs. Her "shyness" was a good excuse for not having to bring her out in company where her lack of facility in the local language would have otherwise given her away to the police as being from "outside," notably from Bengal. Sonal's "knowledge" of these practices of dissimulation were quite widely shared among middle-class Hindu society in town, drawn in part from the voluminous media discourse on the subject, as I was to discover.

In contemporary Kutch, there is much media and political interest in women designated as "Bengali" who move to Kutch to marry, or after their marriage to, local men. I first started ethnographic research in Kutch in 2001; often while traveling through isolated villages in Banni, I heard someone or the other mention a "*kalkatta bai*" or *Bangalan* (woman from Kolkata or Bengal). It turned out that these were women brought from "Kalkatta" or somewhere farther east to marry locally, much as Sonal had explained. "Kalkatta" was typically a euphemism for the fact that they were from Bengal. None of the women I ended up interviewing were actually from the city; some, although certainly not all, said they were from Bengal. All the women I interviewed identified themselves as Muslim and were married to Muslim men in Kutch. I did hear cases of "Bengali" Muslim women married into Hindu families in Kutch, although I did not find instances of the reverse—that is, Hindu women migrants married to Muslim men. Further, to ask whether they are "actually" Hindu or Muslim, West Bengali or Bangladeshi, Indian or Pakistani is not really the point, as that would be to limit our frame of analysis to terms naturalized by the state (see, e.g., Bourdieu 1994). In addition, it is in fact to replicate the forms of policing that emanate from the state as it attempts to "fix" the identity of those women in Kutch who are deemed to have transgressed some form or other of the social and moral code—that is, they are adult women who have traveled into Kutch from elsewhere, usually unaccompanied by men (such as husbands) from their home regions; they have not migrated in search of "work" but marriage; their marriages violate accepted social codes of religious, caste, and regionally endogamous marriage. Thus, I follow the local use of the category of Bangalan (Bengali woman) as a term that designates a particular sociological category of person rather than a specific designator of place or region. The "Bangalan" is, on the one hand, the subject of policing by the state and border security forces, for she indexes the fear of the "illegal Bangladeshi (i.e., Muslim) migrant"; on the other hand, the designation by ordinary people of a host of migrant women as "Bangalan" points to the difficulty of asserting in any "accurate" way who is the target of censure and by whom.

This chapter unpacks the myriad ways in which migrant Muslim wives in central and northern Kutch are the subjects both of a heightened visibility and a dissimulated presence. It is generally believed by the largely Hindu middle-class, newspaper-reading public in Bhuj such as Sonal that these migrant wives are "hidden" at home, away from public interaction until they can demonstrate a facility in the local language and customs in order to "pass" scrutiny. This acquiring of local cultural capital is also seen to be premised on a "forgetting" of existing practices, such as reading and writing, and their fluency in other languages (Hindi, Bengali) in order to more effectively "blend" into their new environment. Although the "Bangladeshi infiltrator" is made visible through sensational news stories and gossip networks, the chapter argues that "detection" by the police or media is not the only challenge that "Bengali" women migrants are faced with as they choose to manage their visibility to others. Even though the opening vignette suggests that the family is complicit in "protecting" these women through the mechanism of the public secret, for instance, this is not to suggest that the family/community does not engage in its own modes of policing, as will be seen. Further, as many of my interactions with the family that are presented in this chapter were mediated through the NGO's outreach activities in these villages, it will become apparent how various, often competing demands for visibility (for the police and border patrol, for NGO-led development work, or for the anthropologist) are managed with the need for privacy within the family.

Donor agencies require the process and results of development work to be made transparent. Here, transparency is accountability. This produces practices—not unlike the anthropologists'—that may mimic forms of biometric surveillance associated with the state such as taking photographs or thumb impressions (see, e.g., Garriott 2011, 138). Further, the ubiquitous anthropologist—whether or not she asks tricky questions—observes, takes photographs and notes, and may be drawn into family dynamics that unfold over time. The presence of the anthropologist may court exposure for those who are cast within her reach. This exposure may be welcomed as a source of social capital—in the case, for instance, of Nizam, the maulana who derived some stature among his peers through his attempts to direct my research—but it may also bring unwelcome attention, as we will see in chapter 4 with Bano, a "Bengali" wife who uses her interaction with me to "defend" herself against charges of wrongdoing. The family-NGO-state-anthropologist network pushes people to dissimulate differently, even as they are required to make themselves transparent—albeit in different ways—to each of these institutions and people. How migrant wives and their families manage the terrain between "detection" and "deception," determining how much to reveal or conceal, from whom and to what end is the subject of this chapter. The ethnography suggests that the law or police are not the only sites that court heightened visibility while the family is a site of interiority or refuge from the law or its agents. The possibility of exposure lurks on the edges of every interaction, inside or outside the family. The idea of the family as a "safe" space or a site of refuge from the state is tested throughout as "Bengali" women move in and out of focus through multiply mediated interactions and encounters. Ideas of insider/outsider and of legality are rearticulated, negotiated, and acted on constantly, both by the police department and the family.

One of the sites where the margin between legality and illegality is produced in the evaluation of women's mobility is its designation as either marriage or trafficking, as the two possible legal registers for women's mobility—the one a legal and aspirational social status, the other a dreaded social evil. Surveillance and policing of women's mobility exists both at what are assumed to be more "cosmopolitan" and "global" sites such as airport immigration counters and visa offices (e.g., Maunaguru 2014) where women are asked to "prove" the nature of their relationship with the men accompanying them on their travels, much as women like Razia may be accosted by police in Kutch on the merest suspicion of too much (or not enough) fluency in a particular spoken language, to determine the legitimacy of their presence in the region. When I decided to systematically track down more "Bengali" women, Mohamed Hosain was uncharacteristically hesitant; he finally asked me outright whether my meeting them would threaten their carefully strategized subvisibility.[2] Apart from the fact that I have changed their names, this is another reason why the book is not taken up with the question of origins and my references to "Bengali" women migrants are presented not as a fact of their identity but to index the manner in which they were referred to in the field. My challenge in writing up this ethnography was to try and retain the element of uncertainty and the constant play between "truth" and "falsehood," "detection" and "deception," "visibility" and "invisibility" as I encountered it. As in my encounters with Razia, Nizam, and a number of others, my fieldwork was riddled with instances of conversations that did not add up. People said one thing at one time, and they were quite often contradicted another time, often constituting the realm of the public secret. News and information seemed to circulate ahead of me; what I thought of as my sudden and unannounced visits in the remotest of villages were often anticipated. "Oh, so-and-so mentioned that you might show up," "X mentioned that you had come around, asking questions," making it more and more apparent to me that I was not the only one piecing together a story. Nizam had become keenly invested in my fieldwork, to the point that I had begun to feel distinctly uncomfortable about what I felt was his way of managing my access to people and information. When contradicted publicly, my interlocutors were not embarrassed to have their "lie" caught out as I initially thought. Instead, everyone was participating in various forms of the "public secret" (Taussig 1999; Robinson 2013; Jusionyte 2015). So when Sonal referred to Razia as "the girl from Kalkatta" in a room full of women who had said otherwise to me, there was none of the embarrassment that I thought would ensue from their being "caught out" in this—what appeared to me to be—blatant "lie": for had they not just the other day told me that she was from Rajasthan? Yet, this was not the case. We became part of a shared system of knowledge that decreed how much we knew and what we had to agree to not know publicly (Robinson 2013).

These incidents allowed me to recalibrate my encounters with various informants along the scale of honesty versus subterfuge, truth versus lies, or transparency versus deception. Instead, each of these categories was constantly shifting in relation to what was being said when, about whom, and most importantly, *to* whom. Agents of surveillance were not just to be encountered in the form of the police and the border security forces but also as journalists, development workers, tourists, and the roving anthropologist, as argued in chapter 1. When a woman designated as "Bengali" married into a family, she—and her affinal family—worked to manage her appearance and disappearance across interactions. The following sections explore some of these interactions and highlight some of the tensions that often built up in these carefully choreographed social dramas that nonetheless sometimes veered off script as when Razia broke out of the social role chosen for her (of invisibility) to track me down in a public street and strike up a conversation in full public view. In the sections that follow, I present some of the everyday interactions that took place in Sonapar between Muslim families and the anthropologist, in this case mediated through NGO activity. Each of these actors brought their own desire for information gathering into their encounters and were managed within the overall context of policing the "illegal" migrant as set out by police and media discourses.

Exposing the "Illegal" Migrant

Police and media reports regularly report the arrest of "Bangladeshis" from Kutch; in these reports, there is little by way of contextualizing the "illegality" of border crossing or migration. Men apprehended in the border areas of the Rann who cannot provide a good enough reason for their presence are often declared to be "Bangladeshi" citizens. Police rely on intuitive sartorial and linguistic markers to "recognize" them in the absence of documentary evidence of their nationality. For instance, a news report titled "Bangladeshi Held from Kutch" mentions that the man arrested and sent to the Joint Interrogation Centre in Bhuj "has no documents on him. He was wearing a lungi, shirt and skull cap," the *lungi* supposedly giving him away, as men in Kutch tend to wear *shalwar kameez*. It adds, "He is acting as if he is not able to speak. . . . Policemen say there are many Bangladeshis in this region and when they are caught, they *pretend to be dumb*" (Yusuf 2011, emphasis added). These media practices are also instructive and pedagogic in nature: they enumerate the practices of deception used by "illegal" border crossers, thus schooling the reading public how to "recognize" or "read" practices designated as "suspicious." This includes imbuing general personality traits (such as a new bride's "shyness") or presumed disability (inability to speak) with suspicious intent, resignifying these as symptoms of illegality within a field of police practice (Garriott 2011). The newspaper-reading public is then complicit with the police in the identification of these traits as suspicious and as markers of illegal cross-border activity. Another report, titled "Exfiltration: The New Threat to Border Security" (Nair 2007), describes how there is a growing trend of Indian and Bangladeshi Muslims crossing the western border illegally to enter Pakistan from where they hope to go to the Middle East in search of employment. It describes some of the strategies they follow to escape detection: "posing as cattle grazers; some pretended to be mentally unstable when the security persons caught them loitering near the Great Rann of Kutch" (Nair 2007). Another reports, "the 'foreigner' catching 'spree' in the bordering [*sic*] Kutch district of Gujarat continued with the arrest of a Bangladeshi lady in Kharinadi area of Bhuj town late last evening" (*Desh Gujarat* 2015a). "Mental instability" is a frequently recurring trope in these stories (e.g., *Desh Gujarat* 2015b). Police reports emphasize that "mental instability" (usually referred to in scare quotes) and the inability to speak are ruses to get by without detection. It is significant that "mental instability" is thus marked out for evidence of criminal intent. In my travels across Muslim settlements across Banni, I discovered that due to generations of consanguineous marriages, it was not unusual to find occasional cases of mental illness that was likely the consequence of a highly in-bred population. This was more visible among some communities than others. However, this became resignified in police-speak to indicate a deliberate pantomime of mental illness/playing dumb to avoid having to speak and be caught. The news story titled "Bengali-Speaking Girls Being Trafficked to Kutch District of Gujarat" (Bhattacharya 2012) seamlessly moves between "Bengali-speaking" women and "Bangladeshi" women; in effect, this conflates all Bengali speakers as Bangladeshis (therefore "illegal"), regardless of the fact that Indian citizens from the state of West Bengal are also Bengali speakers. The news item is imbued with a strong sense of moral panic: "The coastal district of Kutch in Gujarat is witnessing a *sea change in its demographic profile.* Hundreds of Bengali-speaking Muslim women are being trafficked from Bengal and Bangladesh to Kutch, where they are sold off as brides. . . . A large number of these women are even pushed into flesh trade [*sic*]" (Bhattacharya 2012, emphasis added). Although the women interviewed in the story say they are from West Bengal, the reporter takes recourse to their "Bangladeshi dialect" as evidence of their illegality. The article concludes, "for the authorities, the biggest challenge is in detecting the alleged Bangladeshi women as their nationality is shown as 'Indian' on government papers. *'Even if we suspect them to be Bangladeshis*, we can do nothing as they hold valid Indian papers,' a senior police officer said" (Bhattacharya 2012, emphasis added).

The "suspicion" of being Bangladeshi is thus tied into nondocumentary forms of life: skin color, clothing, and speech (or its absence). Through these rhetorical devices, the "Bangladeshi" migrant is then produced as an object of social and moral disorder through media practices that sensationalize the "trafficking" of women and the "infiltration" of men from Bangladesh into Kutch. The "Bengali" woman in Kutch is designated as cultural "matter out of place" by the police regardless of where she has actually migrated from. Almost every family I knew in Kutch was acquainted with or was related to someone who was married to a "Bangalan." Some of the women I met with and interacted with over time said they were from Bihar or Jharkhand, other Indian states east of Gujarat, even as our mutual acquaintances—if they were present—shook their heads incredulously: "Oh, you are not from Bengal? We always thought you were!" The "Bangalan" thus indexes (il)legality and visibility more than region of origin. On the one hand, this discursive strategy ends up illegalizing Muslim women migrants in Kutch as "illegal border crossers," "trafficked women," or as victims of "forced marriages" from the point of view of various state law enforcement agencies. These varied constructions of illegality coalesce for the most part into the figure of the Bangladeshi migrant in India who is the "iconic illegal migrant" in India, much as the Mexican migrant is in the United States, her illegality inhabited as a perpetual condition of "deportablity" (de Genova 2013). Illegality is not a fact given in law—attested to by the presence or absence of paperwork, for instance—but is actively produced through encounters between various forms of regulation and policing that generate the legal and illegal as relational rather than fixed categories (Poole 2004; Jusionyte 2015). Language, religion, sartorial practices, and skin color became clues to the identity—and thus the presumed legality—of migrants in the region.

On the other hand, the "Bangalan"—the collective designation for a host of women who migrate into Kutch from outside—are also received by the Muslim families that they marry into as desirable outsiders. There are different moral codes in operation as the presence of the "outsider" is evaluated. On the one hand, the "Bengali" Muslim woman is feared as a reproductive being that threatens the nation's demographic balance away from the ideal Hindu-majority population, desired by right-wing nationalist parties. On the other hand, she is read through a different moral index for Muslims who see her as the bearer of an Islamic civility—although poor (therefore, sent far away in marriage by parents who cannot afford to provide her with dowry), she comes with cultural capital—that is, knowledge of reading and writing and of Islamic values—which she can then disseminate in her new environment.

Forms of action or states of being that are marked out as constituting "suspicious activity" by the state may be read quite differently by families who choose migrant brides.[3] This does not, however, mean that borderland residents are not discerning about what it means to have "others" in their midst. It is just to point out that the moral axis along which this distinction is made is different from the policing that emanates from the state.

The Bengali Migrant and India's "Citizenship Regime"

The migrant has been crucial to legal debates on citizenship in India from the very beginning, as seen in the foundational debates on citizenship after Partition. Although migration enabled the acquisition of citizenship during the immediate post-Partition period, when it "provided the condition of passage into citizenship" (Roy 2010, 27), it was precisely the figure of the migrant that became a mark of illegality by the 1980s, the "illegal migrant" from Bangladesh becoming a key site of nationalist insecurity (Roy 2010). Although the Bengali Muslim immigrant from Bangladesh became a particularly charged policy issue only in the 1980s when India's "citizenship regime" (Jayal 2013) began to move toward a more exclusionary definition of citizenship, it had been biased against Muslims right from its inception following decolonization. In the immediate aftermath of the 1947 partition, Constituent Assembly debates already reveal an inherent bias as they attempted to keep out Muslims, with Hindus regarded as somewhat more "natural" citizens (Jayal 2013, chap. 2). Legal judgments and cases indicate this double-speak by the Indian state on the question of migration into India from Pakistan, reaffirming in the process the "ethno-cultural and gendered bias of citizenship in India" (Roy 2010, 61). Especially in the period between the enactment of the constitution in 1950 and the commencement of the Citizenship Act in 1955, a period characterized as one of indeterminacy and liminality (Roy 2010), there was a notable distinction between policies pertaining to the granting of citizenship to Hindus coming to India from Pakistan and those that concerned themselves with the admission of Pakistani wives as Indian citizens. The latter, as Roy's (2010, 62) survey of archival documents reveals, was a far more "grudging admission" while there appeared to be an official understanding "that the legal confirmation of Indian citizenship of displaced (Hindu) minorities from Pakistan was to be facilitated and expedited" (74).

Chapter 5 will revisit these concerns ethnographically through an examination of cross-border migration from TharParkar in Sindh and the role of marriage and kinship networks in facilitating the transition into citizenship for those who chose to migrate in and around 1971. Current debates over who has more legitimate claims to citizenship and residence rights in India thus bear the shadow of these early debates. The Citizenship Amendment Act of 2019 legalizes the status of certain religious "minorities" from neighboring countries (to be read as all except Muslims—"Hindus, Sikhs, Buddhists, Jains, Parsis and Christians from Afghanistan, Bangladesh and Pakistan") who, it is proposed, "shall not be treated as illegal migrants for the purposes of this Act."[4] This is the third amendment to the Citizenship Act, with earlier changes incorporated in 1986 and 2003, each of which was formulated as a response to the crisis of potential Muslim migration into India. Muslim migrants from neighboring countries (or, for that matter, even from other states within the country as seen above) are designated as "infiltrators." Migrants' status is thus "illegalized" (Jusionyte 2015) through such discursive exercises: the designation of refugee or infiltrator.

Moral Panics and the Migrant Woman

In late-colonial India, women's chastity and appropriately managed conjugality was the idiom for the construction of what was deemed to be an authentically indigenous (and therefore Hindu) nationalist response to colonial modernity (Sarkar 2001). The upper caste Hindu woman was "the metaphor for both the unviolated, chaste, inner space and the possible consequence of its surrender" (Sarkar 2001, 265). Sexual moralities in the late-nineteenth and early twentieth centuries were reconstituted within the idiom of an upper caste, bourgeois respectability. Hindi literature was canonized into a properly respectable genre; the depiction of Hindu women consequently shifted "from the sensual to the virtuous. . . . The woman was gradually transformed from a figure of eroticism, sexuality, excess and playfulness to a classic, calm and perfect figure in most of 'high' literature. The assertion of a moral code in a canon of literature became a national virtue" (Gupta 2001, 40–41). The Hindu woman had to be protected from the Muslim male, portrayed in newspapers and popular literature of the time as aggressive and lewd. A spate of "abduction" stories circulated in the popular media in the 1920s enabled the consolidation of the "Muslim" as the chief threat to the emergent Hindu community as they targeted the Muslim man as the lascivious aggressor who set out to "abduct" the virtuous and innocent Hindu woman who must be kept safe from his clutches (Gupta 2001).

With this high value placed on chastity and domesticity in the evaluation of women's character, migrant women have been marked out for particular censure in the subcontinent, much as in other parts of the world (Andrijasevic 2010). Women's migration in general—regardless of religion or ethnicity—is often designated as "trafficking" in the domains of law and public policy. This is also the result of a tendency to equate women's mobility with questionable morality (Kapur 2010). Thus, many distinct types of labor migration undertaken by women are often collapsed under the single framework of "sex work" and all sex work is then equated to trafficking. This problematic set of assumptions not only ignores other instances of exploitation and potential trafficking of women in factories and domestic work but also assumes that sex work is "immoral" and that as such, no woman would willingly choose it as a form of labor (Kempadoo 2005). In the ethnographic sections that follow, it will be seen that although law and policy may criminalize or illegalize women's migration due to a particular evaluation of "normative" women's work, the family makes its moral evaluations on a qualitatively different register. While policing the moral boundaries of the family, its interests do not always dovetail with the state and law.[5]

A Watchful Eye: Maintaining Domestic Order

In Sonapar, women artisans are crowded into the house of the "field representative" of a local NGO that works to preserve and market the region's traditional handicraft. Hasham is the chief go-between for this village and the NGO. The previous day, he had attended the weekly meeting at the latter's office where he, along with all the other field representatives from the various villages they worked in, went to deposit finished embroidered products and to collect new raw materials: thread and cloth. Back home, he has lists of items that need to be produced—cushion covers, shawls, skirts, jackets, and spectacle cases. He cuts the cloth for each item and distributes it among his kinswomen, for everyone in this village, as with other Muslim settlements that I have worked in in rural Kutch, is related to everybody else. As with other Muslim communities I met, they practice consanguineous marriage, often making it hard for the anthropologist to keep track of kinship as there were so many doubled-up relations. By the time I arrive at Hasham's, most have already left with their assignments. It is 1:00 p.m., and he tells me he has been at it since 9:00 a.m.! "What do you want to embroider?" he asks a young woman whose turn has arrived. She says that she would like to do a shawl. "No," he replies, "you already have a lot of work that you still have not finished; you need to bring that in before you take anything else. If you want something small like a spectacle case, you can have that." She looks doubtful and is too shy to pursue the matter, perhaps because I am sitting right behind her. Turning to another woman, he tells her to embroider three cushion covers and that he wants them done by Friday. "By Friday!" she exclaims. "But that is only three days away; I couldn't possibly do that. Why not give me one or two?" "Because," responds Hasham, "they are a part of a *set*; they have the same design, so it is better to have one person do them. This is a new design and it will look better if one pair of hands works on all of them." He hands her the embroidery threads for them. The fabric is orange, and it will have a beige and brown pattern on it. She still looks doubtful and says she cannot take this on; she does not have much time. She settles for spectacle cases instead. Mehreen, who is Hasham's sister, gets the cushion covers instead. Who decides on the patterns and the colors? I ask Hasham. "I do," he declares with a grin. He is still trying to persuade the young woman to do the cushion covers: "People in big cities have liked these products," he tells her. "When a woman from *Dilli* [New Delhi] came to the [NGO's] office, she looked around for things to buy and didn't like anything as much as our products; people like them, they will buy them, you should be happy to do this work," he adds. Still unsuccessful, he gives up. Why not give her what she wants? I ask. He replies that he knows each and every woman's embroidery by heart; he can recognize the singularity and uniqueness of each's work and that he knows who is capable of what, whose work is likely to be better appreciated than others. He keeps a strict watch on the progress of the embroidery even as he is doling out new tasks and chatting with me. Women stop by occasionally to show him their works in progress, and he checks and comments on each one. "A stitch in time saves nine, isn't that so?" he asks.

Meanwhile, Mehreen, with orange cushion covers in hand, asks me to come with her to her house. "I will sit and work, and we can keep chatting, OK?" We settle down on the porch in front of her house where there are about six women of all ages embroidering away. She introduces me to her daughter-in-law and two of her young daughters who are still too young to embroider professionally but have begun as apprentices to their mother. She begins to measure the orange fabric designated for a cushion cover. Hasham has drawn out a pattern and she will follow it. But when she measures across, she demonstrates that the design is not accurately drawn. "Basically, his markings are just to give me an idea. Now I will measure and find the center point from which to make a symmetrical design." The embroidery is geometric and relies a great deal on accuracy of the counted spaces between each stitch. "How will you mix and use the colors you have been given?" I ask. "Oh, that is up to me," she says. And what of the decision as to what stitch to use where? "That, too, is up to me," she responds.

Hasham prides himself on being able to "read" everybody's stitches; he has a keen sense of his kinsfolk and indicates that nobody can escape his eagle eye. He knows who is visible and present when the anthropologist and the NGO team visits and who is not. He works hard to manage the public face that the artisans of his village present to the outside world: the quality of their embroidery, their punctuality, and their attention to detail in their work: *hath ki safai*, which translates as a clear (i.e., skilled) hand, but importantly, it can also indicate a "sleight of hand," depending on the context. He also took it upon himself to organize the "rebuilding" of the village using donor funds in the aftermath of the Gujarat earthquake of 2001.[6] Although the police are focused on aspects of dress, demeanor, and language to determine the boundaries between the insider and outsider, in the determination of "illegality," they are not the only ones keeping an eye on those activities or persons who are seen as rupturing the smooth flow of everyday life. The family also keeps a keen eye on the management of legitimacy, between those seen as insiders and outsiders. Skills and general good breeding, such as reading and writing, and knowledge of the Koran and a generally "Islamic" way of life are also central to the manner in which boundaries are drawn up between those who are "local" and those who may have come in from the outside and therefore the locus of potential suspicion. Family and kinship networks are once again crucial in the way in which these boundaries are negotiated.

Further, this brief vignette suggests that the family does not denote a space of "interiority" from the gaze of the state, law, or the police. What the law threatens to expose ("illegality" of citizenship status, for instance), the family does not necessarily cover up in the folds of intimacy and kin relations. Exposure is threatened at each level, just as one is being scrutinized even when within the ambit of the "domestic." In the above examples, embroidery is being distributed through domestic networks, where women's individual style and skill is known to their kinsfolk. Hasham is the uncle who knows familial secrets, but he is also its conduit to the outside world through his official designation at the NGO. Watchfulness and knowledge of the domestic can segue into surveillance and the deployment of information about the family by others as well.

Islamic Civility and the Strategic Incorporation of "Outsiders"

Hasham's sister is married to a man of another caste in a different village. She has a physical disability, and it had been difficult to find a match within the village. A marriage was fixed in a village in Banni among a different caste, more socially backward and poor. One of her sisters-in-law—her husband's brother's wife—is a "Bengali" woman, Halima. She stands out in her affinal home by virtue of her (very elementary) education; the others are steeped in illiteracy and ill health. Halima knows how to read and write; over the sounds of her rolling out and cooking *rotis* (bread) on a tiny wood-fired stove in the corner of her single-roomed hut and her children crying occasionally, I catch fragments of sound as voices reciting the alphabet in Urdu float in on the breeze: "*aliph, be, pe . . . sin, shin . . . toe, zoe . . . lam, mim, nun,*" the children are chanting rhythmically, strong gusts of wind carrying away bits and pieces. Do they go to school? I ask Halima. She teaches them the Urdu alphabet and the Koran. They come to her every morning and study until the afternoon with a break in between. "What is the point of a school?" she says. "What is there to learn in a jungle?"

"You never can tell," she says, concentrating on the *roti* she is rolling out, "where your destiny [*kismat*] will pick you up and leave you." Her husband is completely unlettered; he did not even know how to be a Muslim, said Halima. "The atmosphere [*mahaul*] here is completely different from where I grew up." Her husband was named Moti (pearl), after his grandfather. When he was to get married to Halima, her parents said that this "Hindu name" would not do; he should get a "proper" Muslim name. So he changed it to Mohammed Ali. Halima has brought some "*Islami tariqa*" (Islamic ways) to the family but was soon disheartened. On my next visit a couple of months later, she said she had stopped teaching the children. Her mother-in-law had died in a road accident in Bhuj, and it was difficult to manage all the work at home. In any case, she felt that the "atmosphere" (*mahaul*) in a "jungle" was not easy to change. "Look at their names: most of the time, they just name their children after the day [of the week]."

Hasham's sister wants to bring Halima, who is her sister-in-law, to Sonapar on one of her visits home. "I want to show her a different place," she says to her brother, Hasham. "We have fields and some *kheti* [cultivation; agriculture] in Sonapar. Sonal comes once a week, and the women get to meet others when they go to the NGO office now and then." Hasham told her off in no uncertain terms: "You think I don't know what is going on under my nose? I will not allow it. In fact, you have had too much freedom. I don't know what your husband calls himself [a reference to another un-Islamic and, according to him, 'odd' name], but it's time he stopped letting you out and about. I don't want girls from here and there hiding under my roof." Later, Hasham explained to me out of his sister's earshot that he did not want any *lafda* (problem or scandal) over the presence of women he could not vouch for personally. It occurred to me through the many visits I had with Hasham that he had never mentioned Razia, who had spoken to me at the village's bus stop. Although he and I met and spoke at length over the course of a couple of years, he never once raised the question of "Bengali" women in his own village, even though he did not have any hesitation in discussing Halima, the "Bengali" sister-in-law of his own sister. Although the women of the village appeared to acknowledge her existence, even if they did not wish to clarify her biographical details—if in fact these details were public knowledge—I was never able to meet Razia again to interview her directly.

Ways of Seeing

What a particular category "looks" like as it is enumerated is typically an anthropological/state concern that does not always mirror the blurriness in practice. Although the overarching theme for the police's search for "outsiders" in this border was evidence of being Muslim and/or Bengali, Hasham constantly made references to various "others" from whom he chose to distinguish his people. These "others" were typically *adivasis*—a generic term used for the freelance migrant labor that came into Kutch after the earth-quake in search of work in construction. What is also noteworthy is that Ha-sham's own self-reflection on what it means to be Muslim also complicates ways of seeing that are naturalized by the police and the state that uses cer-tain markers such as clothing or given names to make an assessment over identity and from there jumps to conclusions about legality, as is done for "Bengalis" on this border.

The theme of given names came up often in conversation, along with what were seen to be forms of behavior that were deemed to index a certain "Is-lamic" civility. Driving with me to visit his sister in Banni on one occasion, Hasham explains to me the rudiments of their faith: "We are not Muslim [*mussalman*]! 'Mussalman' means those who pray five times a day and who read the Koran; this is what it [the Koran] says; you must have read this there. We don't read *namaz*, nor do our children. And after all, if we don't, then how will they follow our example? Look [pointing outside the car at pass-ing herds of cattle]! Allah has made a cow different from a buffalo, a goat different from a camel. You can spot the difference as soon as you set eyes on any of them; you would never mistake one for the other. But he did not make any difference between human beings, between a Hindu and a Mus-lim. There is nothing to distinguish us. By keeping a beard, we think we become Muslims! But a true Muslim is only he who prays regularly and reads the Koran. We don't do that, so we cannot lay true claim to being Muslim."

Hasham was able to detail for me his ideas of who constituted a "real" Muslim, thus distancing himself from a full claim to the identity. Even though Islamic practice was an aspiration that was worthy of emulation, there was also a very real recognition of human frailty and the difficulties of achieving a perfect congruence with this ideal that was now available in the person of the "Bengali" bride who often displayed a fluency in Koranic education, as Halima had. Similarly, there was also an understanding of what forms of practice they wanted to distance themselves from. Who was allowed entry into the circle of kinship and residence in the village was the outcome of a process of vetting that Hasham declared crucial to maintaining social order. *Adivasis* were universally reviled by most Muslims as being of a particularly uncivilized form of life. Bengali brides, on the other hand, were poor and came from destitute families ("They are so poor, their parents have no choice but to sell them—*bech dete hain*—to far-off places") but had capital in the form of more "properly" Islamic ways that could contribute to the uplift and maintenance of the moral order in families and villages they were married into. This made the Bengali woman a desirable wife and mother.

The reviling of the *adivasi* was closely linked to the competition for scarce resources in the region and how the incoming *adivasi* directly threatened Muslims' access to work.[7] In Dolpar, a village of pastoralists in Banni, I never saw any men in the village, whatever the time of day or night. Rumana, a middle-aged woman who kept a feisty hold over her family, said that in all her years she had never seen such hard times as these, referring to the consequences of three consecutive years of drought. "We are traditionally *maldharis* [pastoralists], and we do still have some *mal* [animal herds; also wealth] which the men are currently out with in hopes of finding some water and fodder. They used to work in *kolsa* [coal; making coal illegally by burning wood]. That was good, the going rate was 110 rupees for 40 kilos of coal, but it's been nine months now and that has been closed down. They promised us that they would restart it after the elections, but we are still waiting. It's too dangerous to work in coal nowadays. The police roam about every evening," she says, circling above her head with her finger.

Suddenly struck by an idea, she turns to Sonal. "Why don't you take the coal that we have and sell it for us?" Sonal laughs and retorts that she does not want to go to jail either! She suggests instead that their menfolk travel up to Bhuj and look for work among the newly commissioned construction work in the post-earthquake building boom in the towns. Sonal adds that there are people like the *adivasis* who have come from so far to work in Bhuj, people who have come from outside Kutch even; so why should their own menfolk not be more enterprising in their search for work? Rumana virtually explodes. "These *adivasis* are all over the place! It's as if when the earth moved and shook at the time of the earthquake, these *adivasis* came out of the earth and took over this place! Wherever you turn, they are there!" She regains her composure and adds, "Well, most of our men are away in any case, looking for work; there are only two men in the village, looking after all of us women, and we need them to stay here," she concludes firmly.

Hasham takes me on a walk around his village. The houses are easily identifiable: after the earthquake, the NGO built them 132 houses from their reconstruction grant. Seventeen new houses are being built under a poverty rehabilitation scheme of the government, and fifteen were built under the same scheme before the earthquake. The NGO-sponsored construction stands out—round cement structures with rust-colored curved roofs, whereas the government-sponsored ones are rectangular with sloping tiled roofs. Interspersed with these new houses are old ones, or remnants of old ones, mostly made of mud, with tiled or thatched roofs, repaired after each monsoon. Hasham conducted the post-earthquake village survey himself and decided on the number of new houses required to be built through the NGO. The organization had planned and budgeted to build houses only for those people registered with them as artisans.

This did not suit them, said Hasham, pointing out that at that time, there were only about forty artisans. "How could we say to one brother that you will get a house, but the other one won't? So I made sure that everybody got a house constructed in their name; I even made sure that the names of my young children were written down. Now, if the organization [*sanstha*] is giving us a house, we should make sure that the future is taken care of as well, shouldn't we?" He then made sure that no "outsider" was given the building contract. He convinced the NGO staff that when he had about two-hundred-odd men in the village who needed employment, there was no way he was going to allow outsiders like "*adivasis* who want alcohol all the time, men as well as women," to come into the village and ruin the atmosphere (*mahaul*). "I drink, too," Hasham says as an aside to Mohamed Hosain, "but in moderation, not like these *adivasis*."[8] Turning back to me, he says, "I told the *sanstha*: you may send one person to oversee the construction and give instructions, be a supervisor, but all the labor will be ours. And so it happened [*aisa hua*]; our own people earned good money building these houses." For these Muslims, it was the "*adivasi*" who was the figure of social and moral disorder, a licentiousness and excess that threatened to ruin the *mahaul*. "Bengali" women, on the other hand, were seen to be poor, but they had "good Islamic values," and this was held in their favor.

The Management of Transparency

Expectations of transparency come from various institutional sources. In the context of borderland policing and the maintenance of various boundaries, NGO-led development work creates new layers to the management of deception and detection. I am at Sonapar with Sonal; she has come for a follow-up workshop with the women on safe pregnancy. We sit in a newly constructed office building and wait for the women to arrive. It is the middle of the afternoon, four o'clock and blisteringly hot. Prior to parking in front of the office, the jeep did a round of the entire village, sounding the horn loudly, announcing our arrival. About fifteen women show up and they are of all ages, many of them young unmarried girls and some older women among them. Sonal begins by asking them—as she did with the other groups in different villages—how they cleaned the cloth they used during their menstrual cycle, emphasizing how it should be washed, dried, and then stored in a clean place. The women responded that they knew how to do this. They are not like Rabaris (a Hindu pastoral community); they do know better than *them*! "They consider themselves above the Rabaris," Sonal feels the need to explain, underscoring to me once again the constant need to distinguish one's own people from "others" who are considered less "civilized." When she displays the illustrated book on pregnancy and childbirth as well as the male and female anatomy, they giggle but only sporadically. Mostly, they listen well, and I am impressed at their attention and engagement. Finally, Sonal takes out chart paper and pens and asks them to convey through illustrations what they learned today, while she will take photos to show the workshop sponsors. As soon as they see the paper and pens, they scuttle into a corner; fear grips them.

Sonal says, "You do such beautiful embroidery. Can't you draw a bit? It's not to judge you, just to get a sense of what you learned. Since you can't write, why not draw? Look, all the other villages have drawn something." And she shows them the drawings; some of the charts have a lot of written words as well. I am intrigued to see the fear of the paper and pen in this village. When the camera came out, Fawzia objected vehemently. She is educated and young; she joined the group late but interjected vehemently. "This is not right," she announced. To be showing such pictures and talking like this, and then to have them draw and talk about it—it was not acceptable to her, and she stormed off. The NGO's need for transparency is dictated by the terms of their donors who demand visible proof of the development process as well as the tangible outcomes of activities they have funded: in this case, a workshop on maternal health. These activities may bring in their wake a need to make themselves visible that is not always desired; they may also unintentionally stage or highlight some of the latent tensions within the community in their management of privacy under conditions where transparency is demanded of them.

The NGO has a newly inaugurated office building in the village, where the weekly sessions with the health and education outreach team are to be conducted. The keys cannot be located, so we all congregate in Hasham's one-roomed house once again. Like the last time, the room fills up with women, not to receive embroidery this time but to work at whatever task their teacher, Harilal, has planned for the day. A mat is spread out on the floor for me; Harilal sits on a quilt spread nearby while all the women squeeze themselves onto the floor space opposite us. Except for my tiny corner of the mat, the rest of it is scrupulously avoided by all the women. Come and sit next to me, I coax them, it is so crowded over there. But they only giggle. Finally, Harilal tells Fawzia and Mehreen to come and sit with me so that others would follow; sure enough, four women came and sat down. Once the children had been shooed away, there were about fifteen women roughly between what I imagined were the ages of about twelve to forty-five. Harilal announces the project for the day. He hands out sheets of paper to the women and tells them that they will draw their family tree on it—like this, he demonstrates, drawing one. He draws lines, each culminating in a circle that represented one person. "If you can write, put down the names of the family members you are representing in each circle; if you cannot write, at least you can draw lines and circles, can't you?" he asks them. As he demonstrates a family tree, pointing out the base for the grandfather, then branches going upward for each uncle and the father, there are stifled giggles at the prospect of drawing a circle and saying, "This is my uncle." There are not enough pens to go around, so they have to take turns at this. "Where are your notebooks and pens?" Harilal asks. There is no response except for more stifled giggles.

It takes an age for the women to come up with their charts. The broad contours of the kinship network of the village have been sketched: each chart starts with a grandfather and shows all the male members of a family. I tease Harilal, "What about the women? Why do the charts only show men?" There are more giggles, louder this time. "OK, let's put in the women, then: start with your *dadi* [paternal grandmother]," he instructs. Now there is more confusion: many women have the same name, across generations. "But they can't be the same person," I argue. More laughter. "No, but we keep the same names across generations," says an older woman. Fawzia has identified a circle with a very different-sounding name from the usual pool: Shehzadi (princess). "Now, that's a nice name; who is Shehzadi?" asks Harilal, holding up Fawzia's chart. There is an uncomfortable silence. The younger women cover their mouths with their *dupattas* and look intently down at their charts. Fawzia's mother reprimands her, a short sharp sound that I cannot decipher. Turning to me, she says, "This is why we have banned television in our village. We don't like people watching films; this is the kind of thing that happens. She is confused between real life and TV life." Nobody speaks after this; the general bonhomie has broken. Harilal and I gather up the charts and prepare to leave. An unspoken tension leaves a mark on the room, regardless of whether there is *actually* anything to hide.

Is Shehzadi a fictive character—from a television show, as Fawzia's mother's reprimand indicates—or is she someone whose public identity must be fictionalized in order for everyday life to go on? From the ethnographic vignettes recounted above, it is clear that Muslims in villages across Banni are engaged in the everyday policing of boundaries. These are social and moral enumerations that allow them to articulate their terms of belonging to a community, even while Hasham reflects pertinently that it is not always easy to demarcate the objective boundaries of a group. What does it mean to say we are Muslims? he asks—a question that is of more than passing importance to the anthropologist. These boundaries determine who is an acceptable or desirable member of the group—regardless of their language, skin color, or region of birth (thus, women from the east are desired for their "Islamic" values) and who is the "outsider"—for example, Rabaris and *adivasis* who are endowed with a social and moral bankruptcy. These evaluations of insider and outsider do not map onto the state's policing of border communities, but they take active cognizance of them. Thus, the fictionalization of Shehzadi is an acknowledgment of the multiple regimes of policing that encounter one another in this complex and multilayered terrain. When these regimes of policing come up against regimes of transparency— the NGO, the anthropologist, or the state—they produce unexpected social outcomes as recounted above.

Demands for transparency were also negotiated at a physical level of presence/absence. I noticed with the NGO outreach programs that they struggled to acquaint Muslim women in border villages with the rudiments of reading and writing. A grassroots worker in an organization dedicated to Banni's development said, "It's hard to organize anything in Banni; women will not come to any kind of public meeting." Sonal tells a group in Dolpar, "Reading makes your life easier. You can read nameplates on buses to know which one to take; you can sign your names and can keep track of your embroidery work and how much money you have earned." Often, the "Bengali" woman is better educated, albeit in Urdu. This is a fact that must be kept hidden, for it is an avenue to detection, much like reports of men being rendered "speechless" when accosted by the police.

In another village tucked away in Banni, I am introduced to two young women who—it is said to me—are from Kolkata. Over conversation and tea, Rabia tells me that she is from Patna (Bihar), that she has lived in Banni for five years now. She speaks fluent Kutchi, as does Salima who confirms that she is, indeed, from Bengal. Rabia and I had established a friendly rapport before Salima joined us, during which time she told me that Salima was from "Bangladesh" and had six or seven others from her area in nearby villages, unlike she who was all alone here; nobody from Patna had married anywhere in the region, to the best of her knowledge. Salima "corrected" Rabia's observation when she joined our conversation, stating that she was from (West) "Bengal, near the bone glass factory at Asansol." "We can't go to Bangladesh," she chides Rabia. "You need a passport for that." Turning to me, she clarified, "Where I come from, there is a border; here, too, is a border." I asked whether she spoke Bengali, and the others immediately chorused, "She has forgotten her language!" Only Rabia laughed and commented astutely, "How can you forget your own language? You can never give that up, can you?" When I ask her to, she writes her name on a piece of paper, in Hindi and then in Urdu, the two languages she learned in Bihar.

I noticed that she had written down her name as "Roohi" and I looked up, puzzled. "I was Roohi there, wasn't I? I was given the name Rabia after my *nikah* [Muslim wedding ceremony]," she clarified. In this narrative, there is a melancholic longing expressed by women that is no different from the leaving of a natal home post-marriage in the South Asian context more broadly but compounded here by the additional demands of being a border area where difference in language and culture mark one out as "different" and with differing moral contours depending on who is doing the work of seeing.

Policing the Social Order

The above ethnographic vignettes dwell on some of the ways in which boundaries are assessed between insiders and outsiders by those who have a stake in the maintenance of social and moral order along this national border. The police make their assessment of the legal and the illegal, not on the basis of paperwork—as is often assumed for a rational, bureaucratic form of governance—but on an "intuitive" sense of the "outsider" that is based on clues such as language (even dialect) spoken, clothes worn, and skin color. Although on the one hand, for police and media discourses, the "Bengali" indexed a fear of Bangladeshi infiltration and triggered a moral panic oriented toward the containment of social and moral disorder thought to ensue in the wake of the Bengali migrant, on the other hand, the family was invested in a very different kind of order based not on "legality" but "legitimacy." One of the markers of being from the "outside" was any evidence of an educated woman among an almost completely unlettered population. Similarly, marriage to a "Bengali" woman was often the recourse taken by men who were regarded as not particularly attractive partners: they often suffer from a range of social or psychological deficits (they are often unemployed, ill, or old). As a consequence of their marriages, they came to lead more structured, ordered (even Islamic, as Halima felt of her husband) lives. This was often the case in town as well.

Although Zain came from a respected Muslim artisan caste in Kutch with long-established urban connections across the region, he was nevertheless considered to be somewhat "useless" (*bekar*) by the community. He could not hold down a job; after his parents died, none of his brothers wanted to look after him as they were "fed up" (*bezar*) with him and his slovenly ways. He lived alone and ate at local eateries (*hotel ka khana*), a sure marker of undomesticated ways. People tut-tutted and expressed sympathy for him but were not moved to help him out in any way ("his brothers have washed their hands of him; what is it to us, then?"). One of his usual haunts for meals was a restaurant run by a family from his caste. It was well located near the main bus station in town, and he often managed to get meals at a discounted price, catching up on the day's gossip and news. The restaurant owner realized suddenly that it had been a while that Zain had not shown up. Then others began noticing a distinct improvement in his appearance. Women commented that his clothes looked clean and mended. Something was clearly up. What kind of job had he landed? Rumors began circulating of possible nefarious connections and "illegal" activities (*do number ke dhandhe*). Was he dabbling in one of the illegal trades in liquor or coal? Was he helping the "military" out? Some could not quite believe this of him; he was too simple.

Then what explained this sudden turnover? An acquaintance of one of his sisters-in-law found out that Zain was now married and leading a life of quiet and respectable domesticity. It turned out that his *bhabhi*'s (brother's wife) parents had suggested a "Bengali" wife for him. After his marriage, he found a job working as a cloth dyer in someone's *karkhana* (workshop) and was doing reasonably well. As they said of him now, "He is poor but always well turned out in clean clothes and fed and looked after by his wife."

Conclusion

Boundaries between insiders and outsiders, "legal" and "illegal" residents were drawn continually by agents of law enforcement as well as the community. When the police struggled with "illegality" as a stable, documentary attribute, they made up for it using forms of intuitive wisdom drawn from the region: who belonged and who did not was ascribed to the ways in which people looked, spoke, dressed, and behaved. "Look at the features of these people in Banni," a police officer pointed out to me. "They are tall and fair; many of them have light eyes. Bengalis are short and dark. You can *immediately* tell them apart. I don't have to talk to a *Bangladeshi* to know one; I can see him and tell you *immediately*."

Yet, pastoralists in Banni reflected on the irony of such "intuitive" wisdom deployed by a force that was also ambiguously related to the local, evocative of colonial forms of policing that produced distinct social "types" as the objects of policing (Nigam 1990) by a state that was simultaneously disconnected from those they were supposed to police; they said it was strange how the police and *military* people thought they could read the local landscape. According to Ismail in Sonapar, "These military people are all from outside, mostly from Kerala [again, not to be taken literally; here, the southern Indian state of Kerala signifies the south and non-Hindi-speaking regions]. They cannot even speak Hindi properly; what do they know of our language? They don't have a clue and then they harass us, suspecting all Muslims of being terrorists." The community was also constantly engaged in the evaluation of legitimacy and illegitimacy for those whom they decided to incorporate strategically into the family.

Women designated as "Bengali" were conduits to an "Islamic" way of life and they brought domestic order to men who were lacking these attributes, therefore seen as social outcasts, regardless of how they were perceived by the law enforcement authorities. The enumerative practices undertaken by the state, as it attempts to "fix" identities—"citizens" or "infiltrators"—are not always the outcome of rational bureaucratic practices. They are quite dependent on the ways in which particular police officials deploy this information and on how they determine the attributes of those who are deemed to "not belong" to a particular context. As we saw, this is often based on subjectively evaluated criteria of religion, dress, skin color, or language. On the other hand, the family or the community is also engaged in similar enumerative tasks, even asking, what does it mean to be called a Muslim? These ways of reading the landscape and the people within it alert us to be wary of the use of categories, forcing us to ask what is the content of these categories and how are they contextualized within the particular contexts and the agents through whom they are deployed.

Chapter 4

BLOOD AND WATER

The "Bengali" Wife and Close-Kin Marriage among Muslims

The previous chapter argued that notwithstanding forms of bureaucratic rationality that are believed to structure state practices of which policing is a key component, the police depend on modes of seeing that often rely on intuitive assessments of who is inside or outside the law. We saw how these assessments were made on the basis of languages (un)spoken, textures of silence, and types of dress. Forms of documentary evidence for citizenship may be summarily rejected as being "forged" and therefore "inauthentic." Paperwork is not always a guarantor of political belonging, a theme that continues into chapter 5. We saw how identification of the "authentic infiltrator" was often for the police just a matter of knowing "at first glance."

In this chapter, I will broaden the scope of policing away from formal state institutions and include in it other forms of knowledge creation engaged in by institutions and persons outside of the state apparatus, strictly speaking, with a particular focus on the family. "Bengali" women migrants were threatened by exposure not only due to the work of the police who attempted to track them down using techniques of identification mentioned in the previous

chapter but also through the activities of journalists, nongovernmental organizations (NGOs), the anthropologist, and the family, each of whom demanded
transparency and brought in their wake degrees of exposure, whether in-
tended or not. My interaction with Bano—a "Bengali" wife who also operated as a matchmaker for other "Bengali" migrants whose marriages she
networked and facilitated—will help understand how the presence of the
anthropologist—as we saw with the NGO in the previous chapter—may
even inadvertently threaten exposure; under these circumstances, her ethnographic mandate may end up mimicking more active forms of policing that
are undertaken in pursuit of detecting the "illegal" migrant in this borderland. In the second half of the chapter, I will show how ways of seeing that
are seen as particular to the police (e.g., suspicion and surveillance) are not
discontinuous with modes of policing that operate within the family especially with regard to the reevaluation of close kin marriage within Muslim
households.

The Reluctant Matchmaker

Mohamed Hosain, who was always courteous and eager to help me in all
my research pursuits, was uncharacteristically reticent when I mentioned my
intention to meet more "Bengali" wives. Eventually, he agreed to introduce
me to some but shared his apprehensions: "Tell me [*batao*], they won't face
any problem or harassment afterward, right [*hain na*]? You will be observed
visiting them at home; then the police should not land up at their doorsteps
in pursuit [*peechhe peechhe*]." This section describes my interactions with
Bano who, by making transparency the central theme of her narrative, used
her conversation with me almost like a defense against charges of illegality
that I did not make, but my presence may have triggered. My seeking her
out for an interview brought her into focus in a way that was not unlike interrogation she may face through formal law enforcement agents (see, e.g.,
Garriott 2011, 138). Her narrative emphasized legality and transparency and
was no doubt crafted for me but was also designed to reach beyond me, offsetting her vulnerability to exposure as a "Bangalan."

  I was taken to visit Bano and her husband, Haroon, by a mutual acquaintance who wanted me to meet an older "Bengali" wife—someone who had
been in Kutch for over ten years. Bano was described to me by those who

knew her as "very well settled." She used her extensive networks in Kutch and West Bengal to broker new marriages with migrant women. Although this is technically what *dalals* (in this context, marriage brokers) do, she was quick to distance herself from the term. Reminding me of how the presence of the anthropologist produces encounters that may court exposure, Bano took charge of the narrative by choosing to talk of transparency and of how she and Haroon had "nothing to hide."

According to Bano, Haroon visited her natal village in Bengal personally and "hid nothing from us." He is significantly older than Bano and terminally ill, in need of palliative care. He had not divorced his first wife, someone described by Bano as "mentally unstable" (*dimagi halat thheek nahi hai*). Bano underscored the transparency that, according to her, was the bedrock of her marriage: "He hid nothing from us. The entire village [her natal village] knows [*sara gaon janta hai*)] that I have come to take care of him [*seva ke liye*]. There is nothing wrong in this [*isme kuch galat nahin hai*]."[1]

Bano thus begins by placing her marriage squarely within the scope of social normativity. Although she is her husband's second wife, by attributing mental instability to the first wife, she is able to retain her primacy in the conjugal unit with her husband. Foregrounding care instead of sex and procreation as the bedrock of a successful marriage, she is also responding to the discourse that attributes women's migration to trafficking and sex work (Kempadoo 2005; Kapur 2010). In her stress on public knowledge and transparency, she preempts the media and police discourse of young women being duped and trapped into marriage by unscrupulous men.

Once she establishes for me a context of consent and transparency within her own marriage, Bano broadens the scope of the conversation to the more general question of cross-region marriages and the role of *dalals* in mediating these *rishtas* (relationships, specifically used to describe prospective marriage proposals).[2] In the police's understanding of such marriages, as presented in media and police reports, the *Bangalan* is brought in groups to Kutch by a typically unscrupulous male *dalal* who then "sells" her to the highest bidder, making a tidy profit for himself. Families with "Bengali" brides that I interviewed did not make a secret of the fact that there was a transactional element to the process of fixing a *rishta* with a Bangalan. Yasmin, one of my friends in Bhuj, accompanied an aunt to "select" a wife for the latter's son; they went to the home of a woman known to them as a local *dalal* where they were presented with three or four "Bengali" women from among whom they were asked to choose. The woman's family was paid about 15,000–20,000 rupees (in 2013) with the *dalal* taking the rest of the payment. Rates were higher for fair-complexioned women who were in greater demand.

Bano uses her networks in Bengal and Kutch to fix marriages for those Muslim families in Kutch who increasingly want "Bengali" brides for reasons that are explained below. However, she was very firm about distinguishing her work from the operation of professional male *dalals* who, according to her, were "real bastards [*harami*], telling all kinds of lies for the sake of money. They often hide the fact that the 'boy' [*ladka*] is mute or lame, or that he has a mental problem. In cases where the girl's [*ladki*] parents cannot come down themselves to see the prospective groom, they send their daughter with the *dalal*; when she finds out the truth about the man she has married, her life is ruined. Some lose their minds [*pagal ho jatey hain*], some run away." These *dalals* also engineered fake or "scam" relationships (*farzi rishtey*). It is not only the *dalals* who are duplicitous, she adds. People can also withhold the truth just to get their sons married. Bano is upset at her own husband's sister. Their son is paralyzed, and his parents lied about his disability just to find a bride for him. "This is absolutely wrong [*bilkul galat*]," she emphasized.

Distinguishing herself again from a professional *dalal*, Bano indicated that the matchmaking she did was free of charge. Money was paid directly to the bride's family. Bano has facilitated two marriages (*do shadiya karwaiy hain*), one of them for her neighbor's son. She strategized and chose a childhood acquaintance from her own home village, who is now a friend and companion for Bano in Kutch. They plan their trips home together so they can have each other's company on the long train journey. The other marriage she fixed was for her sister. Apart from these, she says, she is a reluctant marriage facilitator because she does not want to get too involved: "What if the marriages don't work out? Then I will have to bear the blame." She describes how a number of people, including Hindus, show up at her door asking for "Bengali" women to marry to their sons or brothers. "Some of them say we don't care if the woman is Muslim or Hindu, we just care about the girl [*hamein to sirf ladki se matlab hai*]." But Bano is horrified at this proposition: "Who will be responsible for her if she is unhappy?" She firmly turns away Hindu "clients," saying she is networked with only Muslim families in Bengal and will not be a party to what she sees as deception. "This is not a *dandha* [business; the term also colloquially refers to sex work]; it is a question of the girl's life [*zindagi*] after all," she says disapproving of professional *dalals*. On one

of the occasions that I was visiting at her home, Bano was expecting a prospective "client" from Bengal: "They must be on their way here now. A family
from [a village close by] was interested, so I arranged the meeting, which will
take place in my house this evening. They have said if they like the girl, they
will take her and pay, but not otherwise. I told them, 'That's fine'; after all,
we are hardly dalals *to strike a deal [hum dalal thodi hai ki sauda karne lage]*"
(emphasis added).

Bano uses her interactions with me to emphasize the lack of deception in
her own marriage and the ways in which her matchmaking distinguishes
her from *dalals*, whose existence she does not deny but distances herself from.
By presenting her work as a reluctant matchmaker, she is also able to distance herself from allegations of corruption and monetary self-interest, as well
as from failed marriages. In these conversations with Bano, it is clear that
"detection" of the "Bengali" wife is not only at the behest of the police or
intelligence services but may be enabled by the anthropologist's probing. In
this example, Bano uses the conversations to draw a picture of legality and
consent, a far cry from the media and police discourse around "Bengali"
women in Kutch.

Family Secrets

So far, I have discussed the play between the overt and the covert that structures interactions within and outside the family, especially when it concerns
the exposure of the "Bengali" either as "trafficked woman," "forced bride,"
or "illegal infiltrator." I have suggested that there are many interactions that
can "expose" the "Bengali"; the formal institution of police are not the only
ones who may "uncover" them. Here, I show how it is not just families with
"marriage migrants" that are riven with suspicion and bear the burden of
being transparent to others. An overview of a borderland society like this,
saturated with multiple forms of police and military surveillance may suggest that women are under surveillance primarily by the police, but the view
from the ground reveals that suspicion and surveillance permeate a whole
set of relationships even within the family. Although at first sight, it may appear that allegations of deception and suspicion are attached only to those
rishtas that are engineered by *dalals* or involve migrants from other regions,
the regular—so-called normatively constituted family in Kutch—could also

be thickly layered with suspicion. Information, its possession and trafficking, could create alliances and rupture others in ways that mirror forms of behavior and suspicion that attach to marriage with "Bengali" women. The idea is also to suggest that forms of practice that we associate with police work in the manner in which they deal with the apprehension of the "Bengali infiltrator"—suspicion, observation, and exposure—are also operative within closely guarded circuits of the family that is otherwise seen as the epitome of trust and understanding. Even though the "Bengali" wife was the object of policing for the state, the desirability of the Bangalan as a "good wife" is tied to modes of policing the Muslim family. In chapter 3, we saw how in rural families the "Bengali" woman indexed a certain kind of Islamic civility especially in a context of growing state Islamophobia where people like Hasham ruminated openly on what it meant to be a Muslim. In urban Muslim families, the "Bengali" wife became a preferred marriage choice in order to circumvent the hazards of too much proximity entailed in marrying close kin. Rumors, past misdemeanors, and the management of "poisonous knowledge" (Das 2007) were significantly amplified with consanguineous marriages that, because they were based on a "double *rishta*" (Charsley 2013, 108–111), entailed the collapsing of blood and affinal relations when first cousins married each other. This could have disastrous consequences for the family as it threatened to tear apart the familial order from within. The "Bengali" wife was the "outsider," the affine who could be "made local" and thereby incorporated into the family (Carsten 1997). Due to pressures already alluded to— the dangers of speaking her own language, dressing or eating in culturally distinct ways—due to the possibilities of being "detected" by the police, "Bengali" women were said to make particularly docile wives, their "blending in" evocative of the "good old days" when women were more easily controlled and "adjusted" within the family.

Even though the presence of the "Bangalan" was an uncomfortable subject, usually glossed in conversation, marriage in general was a favorite topic, particularly with women. As an unmarried woman, I was constantly advised to marry and "settle down"; as I got to know families better and more intimately, older women did not consider the offer to find me a suitable match in Kutch to be intrusive; they felt this was their duty (*farz*) toward someone they considered to be "like a daughter" (*beti jaise*). Since I was received as a Memon of Kutchi origin (my father's community), marriage to a locally sourced Memon was considered to be a highly feasible—and not in the least bit improper—suggestion on their part. Marriage norms as they operate among various Muslim communities in South Asia, although by no means homogenous, play out on a somewhat different register from the normative Hindu marriage system.[3] The cultural ideal of endogamy and more particularly of consanguinity strongly discourages intercaste marriages among Muslims in Kutch.[4] The normative Muslim marriage specifies the limits of endogamy as the caste (*atak*) or the family (as consanguinity), and in my experience, this was an ideal that was largely adhered to, discursively if not always in practice. The normative practice was explained in the following terms: "first we look for a son-in-law in the same house [i.e., a cousin marriage], then we turn to the next relative, then generally in the village, moving outside the village only if absolutely essential."

As a consequence of this, many Muslim women do not leave the natal village after they are wed; in urban areas, consanguineous marriages combined with occupationally demarcated neighborhoods in the older parts of town meant that some women moved only a couple of houses up or down, effectively living on the same street their entire lives. Endogamy was also a measure of social status, used to evaluate relative position vis-à-vis others; the more effectively a caste group was able to police the boundaries of its marriage practices, the higher a social status it could claim. Thus, people like Hasham could talk disparagingly of the pastoralists in Banni who were said to be in the habit of "buying" women from other Muslim castes in the region, due to their "*lalach* [greed] for money." Hasham's sister, it will be recalled, had been married into a family in Banni because of a physical disability; such practices ensured the reproduction of caste hierarchy among Muslims in the region. Significantly, marriage with the "Bengali," precisely because she existed outside of local caste hierarchies, could be engineered without the loss of prestige that might have been incumbent on an exogamous "intercaste" marriage within Kutch.

Although consanguineous marriage is the normatively prescribed form of marriage, these marriages do not preclude elements of choice, or indeed of "love" and self-arrangement (Charsley 2013, 75–77). Even within this genre of marriage, considered to be the most socially appropriate and morally legitimate form of marriage, I found that there was plenty of scope for the exercise of self-choice and individual agency that often mimicked the performance of illicit romances between young people.[5] Further, not all consanguineous *rishtas* were those that accorded with parental approval. Knowledge of

romantic relationships between cousins and "illicit" communication between cousins who were betrothed to other cousins became sources of information that could be deployed to maintain various forms of order within
the family.

These knowledge trails operated as a means of "lateral surveillance"
among cousins. They became a way of keeping track of others' behavior, the
threat of exposure becoming a key means through which familial order was
maintained, not through a patriarchal diktat from older relatives but via lateral surveillance within a generation. My use of the term *lateral surveillance*
proposes a modification to Mark Andrejevic's (2005) concept. The latter is
essentially a form of surveillance that is a product of the digital enclosure
where, Andrejevic suggests, surveillance becomes individualized as people
take charge of their own security and sever their dependence on traditional
circuits of information management. Crucially, for Andrejevic, these forms
of surveillance "amplify" and "replicate" forms of top-down surveillance that
emanate from the state; the result is an "injunction to embrace the strategies
of law enforcement and marketing at a micro-level" (Andrejevic 2005, 494).
On the other hand, I suggest that these techniques of lateral surveillance operate as forms of policing that operate in conjunction with, rather than the
supersession of, more traditional networks of information flow such as kinship flows. Here, it is not the democratization of technology that enables
people to watch each other and have access to information about each other
through Facebook or Google, for instance, but the *social* proximity that is
engendered through consanguineous marriages, which makes people privy
to certain kinds of information that may otherwise be compartmentalized
(e.g., between one's natal and affinal families).

More crucially, because of the doubled-up relationships (the "double
rishta") that are entailed through consanguineous marriages, proximity and
trust are overdetermined, made more complex through the layering of relationships over time. In her ethnography of transnational marriage among
British Pakistanis, Katharine Charsley (2013) writes that close-kin marriage
among cousins is a way to offset the risk involved in arranging a transconti-
nental marriage. "Migration has introduced additional risk by undermining
the trust based on knowledge of one's kin" (Charsley 2013, 103). In her ethnography, marriage with close kin is desired not only to strengthen the bond
between siblings but to also ensure that preexisting networks of trust and loyalty are strong enough to withstand the possible strains of a transnational

marriage where one spouse migrates to another country. Thus, Charsley (2013, 103–104) finds that "transnationalism and close kin marriage may be mutually reinforcing."

Here, we will see that bonds between siblings may grow deeper—but may also be torn asunder—when they become affines. As Janet Carsten (1997, 196) says about her fieldwork in Langkawi, her Malay interlocutors told her, "We like to marry relatives, but if they quarrel, it's finished, everything goes sour." She describes how the possession of potentially harmful information about others may circulate within the kin group, showing up the fundamental "fragility of affinal groups" (222). It will be recalled in chapter 1 that one of the reasons why the visiting inspector general of police did not think Kutch needed a separate border police force was that people living along and across the border were Muslims who were related to each other. This kind of society, he believed, was a self-regulating one because of a degree of internal coherence and trust that would derive from kinship ties. In the following sections, I argue that consanguineous marriage—although traditionally a preferred form of marriage due to the familiarity of all parties concerned—can also jeopardize the social fabric precisely because of this familiarity. In these circumstances, the Bangalan is preferred because she is a stranger.

"Bengali" women are often chosen as preferred marriage options for a number of urban Muslim families. Yasmin who, it will be recalled, accompanied an aunt to "select" a wife for the latter's son to the house of a *dalal*, said of the aunt, "She is very happy with her daughter-in-law." The "Bangalan" had fit right in; "You would never know by looking at her today that she was not born here," she added. Yasmin's mother-in-law chimed in: "And you should see how she takes care of her parents-in-law! She does real *seva* [care], takes care of all the housework, the cooking and cleaning without a single complaint [*haste haste*, literally, with a smile]. They just don't make them like that here anymore," she sighed. Although some of this was doubtless meant for Yasmin's ears, it provides an instance of some of the ways in which "Bengali" women are seen as more attractive daughter-in-law material than women chosen from within the family whose proximity to the family could become a reason for familial conflict. "Bengali" women are seen to be more docile and accommodating. The distance from their natal homes means they cannot go home at the drop of a hat, making it incumbent on them to make the marriage work at all costs. Women within the family were more likely to "stalk off" to their mothers in the event of an argument; these marital tiffs inevitably spread across the generations and could not be confined to the conjugal couple alone, as the examples below will indicate.

Ashfaq, the oldest son of a middle-class family *liked* Maliha whom he first saw at a *mela* (fair), the annual celebration at a well-known *dargah* in the city.[6] She belonged to the same Muslim subcaste, but the two families were not known to each other and were not linked through previous affinal connections. Ashfaq and Maliha conducted a clandestine *romance* facilitated through *love letters* that were exchanged with the help of one of Ashfaq's female cousins on his maternal side (his mother's sister's daughter), Sameena. Although the match was not in strict violation of the social code (the two families belonged to the same subcaste), it violated an unspoken moral code because of the manner in which the young couple conducted their romance.

Nonetheless, knowledge of the young couple having met at a fair and thereafter written letters to each other was not made public. The *rishta*, when it happened, was proposed through one of Ashfaq's uncles (his father's older brother), who in turn had been approached through an aunt who had overheard her daughter "happen to mention" Maliha's name as a potential prospective bride for Ashfaq. Ashfaq's parents were not thrilled at the prospect of a marriage with Maliha for a number of reasons. The latter's family was not personally known to them, and Maliha's father worked in the Middle East, her mother raised the children singly in Kutch. Nevertheless, the marriage took place and the self-chosen aspect of it was more or less seamlessly converted into a socially approved arrangement (see, e.g., Mody 2008), eased along by the fact that they belonged to the same subcaste and no real endogamous boundaries were breached.

Two years into the marriage and after the birth of a daughter to the couple, however, Maliha had an altercation with her mother-in-law and left her marital home to return to her mother's house. Her father-in-law suspected that Maliha had been *provoked* by his younger brother (Ashfaq's uncle) and sister-in-law who lived next door. The father-in-law alleged that his brother was *jealous* of their success and relative prosperity and wanted to ruin their family. He suspected that this brother was the key figure with whose abetment Maliha's brothers filed a police *case* against Ashfaq's parents, alleging harassment for dowry. Some years after it had become clear that the older generation was embroiled in a stressful situation vis-à-vis each other, Sameena revealed, under dramatic circumstances, the history of Ashfaq and Maliha's love affair. Maliha's parents threatened Ashfaq's parents (Sameena was his maternal cousin) with defamation: "we have already filed one case against you; we will add one more to it"). Sameena cited "evidence" of the letters she had once ferried, claiming that she could produce other witnesses to support her. The case was eventually resolved with the intervention of extended family members, but it revealed a lack of connect between the generations: Ashfaq's parents were helpless in the face of allegations of "love letters"; for them, this was a scandal greater than the fact that their daughter-in-law had walked out of her marital home. The secret knowledge of the letters was leveraged by Sameena to balance another scandal as it began to float like scum to the surface.

Some years after the Maliha-Ashfaq fracas and after Maliha had returned to stay with her in-laws, Ashfaq's brother Bilal became engaged to his father's sister's daughter Yasmin at a ceremony in the latter's home. Ashfaq and Bilal's parents said they had had enough of self-chosen marriages and the experiment with Maliha had not gone particularly well. Yasmin lived three doors down the same street; Bilal's father was extremely fond of his younger sister, Yasmin's mother. The *rishta* was fixed and a simple engagement ceremony conducted. Almost exactly a year after the engagement, the *nikah* was performed and Yasmin moved to her mother's brother's house as the new daughter-in-law. Although Bilal and Ashfaq's family had suffered significant losses in the devastating earthquake of 2001, many of their savings diverted into the repair of their house, no expense was spared on the wedding. The bridal couple had a newly renovated private bedroom and attached bathroom to themselves on the upper story of the old family house, which had been specially painted and decorated in honor of the wedding. I returned to Bhuj after a year's absence just two days after the wedding only to find Bilal's family steeped in gloom. Nobody was talking about the wedding. I had attended the engagement ceremony a year ago and could not fathom what could have transpired to convert the euphoria of that event into the funereal atmosphere of the present. Bilal's mother—whom I had never seen offer *namaz* (prayers) in the past—practically did not stir from her prayer mat, her fingers telling the beads of her *tasbi* (prayer beads) constantly. It felt like a house that had suffered a recent bereavement rather than a wedding.

As the days passed, I pieced together the story from various members of the family. Bilal, it turned out, was in love not with Yasmin but with Fariha, also a first cousin but from the other side, his mother's sister's daughter. The two had *liked* each other for some time but had not made their desires known to anybody. Fariha was already engaged to a young man outside Kutch who belonged to the same caste but was not a cousin. Bilal confessed to his father, the day after the *nikah* ceremony that he had wanted to marry Fariha instead of Yasmin. This confession, a mere twenty-four hours after the *nikah*, erupted into a diplomatic war of tremendous intensity between Bilal's and Yasmin's families. At the center of the crisis were Bilal's father and his very own sister, Yasmin's mother. Bilal's father said he had "lost face" with his sister who in turn threatened him with ruining her only daughter's life. She further alleged that it was all Bilal's mother's (her sister-in-law's) fault; she accused her brother of being controlled by his wife who was not well intentioned and that she had always been suspicious of her intentions (*neeyat*). Bilal's father confessed that his son had not done the right thing. "I have raised him with good values; I have never denied him his wishes. If he wanted to marry someone else, he should have only said so. Even if he couldn't say this in public, he could have confided in me at least." It was one thing to have ruined young Yasmin's life from the first day of her married life, but he added with tears in his eyes, "My relationship with my sister is ruined forever."

While the parental generation bickered on and off, Sameena—who was Fariha's sister—decided this was the moment to reveal the clandestine correspondence between Maliha and her cousin Ashfaq. This was a way for her to get back at Bilal's family for the way in which the two brothers evidently conducted their romantic lives to the detriment of others' interests and reputations—her sister Fariha's reputation was at stake—and to deflect the public eye away from Fariha's complicity in the scandal (of being in love with Bilal).

Peer Surveillance

Young urban Muslim women in Bhuj were governed by an unspoken set of norms that dictated the extent of their participation in the urban public sphere as "modern" women. Thus, although driving two-wheeled "scootys" was socially acceptable, driving a car was not considered to be "proper." When I visited on fieldwork and stayed with families I was acquainted with, one of the ways in which their gradual upward mobility was reflected was in their offers to use their car for my out-of-town visits across the district. In previous years, I would have rented a car for the day and driven off with the driver and Mohamed Hosain in tow. Now more people I knew owned cars; they only lacked someone to drive it. Young men who were capable of driving were busy at their workplaces during the day. Older men did not know how to drive, and it was not seemly for the women to be seen behind the wheel. So it came to be that I was often exhorted to drive and to take them along for company, an offer I never took up but was regularly encouraged to do. Regardless of the fact that many upwardly mobile families owned cars and had moved into well-apportioned houses filled with every conceivable gadget at their disposal, younger women tended to not be as fluent as their husbands or brothers in the use of electronic gadgets such as iPads and phones, relying often on their young children to translate these techniques to them. Those who were well versed with these electronic gadgets tended to downplay their expertise in "public" family interactions especially in the kitchen or living room, reserving their use in the relatively "private" sphere of the bedroom when they went to lie down for their brief afternoon naps.

Similarly, the range of clothing and forms of self-presentation that were considered "socially acceptable" were quite narrowly defined in my experience. Although school and college-going girls had begun to wear jeans and leggings—the term for the figure-hugging tights that had come to replace the looser tailored trousers (*shalwar*)—young mothers all wore the more traditional *shalwar kameez*, their upper bodies draped with a *dupatta* at all times whether at home or outside. Similarly, the use of makeup was not socially acceptable. These rules, although not spelled out in any obvious way, were taken for granted, part of the habitus. One time, Yasmin offered me a couple of brand-new bottles of nail polish. She commented that they were gifts brought for her by her husband's foreign colleagues when they had been invited over for a meal at home. "You know how it is," she said, removing them from the kitchen shelf on which they had been sitting, offering them to me while I waited for the water to boil for tea, "we can't use such things here, but you can." I urged her to keep them; perhaps one day she might feel tempted to try? But she was adamant. "It would be different in another city. . . . If I was in Mumbai, maybe, but even there, it is difficult. . . . We would visit our relatives and then people would start talking. It's better to not start such things. Here, *you* take them." The fact that they had been stored on a kitchen shelf, in full view of anybody who cared to notice them, indicated that even to put them away in the privacy of her own bedroom or bathroom, where she stored toiletries for her personal use, was considered inappropriate, perhaps inviting comment from her husband or mother-in-law. Good manners compelled her to not refuse a gift, but in the same spirit, by leaving them on the kitchen shelf, accessible and in full view to the entire family, she was able to distance herself from the moral implications of having "accepted" such a gift.

As it turned out, she was right about the forms of lateral surveillance young women indulged in. I had been privy to a long-winded saga that had to do with Yasmin's cousin Zainab. It was generally held by the extended group of cousins (that also included in-laws because of their consanguineous marriages) that Zainab had "abandoned" her domestic responsibilities—cooking and looking after her husband and children—and was possibly having an *affair*. Her husband was a salesman who traveled out of the city most days, staying at home at the most three days a week. In his absence, the only male relative holding the fort at home was her father-in-law. The elderly gentleman was regarded as ineffective in keeping a watch on his errant daughter-in-law. "He clearly can't see what she is up to, but it's all there for all the world to see," they whispered together. In support of these conjectures, Zainab's cousins always drew attention to the fact that she took too much care of herself: "Her eyebrows are always plucked, and she gets herself waxed [to remove body hair]; she is always lipsticked and powdered," they declared as ultimate proof of her "wayward" behavior.

In the vignettes sketched above, I want to draw attention to the forms of surveillance and watching that are not the hierarchical protrusions of a mechanism of watching that emanates from a source that is construed as *above* those being watched but as forms of lateral surveillance that nonetheless are not amplifications of the work of the state, nor are they only dependent on the democratization and privatization of technology as Andrejevic suggests. Previous chapters have discussed ways in which the work of watching is dispersed through society, rendering the state as one among many others who participate in the work of information gathering and rendering their interlocutors transparent for a variety of reasons. However, here I would like to push further to suggest for an anthropology of policing that the community engages in: lateral policing (keeping an eye on each other), not only as a way of expanding the sphere of police practice (Garriott 2011) or as a means of replicating the state's security practices (Andrejevic 2005) but to suggest that these forms of practice within the family mimic the state's but do not share in the vision of social order that the state seeks to enforce. The "Bengali" wives are policed as "outsiders" by the state; forms of life that are detected as "deception" by the police allow them to transition into valued "insiders," allowing for a new kind of socially sanctioned marriage among Muslims. In the context of work that draws attention to modes of policing that emanate from the patriarchal state in South Asia (Chakravarti 1996; Baxi 2006; Mody 2008), the ethnographic examples here indicate lateral rather than top-down hierarchical policing in collusion between the patriarchal family and the state (fathers and police, for instance, as in Baxi's examples), but refer to the manner in which the sharing and withholding of information and the deployment of secrets become aspects of familial governance but not only within the rubric of a patriarchal discourse of honor, which is the more usual trope for South Asian ethnographies of family and marriage.

Suspicion and the Family

I have been arguing that a study on policing as a form of governmentality needs to reintroduce the idea of the family and the state as coproducers of the well-ordered society. However, the relationship between the state and the family that I propose here is not necessarily based on "tactical collusion" or "strategic alliance," nor of an intervention by the state into the family (Donzelot 1979; Das 1995). Practices of policing that we identify with the bureaucratic state—suspicion, surveillance, or forms of knowledge creation that emerge from documentary and statistical practices—are also evocative of similar practices that constitute policing at the level of the family. In this more expansive consideration of policing—"police as governance" (Garriott 2013)—it is concerned with the production of a well-ordered society and the social, economic, and moral management of its subjects. Governance concerns itself not just with questions of sovereignty but also of the welfare of the population, which also constitute its primary resource, hence they are to be preserved and managed (Foucault 2001). It is clear that the family is the first line of management of these subjects; the policing of families by the state was also about policing beyond the family (Donzelot 1979). However, this ethnography cautions us that the family is more than just a site of intervention for the state. It does not only govern *through* the family; the family is an active agent of policing, but there is no consensus on the moral order that is a desired outcome of successful policing.

The migration of "Bengalis" into Kutch is not only subject to policing by the state for reasons discussed in chapter 3 but is also a *consequence* of practices of policing that are internal to the family. These two trajectories of policing do not have the same consequence for migrant women in this borderland. The "Bengali" bride is welcomed into Muslim families because she is the bearer of a certain Islamic civility that is seen as a desirable form of moral upliftment not only among rural Muslims (chapter 3) but also among urban, upwardly mobile Muslim families because as a stranger, she is not privy to too many secrets in the family. The practice of marrying cousins—although lauded for the fact that there is familiarity all around and everyone knows the family background—can disrupt everyday relationships that are also based on the selective management of information across the family. Ethnographies on the lived experience of marriage in South Asia relate to transnational marriage migration (Kalpagam 2005; Gardner 2006; Charsley 2013), cross-region marriages due to sex ratio imbalances (Kaur 2012; Mishra 2013), the affective and aspirational dimensions of marriage as a lived experience (Grover 2011), and marriage and the law (Mody 2008; Basu 2015). With very few exceptions (Das 2007; Mody 2008; Grover 2011), these ethnographies do not give us enough of a textured sense of how marriage and family structure the flow of everyday life—of how trust is created and withheld, of how marriage is both a keenly desired social status and a potential means to lose status and self-worth. Taken together, chapters 3 and 4 have addressed the question of how distrust and suspicion attach themselves to migrant wives not only as a consequence of policing by the state. These affects are central to the manner in which relationships are structured between young women and their families, regardless of religion or social class, especially around the subject of marriage and its inevitability. The following examples explain this in more detail and also dispel the impression that suspicion, distrust, and familial infelicities occur only within Muslim families in Kutch.

SONAL

During the year that we were closely associated while I conducted my early fieldwork in Kutch, Sonal and I became friends. Because we were both of more or less the same age and were also both unmarried, Sonal shared with me some of the anxieties that are not uncommon among single women in their late twenties and early thirties across the subcontinent. Sonal lived with her parents and younger siblings in Bhuj and, as we know, she worked as part of the health and education outreach team of a local NGO. She often opined that I was lucky to be able to study and write without worrying about *"marriage"* (she always used this term in English) and marveled at the fact that my parents had "allowed" me to travel to the United States just to study.

The social and parental pressure to marry was a huge burden on Sonal, and I could see the toll it took on her as the months passed. She was turning thirty, well over the age at which young women in Kutch were wed. Although she and her sister were both graduates—Sonal had a degree in law and her sister worked as a primary school teacher—she was beginning to get the distinct impression that her parents were no longer impressed with her academic achievements unless she could save face for them within their larger social and kinship universe. Added to her woes was the fact that a *rishta* had been proposed for her younger sister, superseding her in the family hierarchy; according to societal convention, the younger sister could not marry before the older. Sonal was acutely aware of these accumulated pressures and the duty of being the eldest weighed heavily on her. To make matters worse, her brother had a mental disability. This, added to her education and "advanced" years, made it difficult to find a suitable match. Sonal often said to me that she felt that she had been born under a particularly inauspicious star, her parents also having given up on her prospects.

One evening, Sonal called me on the phone and asked if I would accompany her to a temple. It turned out that she was finally engaged to be married and she wanted to go to the temple of "Mataji"—Ashapura Mata—to offer thanks. She had taken a vow to perform a series of fasts for nine consecutive Tuesdays and that day was the last one. Coincidentally, it happened to be the same day her *rishta* was fixed (*pukka kiya*) with a man who had come to "see" her a week ago. We walked together through the narrow bylanes of the old bazaar to reach Ashapura's principal temple in Bhuj town, stopping to buy a red-and-gold *chunri* (scarf) and some *bindis* (dot worn on the forehead by Hindu women) to be offered to the goddess and then some sweets to be blessed as *prasad* (sanctified offerings). On the way, Sonal made what was to me a startling confession: she could not remember what her fiancé looked like and was unable to reconstruct his face in her mind. Yet the overwhelming emotion she felt that evening was relief: the feeling of guilt and familial responsibility that she has been burdened with for so long had finally eased.

With our ritual obligations at the temple over, Sonal and I walked along the lakefront, savoring the cool evening breeze, a refreshing balm after the scorching heat of the day. As the sun set over the horizon, we walked over to the lake where, sitting on a bench facing the lake, encased in the gathering dark, I could sense that underneath her obvious relief and pleasure at her upcoming nuptials, she was also anxious. Again, she mentioned the fact that she could not recall her fiancé's face despite the fact that he had come over to meet her at home just the previous week. She then said that she was now glad she had asked a good friend from her university days who lived in Junagadh (the city where her fiancé's parents lived) to unobtrusively gather information about the family so that she could satisfy herself about their background. She added that this was because she could not really trust her own parents—"I don't trust my parents: they are just desperate to see me married; they will probably overlook every fault just to get me off their hands." Her lack of faith in her parents made her doubt that they had her best interests at heart. Sonal worked out her own investigative networks to inquire into her fiancé's antecedents.

ZOYA

Zoya was twenty-five years old when I first met her. Like Sonal, she was also already older than most women at the time of their engagements and was frequently told by well-meaning aunts that it was high time she "settled down." She was feisty and entrepreneurial, running a small beauty salon out of one room in her mother's house, which was in a modern and well-appointed middle-class urban housing society. Young, middle-class women from the neighborhood dropped by now and then to have henna put in their hair or their eyebrows threaded. On a rainy August day that I happened to be staying over at their house, Zoya and her younger sister persuaded me to have henna put on my hands; Zoya was an artist and she carefully filled my left hand with intricate patterns. Her mother had invited eight young girls to eat dinner at home, the annual fulfillment of a *mannat* (ritual vow) she had once made for her sister's recovery in surgery. Over a multicourse dinner, some of them joked that they would not have anyone to give them beauty tips and advice once Zoya was married and left her mother's house. Zoya insisted that she would go nowhere, that she did not want to marry.

The following morning, everyone asked to see my henna-anointed palm before I washed it, effectively stopping the color deepening any further. What was the color like? I turned my palm out, now covered with a deep auburn design, and everyone smiled happily. The color was dark and deep; I would have a husband who loved me very much and I would get along with my mother-in-law and have a happy marriage, Zoya's sister proclaimed happily! If the color was faint, I would not have any of these things. "All of this is rubbish," said Zoya to me, "but what do we do? We are constrained [*majbur*] to believing these ideas we have grown up with." Her father and an elder sister had died in the 2001 earthquake; she wanted to live with and look after her mother and two brothers. Her beauty salon business was an attempt to be independent.

At the end of that year, Zoya's younger sister became engaged to be married. Zoya was excited for her but insisted she was going to stay single herself. As time passed, she was pressured by various members of the family to not waste more time and, importantly, to not cause any more *tension* to her mother by her refusal to get engaged. Her mother's sister rebuked her that she should not be selfish or stubborn (*ziddi*): as an older sister, she had to be married first. When none of these tactics worked, she was rebuked that her mother had too much *tension* because of an unmarried daughter growing older by the day, "sitting at home." Having already lost a husband and a daughter in the earthquake, Zoya should not make her mother suffer any more. Zoya still held out; her sister married and went off to her marital home in another city.

About a year later, Zoya mentioned to me during one of my brief visits to Kutch that she could not bear the pressure anymore and had decided to take up an offer of marriage that had come through the intermediation of one of her uncles. The "boy" was coming over, and she asked if I would be present during the meeting. Afterward, she asked what I thought of him. He seemed like a pleasant enough person, and I said so. However, Zoya cut to the chase: she wanted my opinion on whether I thought there was a "*defect*" in one of his eyes, referring to a possible squint. Zoya was no longer considered a prize match. Despite her education, the family's good social standing, and their middle-class urban life, she had to be content with an offer of marriage from an older man, from the same caste but from a poor family. Besides, Zoya could not quite shake off the idea that he had a squint. This is my destiny (*kismat*), she sighed, even as she agreed to the marriage. The wedding took place, and Zoya moved to a small one-roomed house in another town. When I visited her some years later, I found her cooking on a tiny kerosene stove in the corner of the room, looking after her baby son at the same time. She wove baskets to earn some money on the side. The marriage had entailed a steep downward mobility for her for she could now afford none of the pleasures of middle-class life that she had enjoyed in her mother's home and that she had so generously included me in when we went to the movies, shopped for clothes and trinkets, always scheduling a detour to eat *sev puri* and *dabeli*.[7]

Both Zoya and Sonal reposed faith and confidence in "outsiders" to evaluate the extent to which their prospective spouses were suitably matched with their own personal standards. They were unable to trust their own parents or family members because of an overwhelming sense that they were no more than a "burden" to be disposed of in marriage to the first available suitor. Although Sonal contacted a friend from college, Zoya asked me to be present at her meeting and subsequently demanded that I be honest with her about her prospective fiancé's physical appearance. Much as is believed to be the case with "Bengali" brides who are married off to "unsuitable" men—those with physical or mental infirmities—here were instances of women from Kutch—both Hindu and Muslim—who were considered too educated or independent to find husbands before they were considered to be "on the shelf." No longer trusting of their own families, they invoked their own personal circuits of information gathering (in Sonal's case) and judgment (in Zoya's case) in order to independently evaluate the suitability of these men as prospective spouses.

Conclusion

Marriage forces women to tread a tightrope between the demands of visibility and invisibility not just to the state but also to others such as the extended family. The example of Rahila's wedding, described in the preface, when her mother collapsed inexplicably during the rituals was one example of how a key moment in the reproduction of kinship structure also became a dramatic enactment of matters that were internal to the family. Mehrunissa's extended natal family had died during a collective disaster, the 2001 earthquake. Her inability to bury and mourn them appropriately due to the forms of disfigurement induced by the disaster—bodily as well as by way of survivors' displacement from their homes—made this a charged moment that erupted during the wedding of her daughter, making visible something that had not been talked about earlier. On the other hand, marriage migrants are pursued by the censorious gaze of the police and of the media, for it is assumed that they are sold into marriage, lured by deceitful middlemen or by a well-planned strategy to infiltrate by unleashing the equivalent of demographic terror: the relentless reproduction of the Muslim family in India. But as this chapter has argued, trust and security within the family may be hard to come by not just for women who are allegedly "bought" and "sold" by *dalals*; in fact, as Bano's narrative indicated, her matchmaking skills may have enabled her to retain some measure of control over the fixing of these long-distance marriages; the long journey made from the east to marry into Kutch may help women stay in touch with their sisters and friends from back home when they help them come to Kutch as brides.

On the other hand, women like Zoya and Sonal expressed reservations about their natal families, not sure they could trust them to make the right decision for their future. The deployment of suspicion within extended family circuits must be taken into consideration as a type of policing practice that is parallel to and operates along similar modes of detection and suspicion that is deployed by the police in its attempts to detect the ("Bengali") "infiltrator wife" even though they stem from different sources. These examples also highlight that a clear binary between marriage and trafficking is not entirely tenable. The failure of trust is not just a possibility between *dalals* and their clients but also within the biological or extended family. Finally, this chapter should be read as a significant anthropological intervention with respect to Muslim families—on which there is a remarkable gap in the literature. The favoring of the "Bengali" woman by the family—even as she is denigrated by the state as an "infiltrator" from Bangladesh—is also a form of policing within the Muslim community, for it allows certain urban families to reassert dominance in the face of changing sociological conditions in Kutch. Local women who are already part of the family are not the right choice for wives in a consanguineous marriage system because they are thought to be too individualistic, uppity, and not docile enough to be a good daughter-in-law. By this yardstick, the foreigner, who is thought to be pliant, is a better marital choice. In the long run, this is a major shift because it is also changing—in this region—the norm of consanguineous marriage among Muslims, long considered as the hallmark of Muslim marriage structure in South Asia.

Chapter 5

THE WORK OF BELONGING

Citizenship and Social Capital across the Thar Desert

This chapter turns to border crossing narratives of Hindu men who left their homes in Sindh, Pakistan, and moved to India in 1971, more than two decades after Partition. The migration of these men from the west, much like that of the "Bengali" women from the east, enabled them to forge new relationships of kinship and, in this case, nationality. These new forms of belonging were also premised on a reexamination of the efficacy of traditional forms of marriage. The chapter also shows us what it takes to "belong" to a social group, whether the nation, or a caste or a religious group. It shows how "insiders" and "outsiders" are evaluated and policed by the state on the one hand, and how they are received by the family. As in the previous chapters, it is not self-evident that the state and the family constitute similar axes of policing: they are not in direct opposition to each other, but they are not seamlessly allied either. The family is yet again not a space of interiority that may suggest that it constitutes a space of resistance to the state.

Building on earlier chapters that examined the work of belonging that is performed by "Bengali" women, this chapter asks, how do Hindu men who cross into Kutch from Pakistan stake their claim to belonging? As a demographic category, the two are quite distinct. Although the "Bengali" was hypervisible as a "stranger" to the state—language, dress, and skin color constituting a distinct form of "otherness" to the police, regardless of formal citizenship—it was precisely the fact of her being a stranger that allowed her to accumulate social capital as a desired wife within the Muslim family. Marriage within close kin, it was seen, could lead to a crisis of sociality within the family. The social glue and networks of care and intimacy that are believed to structure close-kin marriages (Charsley 2013) can also come apart when too much is known about one's kin, upsetting the delicate balance of power between generations and affines. The management of secrecy, privacy, and the public secret are crucial to the maintenance of kin ties, something that threatens to break down when boundaries between relationships are rendered too transparent. In such situations, it is the relative stranger who is able to restore the balance in the family that may have come undone with too much familiarity. As such, a traditional and normative form of Muslim marriage—marriage between close kin—is being reconsidered in light of the availability of marriage migrants from the east.

The Hindu men of this chapter, on the other hand, are no strangers to the state, who welcome them into the fold of the nation as always-already citizens. The police and local administration abet their border crossings regardless of their formal legality, oftentimes granting permission for entry and residence that are at odds with explicit official orders they have received. Even though as "Hindus," these Pakistani men are welcomed into citizenship by a state eager to manage its border demographics, they do not always meet with a similarly effusive reception among the family, for whom they remain strangers. For their Indian families, these men are kin but are connected through the maternal side: in strongly patrivirilocal forms of kinship, one's mother's kin are not usually the source of political capital. Despite the state's abundant patronage, the stigma of being "from Pakistan" or the corrosion of trust through suspicion of their being "traitors" (*desh drohi*), informers (*sources*), or "*double agents*" makes it much more difficult for these border crossers to be seamlessly accepted within the family or the wider society. Further, their acquisition of citizenship is premised on a reconfiguration of traditional patriarchal—and patrilineal—norms of honor which now have to be rescripted through maternal kin. Mothers, rather than fathers, become the conduits for political and social mobility for men who are at pains to emphasize their patrilineal "Rajput" heritage, laying claim to masculine pride, valor, and staking nationality as Hindu men. Even though the Hindu women *viranganas* resisted the paradigm of national belonging that was offered to them—through the trope of the sacrificing mother—men from Sindh hold on to elements of Rajput valor and pride as a way to claim belonging.

Through the narratives of three Hindu men who crossed the border from TharParkar (southern Sindh) in the shadow of the 1971 war, the chapter reflects once more on modes of policing that operate through the family and the state, arguing that the difference is not merely one of scale.[1] The state does not merely amplify forms of policing that operate within the family, making them more rigid (Das 1995), nor does one necessarily act in collusion with the other (Baxi 2006). "Visibility," "intimacy," or "strangeness" is calibrated differently according to the context. The chapter will argue that Hindu men could cross the border illegally and successfully convert this illegality into legal residence and citizenship because they checked the right boxes for a state that has increasingly sought to legalize non-Muslim migration from its neighbors (as seen in the Citizenship Amendment Act [CAA] passed in December 2019).[2] The chapter argues, however, that the grant of citizenship is not the successful closure of an aspirational border crossing. Vir Singh's words stayed with me long after he had uttered them: "After coming here (*yahan aane ke bad*), we received *nagarikta* (citizenship) *and nothing else (aur kuch nahin)*" (emphasis added). The chapter describes how political belonging and social capital are not necessarily forged in congruent ways, neither for the Bengali wives of earlier chapters nor for the Hindu citizen aspirants from Pakistan.

Migration and Kinship across the Thar Desert

Although "Bengali" women are subjected to specific forms of policing in Kutch, I have argued elsewhere that it is important to situate present-day "cross-region marriage" within the larger landscape of cross-border marriage migration in this particular borderland. In colonial times, Kutch was a princely state governed by the Jadeja dynasty. They originated from Sindh and traditionally married Sodha Rajput women from the Thar region whom, it was said, they could intermarry "without offence to their pride of caste"

(Postans 1839, 52). The Sodhas were remarked upon by colonial observers for the marriage alliances they were able to secure. Marianna Postans wrote of the Sodha that they were a "tribe who inhabit the great desert of the Thurr [*sic*], and are remarkable for the surpassing beauty of their women" (52); they "find their principal source of riches in the beauty of their daughters, for one of whom rich Mahomedans will frequently pay ten thousand rupees" (136). Raikes (1859, 3) wrote in his memoir of Thar and Parkar, "The Soda ladies of the Desert are esteemed amongst the most beautiful women of the East, their virtues and beauty being the theme of many a song—the subject of many a story—and in former days the cause of many a fatal conquest." The princely state of Kutch received royal brides from Hindu Sodhas in Sindh and from other princely states in the region such as Kathiawar or the state of Rajasthan. The uncle of the last crowned maharao, whom I last interviewed in 2003, had a wife from Kathiawar; the rao of Sirohi (1925–1946) married a daughter of the maharao of Kutch, while the Kutch ruler married the rao of Sirohi's sister (Plunkett 1973, 72). Similarly, Sodhas married their daughters into Rajput royal houses farther east that were considered socially superior to them, in order to maintain forms of honor associated with elite Rajput marriage (Raikes 1859). The discourse of honor was central to policing the traditional Rajput family both in terms of managing its gender codes as well as its political ambition. Political expediency dictated the shifting boundaries of the permissible marriage alliance over time. As Ramya Sreenivasan (2004) has argued, marriage practices defined the changing boundaries of the elite Rajput family. Thus, unions between Rajput women and non-Rajputs—particularly Muslims—once accepted as politically expedient, by the nineteenth century gradually came to be redefined as dishonorable, reflecting altered political exigencies. Such narrations, argues Sreenivasan, "must therefore be seen as strategic, seeking to mobilize for their Rajput audience the norms of 'honorable' conduct essential to the maintenance of this political and moral order" (68).

The recourse taken to "honor" in contemporary Sodha narratives must be viewed in this light. In colonial accounts, the Sodha are referred to as a dominant landowning and administrative Rajput caste in TharParkar "where, in the wilds of this almost unknown region, they constituted themselves landed proprietors, acknowledging the Rana of Oomerkote as the head of their tribe, but paying tribute to nobody" (Raikes 1859, 3). As a "superior" social caste, the Hindu Sodhas of TharParkar typically intermarried hypergamously with other "Rajput" lineages to the territories east of them. The border between TharParkar and Kutch was frequently traversed as marriage alliances were sealed throughout the princely period. In contemporary times, the cross-border marriage strategies of the Sodha from TharParkar continue and are explained in terms of the dual constraints of clan exogamy and the need to maintain marriage alliances that would be considered "honorable."

Thus, constrained by hypergamy and unable to marry within their close territories, they typically broadened their search for kin across the border between TharParkar and Kutch-Rajasthan where they had more "marriageable" clans to choose from. These marriages continued after Partition and until 1965 when the border became more rigidly policed in the aftermath of a war with Pakistan. The period 1965–1971, when the next war was fought between the two countries, witnessed a growing restlessness and insecurity among the Hindus in TharParkar due to the heightened militarization of the border; as a result, many of them wanted to cross the border permanently into India. A heavier deployment of border police on both sides of the border and a general climate of fear and distrust of Hindus as being "sympathizers," "informers," or "spies" for India led to strained social relations within TharParkar. This period, which led to the gradual production of insecurity among TharParkar's Hindus, has been described in detail by Sadia Mahmood in her doctoral dissertation. She writes, "The landed and political elites of the Hindu communities were driven out sometimes under the pretense that they were Indian citizens and sometimes under the pretense that they were enemies, opponents of the Pakistani state, or Indian agents. An ecology of fear was also produced and installed among Pakistani Muslims about the Pakistani Hindus" (Mahmood 2014, 123).

The following sections are based on interviews conducted with three Sodha men in Kutch. Each of them has a different migration story and a distinct way in which they interfaced with the military-policing infrastructure, casting themselves variously along the spectrum of the legal or illegal border crosser. They also reflect different classed experiences of border crossing.

Gulab Singh was a middle-class, educated young man who negotiated his own border crossing. He crossed alone, using his connections with a childhood friend who connected him with a border guard along the Sindh-Rajasthan border. He knew the risks involved: this was a betrayal of his country (Pakistan), his home (in TharParkar), and his father (whom he could not take into confidence)—a betrayal of his patriline. Gulab Singh crossed under the cover of the strong winds that whipped up the desert sand into a blinding opacity during the day to slip into Indian territory. Yet, once on this side of the border, he had a hard time convincing his relatives of his good intentions. Border villages are tuned to people coming and going; trust is a scarce commodity: Why would they trust him? Was he a spy? An agent for the Pakistani military? Gulab Singh learned that trust is not easily earned; disheartened with the less-than-enthusiastic reception he received from his kinsfolk on the Indian side, he decided to turn himself over to the Indian authorities in order to claim citizenship and recognition.

Vir Singh migrated with his extended family and caste brethren while the Indian armed forces had established temporary control over TharParkar. His first few years in Kutch were in a refugee camp, in a liminal stage of citizenship as he did not have identity papers of either country. In the camp, police suspicion dogged them as "Pakistanis"; this was a less entitled mode of border crossing than Gulab Singh's had been. However, these masses of migrants still found ways of appealing to administrators in Kutch in ways that the latter found hard to refuse.

My third example is Ram Singh Sodha, the most recent migrant who decided to migrate to India permanently only in 2010, having made approximately five or six visits to India from the 1980s onward. At the time of my interview with him, he was still awaiting his citizenship papers even though it had been almost seven years since he had moved to live in Kutch with his sons. He was among the more high-profile citizenship seekers, having been an active politician and member of the legislative assembly in Sindh. He used his relative influence and political ability to bargain in order to help other potential citizens in limbo in India.

Although these examples indicate the differentiated experiences of border crossing based on the uneven distribution of economic and political capital among the Sodhas, I also stress the point that the specific meaning that migration has for them is not necessarily the same. Notwithstanding the theoretical facilitation of their citizenship by a state that differentiates among Hindu "refugees" and Muslim migrants or "infiltrators," even the most entitled of the recent migrants had not formally received Indian citizenship. Yet, for all practical purposes, he lived in some splendor in Kutch. Even though local police were deputed to maintain strict surveillance and monitoring of his activities as he was still formally a Pakistani citizen, in practice they deferred to him much as they would to a local political leader or strong man. Gulab Singh still struggles to read the Gujarati script; it is Urdu that he can read most fluently: an everyday reminder of his "otherness" with respect to national language and identity. These three Sodha stories highlight the connection between their view of themselves as a socially and demographically entitled group whose marriage practices were closely connected to the maintenance of collective honor for the community and that marked them out as distinct from other groups in TharParkar, and how this honor structured their negotiation of Indian citizenship for themselves. Although narratives of harassment by the Pakistani military and border guards that made the conduct of everyday life increasingly difficult in the years following 1965 should not be discounted, the chapter argues that the relationship between Sodha migrants and the military-security complex of the border does not play out only in terms of a Hindu-Muslim or state-versus-community axis. Even though the Indian state may have found it convenient to approve grants of citizenship based on factors that would be demographically expedient for them, the translation of political citizenship into social capital is much harder to do.

Narratives of Border Crossing

GULAB SINGH

Gulab Singh's narrative subtly points to a price paid to belong: he crossed the border to negotiate an honorable marriage for himself, but in doing so, he left behind his male kin and patriline, central to constructions of honor in Rajput kinship. His father and brother remained in Sindh; the maternal home acquired political significance as he recrossed the border once traversed by his mother as a bride. Gulab Singh was twenty-five years old when he crossed the border into Kutch in March 1970, before the formal outbreak of war. The atmosphere was tense and uncertain; everyday life had become riven with fear and suspicion: "It was like war would break out anytime." He had retired from a Gujarat government position a few years before I first met him and enjoyed spending time with his grandchildren in a house recently built with his retirement proceeds. As a young boy, he lived in Chachro, a town in TharParkar that came under Indian occupation during the

1971 war (Mahmood 2014, 165) where he was born and raised. His mother died when he was a young boy, and his older brother and sister had already established kinship networks across the border in Kutch: the latter had been sent "*illegally*" as a bride into a village in eastern Kutch.[3] His older brother had also crossed over "*illegally*" in search of a wife from Kutch, and he had been able to smuggle her successfully back to Chachro. When I asked how he negotiated his own border crossing, he simply said, "I also came *illegally*," a confession that surprised me with its candor. A Hindu man with valid citizenship papers, a former government employee, he did not have to worry about an act of "illegal" border crossing in his past; interactions with the anthropologist did not threaten exposure as they had done with Bano or the other "Bengali" brides.

Gulab Singh was thus already familiar with the landscape of border crossing without passports and permits. There was a well-established network of agents on both sides who worked closely with border guards on either end. Despite this, it was highly "*risky*," Gulab Singh admitted, even back in the day when things were decidedly less dangerous than they were now. There was always a chance that a friendly "*agent*" was really an "informer" ("*source*") for the other side. The best-laid plans sometimes fell through at the last minute, or people developed cold feet. Crossing illegally once was bad enough, he emphasized, "imagine having to go through the process twice." Men who wanted to bring a wife back to Sindh had to undertake the risky crossing all over again on the return journey. Fully aware of the attendant risks, he hatched a plan: he would leave for India, find a wife in Kutch, and stay on. He did not want to take the risk of returning. Besides, the atmosphere of suspicion had wreaked havoc on daily life in Chachro. It was not easy being a Hindu in Sindh after the 1965 war. So he took the decision to cross the border without informing his father or his brother. I asked if it was difficult for him to have taken this step, and he replied, "I will tell you *frankly*, we had no problems in Sindh. We all lived peacefully, Hindus and Muslims both. But after 1965, things became much more *communalized*. The Indus Rangers, who are the Pakistani equivalent of our BSF, used to *trouble* us a lot. So I decided to cross over into India. I did not want to tell my father and brother of my plans because absolute secrecy was essential. But I was also afraid they would deter me from my plan."

In Chachro, a childhood friend helped Gulab Singh up to the border. This friend, in turn, had a school friend among the border guards whom he approached for help in this clandestine operation. "The question was," Gulab Singh explained, warming to his subject, "how to get me over to the other side. During the nighttime, there was a lot of *vigilance* and the police *chowkis* [posts] and border guards were very alert. In those months [March–April], the desert is known for its strong winds which whip up the desert sand [*reti*] when they blow during the day. So it was decided that I should cross over in the daytime to give me maximum cover. In this way, I crossed the border, aided by hot winds [*loo*] and sand into Barmer [in Rajasthan]. I remember clearly that I celebrated the Holi of 1970 [the Hindu festival that marks the end of spring in north India] in Barmer." Once in Barmer, Gulab Singh decided to contact some of his relatives. Now that he was safely across the border, he wanted also to send a message to his father and brother, informing them of his next steps.

Generations of exogamous marriages with various Rajputs east of Sindh meant that the entire region (primarily Sindh, Gujarat, and Rajasthan) was dotted with kinship networks across various administrative borders. On the Indian side of the border, Gulab needed to enlist the support of his maternal kin; these were people he did not know personally, never having been on this side of the border, but they were not unknown either. Chachro had brides from Barmer, and some of its own daughters were married here; news and gifts traveled clandestinely through well-worn channels of border crossing over the generations. But to his surprise and disappointment, the trust and support of his relatives in Barmer was not a foregone conclusion.

If Gulab Singh thought that crossing the border clandestinely was his biggest challenge and, once in India, he would be welcomed by an extended family of maternal relatives, he was mistaken. In borderland communities, where frequent connections—of goods and people—are made across the border, there is also a high degree of surveillance and suspicion. It is not easy to trust people, regardless of whether they are your kinsmen, explained Gulab Singh. The police and intelligence officers are constantly combing these bordering villages. You can never be sure of a visiting "relative" from the "other side" posing as a bride seeker who may be a *double agent*, reporting to the secret services. When Gulab Singh made initial contact with his extended family networks in Barmer, he was given a friendly enough but wary reception. Although older women were excited to see him, gathering around and anxious for firsthand news of their daughters and nieces in Chachro, they were also restrained from talking with him. Tea was offered, but no further hospitality was encouraged. Gulab Singh was exhausted, hungry, and emotionally spent. The desert sand had caused his eyes to itch and water. The past days had been a whirlwind of activity and tension. Now that he was safely across the border, the initial exhilaration subsided into a knot of disappointment at the base of his stomach: why was he treated like a stranger? He explained to me that at the time, he was young and impetuous—had not his border crossing demonstrated this already?—but he was also *nasamajh* (naive) in the ways of the world. Soon enough, he realized what the problem was.

Given his age, marital status, and gender, it was assumed that he was a *"temporary"* visitor in search of a bride from India, like his brother and countless others had been before. These *"temporary"* border crossers are a dangerous demographic for local residents to befriend "because you have to negotiate the border police twice, you may even be arrested as an informer on either side of the border. It is usually not worth the risk, yet many people did so." The Barmer family preferred to not undertake the risks attendant upon helping out with these temporary border crossers who were chiefly "bride seekers." "Once they became convinced of my intentions (*niyat*), that I wanted *permanent migration* and that I was not there only temporarily in search of a wife, only then their minds began to ease and some of them agreed to help me."

But it was not easy, Gulab Singh maintained. He constantly felt under watch and felt that although they were his relatives, there was nothing stopping them from turning him over to the police. "If I felt that the father was softening, the son began to have doubts about me; when I managed to convince the nephew, the uncle would put his foot down." Gulab Singh realized there was only one way forward: to convince them that his migration was not *"temporary"* in nature and that he wanted to settle in India *"permanently,"* he needed to make a firm statement. The only way to escape the suspicion of being a *desh drohi* (traitor) was to indicate he was here to stay.

Having convinced his relatives somewhat of his long-term intentions to reside in India, Gulab Singh stayed with them but realized it was too dangerous to continue like this, the stain of "traitor" never quite leaving him. So "within a few days," he submitted an application to the collector (the most senior administrative official at the district level) in Barmer stating, "I want to stay in India, in Kutch, and I would like to apply for citizenship."[4] Although he had landed at Barmer, his eventual choice of destination was Kutch because it was where his *nanihal* (home of one's maternal relatives) was. Within the month, he "relocated to Bhuj, got an allotment of land from the government, a job at [a government agency], citizenship papers arrived from Delhi." By his own admission, the process was smooth and easy, and he did not have to suffer the indignities of camp life like those who started fleeing TharParkar for India in larger numbers during the war. It had been so risky to initiate any contact with "home" (i.e., Chachro) while his intentions were being evaluated by his Barmer kinsfolk and while he was trying his best to avoid the tag of *desh drohi*. Thus, he realized that he had not once contacted his father or brother to tell them he was safe. Once he settled down in Kutch, Gulab Singh decided to write to his father to let him know that he was well and that he had decided to move to India where he had now acquired legal citizenship status. The following year, 1971, he further cemented his ties with Kutch by becoming engaged to a woman from Kutch. His mother's family arranged the match for him, and the young couple met for the first time at the wedding ceremony in 1972.

Gulab Singh was never to see his father and brother. The closest he allowed himself to go back to his childhood home was during that liminal phase during the 1971 war "when the Indian Army had taken over [*qabza kiya*] TharParkar. . . . I went up to the village boundary but then turned back. I never returned to Pakistan after that." Perhaps it was not easy to contemplate the emotions that might have assailed him when faced with his father. The guilt of leaving to make a better life for himself but leaving his father behind. Besides, the tag of "traitor" was not an easy one to shake off. Writing letters to family members left behind in Sindh was a risky operation in the period after 1965 with heightened suspicion on either side of the border. Another Hindu migrant from TharParkar said how difficult it was to stay in touch with relatives in Sindh. If you sent them letters from India, they were harassed by the Pakistani police. If they wrote to you, their letters were confiscated by the local post office, opened, and screened before they were delivered to you; sometimes they arrived in tatters and always weeks or months later.

Trying to blend into the new environment was not easy for these migrants from Sindh; it was best to avoid suspicion among neighbors and coworkers and thus easier to shun all contact with Pakistan. For all migrants from Thar-Parkar, written language remained a problem, especially for the educated middle class. Gulab Singh may have avoided the trauma of being in a refugee camp, but he struggled with his lack of ability to read the Hindi and Gujarati script. Gulab Singh had studied in Diplo where he learned Sindhi and Urdu. In the Gujarat government job that he was assigned to after his move to India, it was frequent practice to issue notices and circulars in Gujarati. Although he "tried as much as possible to get by in English," he had to teach himself to read Gujarati through a daily reading of the local newspaper, not unlike I had done when I first began my fieldwork.

VIR SINGH

Gulab Singh was grateful for the fact that he did not have to stay in the "camps" that were set up for incoming refugees from TharParkar during the war. His comfortable middle-class life, bachelor's degree, and a helpful administration on the Indian side of the border enabled him to negotiate citizenship and a new life for himself. The connection with Pakistan was now firmly in the past, interrupted only occasionally with glimpses of recognition embodied in linguistic scripts. Others were not so lucky, making the arduous trek across the Thar desert on foot or camelback, stranded for days without food or water, including women and small children. Although it was not easy for Kutch to accommodate all incoming migrants logistically, these migrants had their ways of negotiating with the administration which claimed to be left "with little option" in their decision to let them in.

Premji Haribhai Bhatti worked as an assistant in the office of the district collector in Bhuj from 1960 to 2003 and was personal assistant to the collector for some years from 1975 onward.[5] During wartime, he recalled the frenetic pace of activity in the office. He was part of a team that was deputed on duty to Chad Bet during the 1965 war, and he traveled to many villages in TharParkar that had been temporarily "captured" by the Indian Army during 1971. In 1972, he recalled, there were scores of Hindus fleeing their villages who wanted to cross the border into Kutch. "They had crossed the border, and we had set up a temporary camp for them at Dhrobana. They had no papers, no permits; we could not let them in. We were under strict instructions. We told the men to go back, but we just could not handle the women. They told us, 'If you want us to return, kill our children first.' They were so desperate and had been suffering so much in Pakistan, what could we do? So we had to let them stay." He was still haunted by these faces of women and their children. They had been told they could not let in people across the border, but this particular officer relented in the face of what he saw as a moral code of gendered kinship and valor apart from a general internalization of the narrative of "Hindu suffering" in Pakistan.

As I have argued above, these narratives of "Hindu suffering" allowed the state to flex their rules of entry and citizenship. However, narratives of military excesses in TharParkar did not always distinguish between the military forces of the enemy nations, both of whom ended up terrorizing the local population. Arif, a Muslim from Bhuj, was a soldier in the Indian Army during the war who found himself in TharParkar in 1971. As a member of the victorious force, he saw that people were terrified of the occupying Indian Army, which was able to instill fear in the local population. Although he felt proud as a member of the Indian force, as a Muslim, he was also troubled at what he saw as the behavior of his fellow troops. He saw them as the perpetrator of crimes against the Muslims in TharParkar who lived in mortal fear of the "invading" Indian Army. His daughter had preserved photographs of him taken at some of the grander mosques in the region that had fallen temporarily under Indian control. "People fled their homes, leaving young women sleeping at home as they decamped in the early hours of the morning; they were so scared of us." In his opinion, soldiers used to often behave quite badly, looting and plundering the houses they came across. Arif brought back with him small mementos such as Korans that were lying scattered around in the melee of soldiers' loot. He picked them up for safekeeping lest they came under someone's feet.

Regardless of the narratives of military heavy-handedness on the civilian population of the Thar region, it was Hindus rather than Muslims who were permitted into Kutch in large numbers. Over time, a number of refugee "camps" sprang up across Kutch. Some of them lasted many years such as the one in Jura village; it is still referred to as Jura camp. Vir Singh is considered to be an elder of the community in a migrant community in eastern Kutch. He recalls that he was in his forties during the war. The collective appellation of Sodha was an important one for him: although all refugees from Pakistan are now called Sodha in Kutch, telescoping under the term a host of Hindu migrants from Sindh, Vir Singh reminded me in no uncertain terms that his family would count as Sodha even in Pakistan.

The idea of a "Sodha majority" (*bahumati*) in TharParkar is an important aspect of community honor and status, as they see it. In Vir Singh's words, "We had a *bahumati* [majority] in TharParkar and Umerkote." He continued, "We were very happy in TharParkar; we had no problems there. Our work was *kheti* [agriculture] and *mal* [animal herding]. The main problem after the *border* came, when India-Pakistan happened [*jab Bharat-Pakistan hua*] was in terms of *lagan vyavahar* [the work of marriage relations]. All our brides used to come from Kutch or Rajasthan depending upon which border applied [*jo border laga, vahan se bahuein late the*]. [Umerkote families tended to bring brides from Rajasthan and TharParkar families depended on brides from Kutch.] Our daughters-in-law [*bahuein*] came from Chavan, Jhala, Jadeja, and Waghela clans in Kutch. After the *border* came, it was difficult to cross, and there were no matches available in TharParkar, so *lagan vyavahar* became very difficult for us." I pressed him to explain the lack of marriageable options for Sodhas in TharParkar, and he spelled it out for me, not unlike Ram Singh Sodha would also do. "Every community [*jat*] has its own social standing in relative terms. We have to weigh our options and can only do *len den* [taking-giving, i.e., marriage] within a social group that matches our own status."

Vir Singh spoke in Gujarati laced with what sound like Rajasthani words. "This is Thari," he said, laughing at the difficulty I had in following his vocabulary, so he kept searching for the appropriate Hindi words for me to note down. When I asked whether they spoke the same language on both sides of the border, he burst out impatiently, "Yes, yes, our mothers were all from here, this side!" Like Gulab Singh, Kutch was the home of his maternal kin, who assumed a newfound political importance in the post-1965 period, as they—rather than the paternal side—became instrumental in the negotiation of marriage alliances and a passport to new forms of political belonging.

This comes through when he describes his border crossing after the 1971 war. They left all their lands behind because "*zindagi* [life] was important, not possessions." "In 1965, during the war, Indian forces did not have the upper hand. But it so happened that the harassment of Hindus by the Pakistani *military* increased after 1965. They constantly accused us of being informers or of spying for India. Daily life became very tough during that time." He clarifies that they had no problems with their Muslim neighbors, only with the "military."

"We had already planned that we would break the *chowki* and escape into India, but as it happened, before we could execute our plan, war broke out in late 1971. The Indian Army took *qabza* [seized] TharParkar, and under their protection, we were able to cross into Kutch. During the war, India held the territory for a while. The collector [of Kutch] used to make frequent trips out into the Thar area." Vir Singh appealed to the collector for a passage to Kutch. In the following conversation that he recounted with the collector, one gets the sense of the kind of meaning and emotion that was attached to the potential migration to India, where they had never been before, but where they had maternal kin. In traditional patrivirilocal marriage, maternal kin are the source of emotional rather than political connection; the nanihal is the space of love but not inheritance.[6] In the 1971 migration from TharParkar to Kutch or Rajasthan, the traditional asymmetry between bride takers and bride givers, so integral to the maintenance of honor in marriage alliances, was reversed. It was the maternal kin, the home villages of their mothers and daughters-in-law, that became the "natural" choice of migration even though they had never been to these places. As they negotiated with administrators for passage, their hopes for the future betray this optimism, as indicated by this conversation reported by Vir Singh with the collector of Kutch on one of the latter's forays into TharParkar.

Collector: So you want to go to India. Where will you live?
Vir Singh: In Kutch.
C: Have you seen [been to] Kutch [*Kutch dekha hai*]?
VS: No, but our relations [*sage wale*] are there; my nanihal is in Ratnal.
C: Your cheeks are red like a tomato [*tamatar jaise gal*] here [you look so healthy with rosy cheeks]; in Kutch, they will become black like a stone [Kutch is also known for its "black hill," *kala dungar*]. Are you sure you want to go there?
VS: (laughing) I don't mind, we will go to our *sage wale* [relations].

Here, the collector is perhaps warning Vir Singh of the travails that lie ahead, of the uncertain life in refugee camps pending the grant of full citizenship. Although they had perhaps envisioned directly settling down with their relations in Kutch, they had to undergo a liminal phase in refugee camps that were set up specially for "Pakistani refugees"; in some cases, their stay in camps lasted as long as 1977. Vir Singh recalls, "We crossed in 1972; about 75,000 families must have crossed at the time, of which 15,000 stayed in Kutch. We chose our migration route based on existing marriage ties. Those who lived in Umerkote had relations in Rajasthan, so they settled there."

In the refugee camps, mobility was restricted. They were guarded by huge police posts to "ensure that they did not run away." They did not have Indian citizenship, and they had to be monitored and surveilled as "Pakistani citizens." They were not allowed to work in waged employment, as they were not yet citizens. One of the oldest nongovernmental organizations in Kutch began to work informally with women at this stage, collecting the embroidery they did at home, and from these early steps, the *soof* embroidery characteristic of TharParkar came to be reproduced among migrant communities across Kutch, enabling many of them to earn a good livelihood from handicraft in the decades to come. Vir Singh stayed with his extended family for three years in the Shivlakha camp, moving in 1974 to his new village. In the camp, he recalled, they were huddled together under the permanent watch of the police. They were impatient; this was not what they had crossed into Kutch for. They wanted to go visit their relatives and begin to chart out their options, begin a new life. "Before we got *nagarikta* [citizenship], we had to apply for a pass to leave the camp and visit villages outside. The pass was valid for three days, issued by the police *chowki* attached to the camp. They kept a heavy eye [*bhari nigrani*] on us. As soon as our three days were up, on the fourth morning, sure enough, the police would show up at our relatives' villages and round us up. They would say, '*You are from Pakistan; we can't let you roam freely*'" (emphasis added). Vir Singh also described the ritual of offering them some money and allowing them to extend their curfews by a few hours or days. Summing up his migration experience after leaving the camp, he said, "After coming here, we received *nagarikta* [citizenship], *but nothing else.* Five thousand to six thousand rupees per family, ten acres of land, ration cards [identity cards that permit a stipulated amount of food grain free of cost per family per month] for everyone; that is all [*bas*]." Although it sounded like a lot to me and I said as much, he responded that "others" were able to get much more and become *ghamandi* (arrogant) in the process, a not-so-veiled reference to those lower caste groups who were able to lay claim to Scheduled Caste status and avail affirmative action. But it is possible to also read his lament in terms of the harsh reality he had to face when he realized that citizenship did not solve the problem of social belonging. As migrants from the "enemy" country, they were potential "traitors" even with the right kinds of papers.

RAM SINGH

The third narrative is from Ram Singh Sodha, who requested the use of his real name. Ram Singh is a well-known name among Hindu citizenship seekers from Sindh. He had been living in Kutch for almost seven years when I first met him. He was still awaiting his formal grant of citizenship, although it is not clear under what provisions his Indian visa is extended repeatedly. Unlike other visitors from Pakistan who have short-term visas and are obliged to repeatedly register themselves with the civil police authorities, Ram Singh's visibility and status were far out of proportion with his formal legal status as a citizen-in-waiting. In Pakistan, he was an elected member in various district bodies in Sindh and eventually became a member of the Sindh Legislative Assembly. His direct channel of communication with the prime minister and Ministry of Home Affairs (MHA) may have had something to do with his extended visa status. He was hopeful that once the CAA was passed, he would not have to run from pillar to post on this official matter anymore (*dhakke na khane padenge*).

I had spoken with Ram Singh on the phone, and he confirmed a morning appointment to meet at his house in Nakhatrana town, an hour's drive west of Bhuj. He requested that I arrive on time as he had a busy day with a number of meetings scheduled. As has been a common experience for me in Kutch, no address was provided; accompanied by Mohamed Hosain, I arrived at Nakhatrana's central bus station where we began to make inquiries. In this case, we did not have long to wait before we were directed into various small alleyways that eventually opened out onto new suburban developments. We asked around in the few shops for Ram Singh Sodha or "Bapu" as many Rajputs are called in Kutch. The *halwai* tending a large vat of freshly frying *jalebis* yelled out to another man, "Where does he live? Ram Singhji Sodha, Pakistan *vara* [the guy from Pakistan]?"

Directed thus, we drove up to his house, an enormous and opulent new multistoried structure with a prominent golden Om (Hindu auspicious symbol) on the roof. Ushered in respectfully by his son, we wait in the living room surrounded by photo portraits of Ram Singh, his father, and his sons—a genealogical display of Rajput status. In their respective photographs, Ram Singh and his father are wearing signature traditional red headgear and long, twirled mustaches, standard sartorial references to Rajput or Kshatriya status. In the same theme, a small glass-fronted cabinet is filled with trophies and mementos inscribed in Gujarati script, *Kutch Zilla Rajput Kshatriya Sangh* (Kutch District Rajput Kshatriya Association). The room signaled elite Rajput caste identity in no uncertain terms; this was an important theme in his discourse.

Ram Singh descended regally from a curved staircase entering the seating area with his hands folded in greeting. In his dress and demeanor—a dark waistcoat over a voluminous *dhoti*—it was not difficult to imagine his past—and possibly future—as a mass political leader. Sitting on the couch opposite me, he settled the folds of his *dhoti*, ordered tea for us, and directed me to write down his full name and title—"Ram Singh Rana Singh Sodha Rajput, advocate, ex-MLA [Member of Legislative Assembly] Sindh." Once again, I had the feeling that this interview was staged as a political interview. He spoke about the Thar region as the most "unique" place, one that "you will not find anywhere in the world"; he also spoke of how life was difficult for minorities in Pakistan. "There is no *protection* there . . . too many shootings and *dakaity*. . . . This made life difficult in Karachi. . . . Things in Thar are better, but *hamari problem kuchh aur bhi hai* [we (Sodhas) also have another problem]." The Sodhas, Ram Singh explained, were somewhat of a "*super caste*" (the highest in the caste hierarchy). "*Hamari hukumat thhi*" (we were the rulers/in power). The problems of a "super caste" that held strongly that community honor was tied to exogamy meant that they had to marry their daughters outside the Sodha group, but other groups in the region such as the Bhatti, Sisodiya, Rathore, Chauhan, and such like were all beneath them, socially and ritually. "How can an 80 percent marry a 20 percent?" he asked in all seriousness. All the "superior" castes, compatible with the "super caste" of Sodhas were across the border in what became India in 1947—Jhala, Jadeja, Waghela, and Chudasama were the castes he referred to. "We were just not able to marry our daughters in Pakistan; *sach poocho to* [if you ask for the truth], this is the *main* reason we have decided to migrate to India—marriage and security."

This reminder of past glories—power and majority status (in TharParkar)—with the uncertain present where they had fallen to the position of a minority (within Pakistan) and were vulnerable to shoot-outs and insecurity of life and property (the lack of "protection" even for an elected MLA) is an important theme that structures Sodha constructions of their move to India and the *necessity* of acquiring Indian citizenship. It is the only way to live honorably and to reproduce the family line (*vansh*) with purity; yet this move is premised on a shift away from the patriline who only remain as portraits on the wall, resplendent in their sartorial magnificence.

Part of the "honorable" life is a strict code of gender segregation (*laj*) that makes it greatly difficult, if not impossible, to talk to Sodha women. Although my interviews with Ram Singh and Vir Singh were conducted in all-male groups (men serving us tea and snacks that must have been assembled by women out of sight), my conversations with Gulab Singh took place with his wife and daughter-in-law at home but in the background. When he asked his wife to come and sit with us, she obeyed him for all of five minutes. Her head demurely covered with her delicate chiffon sari, perfectly matching her gray hair and hazel eyes. However, when the conversation turned to questions of marriage—her own and others—she was as shy as a new bride and retreated hastily to the open doorway between the kitchen and the living room, which is where she sat, head covered and face averted, for the rest of my visit.

Ram Singh clarifies that he had tried to break the taboo against marriage within Sindh for TharParkar's Sodhas, but for the most part, people refuse to change their old ways. Exogamous marriage is a matter of honor, also a way of distinguishing themselves from others in TharParkar—Dalits, Kolis, and Muslims. Ram Singh, whose story by no means represents a "subaltern" perspective, chose to move to India and seek citizenship himself. Referring to him, Vir Singh had said, "Look at him, even he [someone of his stature and connections] could not find *bahuein* [daughters-in-law] in Sindh. He has just recently moved to India because he needs to marry his sons." It is precisely this superior status that determines the necessity to migrate. Vir Singh had added, "Harijans, Kolis, and others like them [lower castes], they have no problems in Thar. They stayed on there; this is because they have no *leti-deti* [taking and giving, marriage relations] problems. They marry within their communities like the Muslims. Our [Sodha] main problem was of marriage." In addition, the loss of *bahumati* (majority) in the context of Pakistani political life and lack of "protection" afforded to Hindus makes the move to India a desirable one.

The language used by each of these men indicates their respective social and political location. Ram Singh speaks like the politician he is—of demographics (80 percents and 20 percents), of the need for security and the stress on "protection" for minorities within a democratic context. Vir Singh spoke of the engagements he had with the state as he negotiated entry into Kutch, but his narrative is redolent of the traditional marriage system—of *leti-deti* (taking and giving in marriage) and the imperative of settling down in Kutch where he got political citizenship but not necessarily the social capital that was left behind in Sindh with the political and social majority (*bahumati*) in the region. Finally, Gulab Singh spoke candidly of being a young, single man who sought to cross the border in search of a new life for himself. The chapter tracked the work that must be done by migrants and citizenship aspirants to belong socially. Although political belonging is granted by the state to people who are seen as having the correct political and demographic attributes, this does not automatically translate into social capital and acceptance by the larger society. The work of belonging involves a reconfiguration of traditional marriage patterns and the place of "honor" in reckoning political lineage in an altered political and social context.

Conclusion

Each of the chapters in this book is presented as an ethnographic exploration into forms of regulation that produce the social and moral order in what appears to be a highly regulated and surveilled borderland society in western India. Taken together, they argued, however, that even on a hostile border between states that manifest an extreme case of "cartographic anxiety" (Krishna 1994), the state and its various arms of order maintenance (e.g., the police, border security forces, the army, and intelligence services) are not experienced as the most salient—or the only—purveyors of order and security. They demonstrate that the state may not always be a privileged site to elaborate the concept of policing as *practice*. Although the Foucauldian approach to governmentality has allowed us to productively theorize a shift from the concept of police as art of government to the broader idea of order maintenance, characterized as the shift from "police as governance" to "governance as police" (Garriott 2013), this very approach has perhaps allowed us to overread homogeneity into diverse forms of police practice. This homogeneity is located in the conceptual and institutional framework of the "police force" which retains a privileged site of inquiry even in an anthropology of police practice (Garriott 2013).

This ethnography of policing on a South Asian borderland opens up the scope of policing beyond the state and beyond the idea of a police force, identifying new sites for an anthropology of policing such as the family, neighborhood, or religious community. Policing is not synonymous with the state in this ethnography, not because of forms of neoliberal governmentality that privatize police functions, but because it argues that the production of social and moral order is a contested, rather than consensual, process. Policing the border in this ethnography is about managing access to cross-border mobility, the acquisition of citizenship, the multiple narratives around war and its memorialization; these actions straddle a fine line between the formally legal and the illegal. Criminalization of activity (such as the illegal crossing of borders and the trafficking of women) is one mode of policing that emanates from the state; this ethnography examined the multiple forms of policing that emerge in the decisions about the modes of filtering and sorting people across the border: whom to include and whom to exclude, whom to trust and whom to distrust, who is a nationalist and who is a traitor. The family is a site of policing, not because it acts as an extension of the state, configuring the public citizen through her intimate life, but because practices of policing that involve ways of seeing and forms of sociality that are based on suspicion and the control of information are also present *within* the family. By making the family as important a player as the institutional police force, the ethnography suggested that sociality within the family is not necessarily devoid of the suspicions and infelicities that are assumed to be active only in the individual's interface with the state.

Having naturalized in modern times the idea that social order flows from the state, this became, in short, a particularly fruitful site to seek answers to the question: where might we look for the sources of social order *beyond* the state (Gluckman 1956)? Unlike other anthropologists working on politically sensitive borders, I did not encounter security and surveillance emanating directly from the state (e.g., Verdery 2014; McGranahan 2016); this did not mean, however, that my presence in the field went unremarked. On the contrary, in fact. However, I soon became caught up in an entire range of activities that were engaged in policing the social order on this borderland by a range of actors, each of whom had their own stakes in observing the anthropologist and through her, each other. The anthropologist became a key player in the way in which information was managed and flowed across everyday encounters. People bestowed information on me—and just as often they withheld it—keeping in mind whom I spent time with and whose homes I was seen to frequent. I became thus interpellated in a sea of sociality and information management that did not necessarily have the state as its center. This ethnography is thus also an invitation to reflect on how the anthropological method may be complicit in forms of policing that are scattered across a field of dispersal—in this case nongovernmental development organizations, state police, paramilitary and armed forces, the family, religious groups, and others. The book suggests that forms of policing do not just "spill over" from the state and circulate within society. They are not only "offloaded" from the state onto others; these techniques are ubiquitous across institutions such as the family and the state.

In villages close to the border, I often found my ethnographic tools mirrored forms of policing that are conventionally held to emanate from the state. Walking on remote and dusty tracks to reach the house of an informant, notebook and pen in hand, I was frequently mistaken for a government official or census taker. Surrounded by people who would begin telling me their problems, I had a difficult time explaining to them that I could not help them in the tangible ways they seemed to expect: a water pipeline, an electricity connection, the extension of a bus route. Yet, I was certainly not the only one interviewing, observing, and assessing. Suspicion circulated within the social fabric, but this suspicion was not only a condition of borderland lives that were interpellated with state intelligence networks (e.g., Ali 2013). Chapter 4 discussed the everyday consequences of suspicion and the breakdown of trust within the family. Although I do not suggest a direct connection between one form of suspicion and the other, the borderland context certainly did provide for an overall ethnographic context that enabled me to articulate them within a larger context of policing.

This ethnography argued that border work is also about forms of policing that emanate from the community, especially those that have a stake in border management because they live in villages dotting the international boundary. Practices of policing this border bring together formal institutional and organizational aspects of police work with other dimensions of policing that operate at the level of the community; these practices create important points of conjuncture between state and community but not in any uniform or predetermined way. The community is heterogenous, as is the state: forms of suspicion, surveillance, and means of policing the social and moral order flow through each of these domains, rendering it difficult to talk about policing as being *either* state or community directed.

On this borderland, the big question for the state is, what are the contours of belonging? Who belongs to the nation and who does not, and how is this to be policed? For the family, the same question is posed and answered differently. Practices of policing involve ways of seeing, learning to see differently, but they also relate to the control of information. If policing is related to a "phenomenology of fear" (Comaroff and Comaroff 2016), then one of the questions addressed by this ethnography is, who deploys this fear? As seen in the chapters, the affective experience of fear, dread, suspicion, or lack of trust is not wielded solely by the institutional arm of the state police. Not only do these affects structure the intimate life of the family, even formal practices of policing are often forged through relations of friendship and cooperation between hosts and guests, policemen and key stakeholders in the community.

By entering into the field of everyday sociality within Muslim families, the book interrogates and challenges the canonical exclusion of Muslims from the mainstream—of academic literature as much as policy within India. Departing from the lens of marginality and exclusion alone, the chapters on the family and policing have examined how everyday aspirations, hopes, and desires configure both middle-class urban as well as rural Muslims on this borderland. An important conclusion of this ethnographic exploration into policing practices in India is to focus on how Muslims are constituted in addition to being targets of the state's policing. Although policing Muslim migration into India constitutes the raison d'être of postcolonial India's citizenship regime (Jayal 2013), this book seeks to examine the myriad ways in which Muslims on the border become subjects and agents of policing in a variety of everyday contexts. Practices of policing—such as the use of suspicion, fear, and the management of information—are attributes that circulate beyond the formal confines of the police as an arm of the state alone: they can be located within families and communities.

Border management practices in India have defined the Muslim as the suspicious "other" from the very earliest articulation of citizenship rules and border control (Chatterji 2007; Roy 2010; Jayal 2013), and more recently, sites of policing such as counterterrorism and the military security network of the state target the Muslim as an always-already suspicious subject (Sethi 2014). On the other hand, I argue that suspicion may also be deployed *within* the

Muslim family and community, thus breaking apart the notion of a homogenous group that is bound together in an intimacy that is produced as a consequence of being policed by the state.

Broadening the scope of practices of policing beyond the state does not intend to overlook the extraordinary reach of the state in its security and surveillance operations, during moments of crisis, but also in the everyday forms of prejudice and harassment of targeted populations in the name of counterterrorism and security (Sethi 2014). On the contrary, it enables us to observe the manner in which suspicion, surveillance, and other components of everyday peacekeeping are forms of practice that are not in *exclusive* use by what we deem to be the "police" or the "military" but are forms of social practice that are more generally disbursed in this borderland society.

The production by the state of the borderland resident by way of the generic term *Muslim* is without a doubt shorthand for invoking a particular vision of demographic management and border policing that has been in place since the late 1940s at least. However, this view does not do justice to the diverse ways in which the Muslim border residents produce themselves or tell us how they do this in relation to which antagonists. What relationships do they negotiate with various competing or adjacent forms of sovereignty? Even though the state produces them as objects of pacification, co-option, even elimination, for the production of order in the borderlands, what does this do for the production of community among a group of citizens thus policed? Does the reduction of the Muslim citizen to "bare life" enable forms of collective solidarity within them as the despised "other"? Or on the other hand, do they emerge not just an object of policing (by the state) but also as agents of policing—vis-à-vis each other but also toward the state? Rather than one homogenous category (the "Muslim"), they appear in a field of dispersal, even when a pragmatic response may appear to be one that would suggest that those who are reduced to "bare life" must stick together. The larger impetus behind this argument is to ask how one might reclaim agency for the Muslim citizen in these times of heightened state surveillance. How totalizing is this articulation of state sovereignty that does not allow the subject to respond in any form other than bare life? The answer may lie in this ethnographic exploration of forms of policing—as a subset of sovereignty—that are adjacent to one another rather than locked in dyadic battles that envision only one victorious side. The family, the religious community, and the state are all sovereign agents—they have power over life and death—and they exercise this power in modes that are not necessarily doomed to be consumed in oppositional conflicts. Muslims on this borderland are interpellated in the state's project of policing, but they also engage the state in their own policing projects. If forms of recognition are critical to the successful performance of sovereignty (Maunaguru 2020), then the manner in which the object of surveillance conscripts modes of sovereign power that are usually associated with the state into its own forms of policing (within the family, for instance, or within the religious community against members of different *maslaks* [sects]) is also instructive.

The book began by setting out the contexts within which border work is constituted as police work—and other way around—from the perspective of the state's territorial sovereignty. If it is in the nature of sovereignty to continually perform itself—with or without the use of violence—then one of the ways in which territorially constituted states perform their sovereignty is by continually iterating their borders. The border provides the limiting frame for sovereignty imagined in a nationalist vein and also throws into stark relief zones of contested jurisdiction (e.g., in South Asia, the most obvious zones are Kashmir or Arunachal Pradesh where India, Pakistan, and China compete for territorial sovereignty). Territorial borders are where the state performs its sovereignty through all the means available to it, ideological (advertisements, tourism brochures, textbooks, maps) or military (armed occupation). It is not only at its borders that the state's sovereignty is vulnerable, but these territorial limits produce special test cases for an analysis of sovereignty: it is here that several adjacent sovereignties may encounter each other, their impulse not necessarily to engage in annihilatory violence toward the other—as is often the case when nation-states encounter each other—but in fact they may choose to accommodate each other in diverse forms of coexistence.[1]

A borderland is unique, therefore, not just for what it can tell us ethnographically about the state, territoriality, and forms of regulation (van Schendel 2004; Gupta 2013; Reeves 2014; Jusionyte 2015; Cons 2016; Ghosh 2017) but also for what it reveals about the flow of everyday life within more intimate spaces such as the family and the neighborhood. How does suspicion and distrust configure itself within the warp of the family's interior life, not necessarily as a response to forms of state surveillance but existing alongside it? How does this particular context allow us to examine forms of distrust, suspicion, and bad faith that occur as part of the normal weave of everyday life within the family? Thus, I suggest not that distrust and betrayal within the universe of kinship are produced as a consequence of living on a border but that this site allowed me to draw certain connections between the *practices* of policing that I observed across domains. The work of policing in this ethnography does not relate only to boundaries that are territorial in nature.

The borderland provides a nuanced understanding of policing as a more general social concept/practice not because it constitutes a geographic margin (as we know, the margin is *not* in fact about geography as argued by Harms et al. [2014] and Das and Poole [2004]), but because it permits a thick description of the various ways in which the circulation of trust and friendship, deception and detection, suspicion and surveillance become forms of capital that are deployed in the management of the legal and the illegal—in the perpetuation of those forms of sociality that are desirable and the disciplining of those that are not.

Citizens of borderlands are thus not only at the receiving end of the state's policies and programs or constituted solely as objects of surveillance or protection, but they are in fact central to the military-bureaucratic regime that produces territorial borders as both objects and instruments of rule. They constitute alternate loci of sovereignty, but these loci are not necessarily either offshoots or oppositional to the state; the book proposes the concept of adjacent sovereignties to understand the coexistence of multiple forms of sovereignty that are not easily sorted out into orders of priority. Although their strategies may mirror each other in terms of the deployment of fear and suspicion or the use of bureaucratic practices such as enumeration and documentation, these forms of mimicry and citation are seemingly endless in scope. The jural, domestic, and religious order constitute themselves as forms of sovereignty that are adjacent rather than nested within one another.

The book should be read as an addition to existing literature on borderland populations' engagements with the state and to ethnographies of policing. It seeks to dislodge the state as the primary frame of reference for borderland studies. It builds on arguments that propose that surveillance is a relation of power that is not always hierarchical but also "lateral," not just a coercive relation but may enable creative forms of practice, and that securitization is a discourse that may co-opt a range of other actors conventionally thought of as "nonstate." It suggests that surveillance and policing come in many forms; the category must be expanded to include so-called "nonstate" purveyors of securitization and surveillance: tourism, journalists, development organizations, the roving anthropologist, and finally, residents of the border themselves.

Notes

Introduction

1. See Ibrahim 2009.

2. Steffen Jensen (2005), in his study of neighborhood and community policing against drugs in Cape Town, argues that sovereignty should be regarded as a figure rather than as an institution. Sovereign power, in his analysis, is the ability to name someone as a threat to the moral community. Legality is a measure not of state law but of community-sanctioned moral norms. This is the manner in which I deploy the idea of policing.

3. Although Garriott (2011) admits that the exercise of police power is a broad exercise in the maintenance of public order in which the state does not have a monopoly, nevertheless he (2013, 9) holds that there is value in retaining the police force as a privileged site of inquiry. Even though I agree that the police force must be opened up to ethnographic analysis, my argument is that by limiting our gaze to what we deem as "public" order and the public institution of the police, we close off possibilities of policing as they play out across a multiplicity of domains including the "domestic." This would entail an examination of how the familial order may also become germane to the maintenance of a more general social order.

4. See, for example, Garriott 2011 and Satyogi 2019.

5. Ward Berenschot (2011, 383) discusses the role of "political fixers" as key to the functioning of Indian democracy, wherein "alien and often unresponsive state institutions" are mediated to citizens through middlemen who act as brokers, bringing the ordinary citizen into the orbit of the state. The ethnographic material in this book will, I hope, challenge this view of the state as set apart from the fabric of everyday sociality. Instead, I argue that the lens of policing is able to encompass both the state and citizen—law and the family.

6. My use of scare quotes around "Bengali" indicates that although this is how they are designated locally, they may or may not actually be from Bengal. Chapter 3 takes up the significance of this in more detail.

7. This argument relates to prenatal sex selection favoring male offspring, especially in the northern Indian states of Punjab and Haryana.

8. See Mulla 2014 for an important discussion on how sexual assault intervention is based on forms of "care" and therapy that serve the technocratic processes of the state and law. Mulla argues that they therefore constitute a form of violence in itself, "the violence of care."

9. In a chilling ethnographic account of rape trials in India, Pratiksha Baxi (2014, 263) argues that custodial violence "straddles the familial and the legal" and is as likely to occur in the police station, remand home, or the familial home. Law, she argues, is the site where the "family articulates its power to discipline and punish" its errant daughters (258). Rape trials are, then, public performances of the "use of criminal law to discipline unmarried daughters [which] points to the dissonance between what is legally constituted as rape and the social uses that rape law is put to" (190). Prem Chowdhry's (1997, 2004) work on caste panchayats in Haryana discusses the use of violence against young men and women whose marriages defy social codes of honor.

10. See Das et al. 2008 for a sensitive portrayal of the domestic as a "modality" that is always imbricated in the nondomestic. The "home" is, then, constituted by a range of domesticities that simultaneously transcend its boundaries insofar as they are constituted in dialogue with events or institutions that exist outside of it—for example, courts, prisons, clinics, and so on.

11. For Hindu-Muslim mixed marriages, see Mody 2008 and Heitmeyer 2016.

12. See Ghosh 2017 for a sensitive account of how the maintenance of kinship ties across the India-Bangladesh border is marked by risk and the labor of women who must constantly balance familial and nationalist affects, thus rendering a fine line between what may and may not be openly acknowledged.

13. A *taluka* is an administrative subdivision within a district.

1. Policing Everyday Life on a Border

1. This is a revised and expanded version of an article that first appeared in 2019: *Comparative Studies of South Asia, Africa and the Middle East* 39 (3): 425–438.

2. See, for example, http://www.narendramodi.in/all-india-conference-of-directors -general-6950, accessed August 31, 2020.

3. The year before he was elected chief minister following the controversial pogrom against Muslims in 2002.

4. See Ali 2019 for an account of state-citizen relations that are characterized in the intimate and emotional tropes of love, betrayal, and longing. In a trenchant critique of James Scott's thesis, she argues that "already out-of-the-way subjects are not trying to run away further, but longing to belong" (4).

5. See, for example, Chatterji 2007; Roy 2010; Jayal 2013.

6. Radhika Gupta (2013, 69) argues in the context of borderland residents of Kargil that they cannot be easily categorized either as "manipulated subjects of the state" or as radical resistors. Their stance, she suggests, is "context-dependent as well as different in relation to various guises of the state."

7. Report of the Inspector General of Police (Delhi and Ajmer-Merwara) on Reorganization of Kutch Police. National Archives of India (NAI)/Ministry of States (MoS)/31(15)—E, 1948.

8. Kutch State was administered by the central government through a chief commissioner during the period 1948–1956, when it was merged into the bilingual Bombay Province. In 1960, it became the largest district in the newly constituted state of Gujarat. Commissioner of Police (CP) H. R. Thakkar to Chief Commissioner (CC), Kutch, dated November 10, 1948, NAI/MoS/31(15)—E, 1948.

9. CP to CC, Kutch, dated December 3, 1948, NAI/MoS/31(15)—E, 1948.

10. *Sanad* is literally a citation. Here, it indicates a formal order from the state that would serve as a statement of police authority.

11. CP to CC, Kutch, dated December 3, 1948, NAI/MoS/31(15)—E, 1948. See Chandavarkar 1998, 180–233, on colonial policing in the Bombay Presidency and its dependence on social networks in the neighborhood.

12. In his account of vulnerable sovereignty, Sidharthan Maunaguru (2020) argues that the sovereign power of Hindu deities in temples of Sri Lanka not only brought the Liberation Tigers of Tamil Eelam to the limits of its sovereign power, but it also forced it to accommodate within itself the deities' model of relational sovereignty.

13. Pastoral groups of Banni are far from homogenous; even though they are all Muslim, they are scattered across distinct endogamously organized social groups that are referred to colloquially as *jati*. Marriage takes place within the *atak* or agnatic group and between *jatis*, they maintain the relationship of *roti* (bread) but not *beti* (daughter)—that is, they may eat together but not enter into matrimonial alliances.

14. The district collector is the most senior bureaucrat in the district, answerable to the elected government; as such, the figure of the district collector epitomizes "the state."

15. Veena Das (2004, 234) argues that documentary practices associated with the state acquire a life of their own when they begin to circulate within other forms of regulation such as caste and community groups that "even in resisting the state reproduce it in new modes."

16. Flight Lieutenant Amit Rastogi in Gulbeg's visitor's book, dated July 7, 1975.

17. There were some concerns that Muslim residents on the border were possibly complicit in cross-border activities and knew of the illegal intrusion of Pakistanis into Indian territory. Chief Commissioner, Kutch to Joint Secretary, Ministry of States (GoI), dated December 7, 1952, NAI/MoS/22(157)—PA/52, 1952.

18. In her ethnography of civil-military relations in Ladakh, Mona Bhan (2013, 128) discusses the ways in which security has long been integral to discourses of development.

Development proceeds hand in glove with counter-insurgency as well as surveillance in the borderlands of Kashmir, leading to the blurring of the "tenuous boundary between militarism and humanitarianism."

19. Visitor's book, entry by Bhomraj Janjani, president of the Gandhidham Chamber of Commerce and Industry, February 29, 1992.

20. She used the word *control* in English.

21. Chinese goods (*chini mal*) implies imported goods and commodities, regardless of their actual origin. Although this is probably not untrue for the bulk of contemporary imports, especially electronics and household items such as crockery and so on, the designation of goods as "Chinese" should not be taken literally.

22. See Berenschot 2011 for a good review of some of this literature.

23. Here, mosque attendance (by men) is seen as a marker of good Islamic practice, and saint worship as a sin.

2. Militarism and Everyday Peace

1. The Patidar (or Patels) are traditionally a Hindu peasant caste in central Gujarat who also emigrated in large numbers to the United Kingdom and East Africa (see Pocock 1972). They formed the core supporters of Sahajanand Swami, the founder of the Swaminarayan sect of Hinduism, which then became the protestant ethic that undergirded their rise as an entrepreneurial class in Gujarat (Williams 1984). Despite their materially well-off status—much of it due to remittances from family working overseas—Patidar women are known in Kutch for a lack of disdain for manual labor that may be expected from those with commensurate levels of social status elsewhere. Early on in my fieldwork, weighed down by my own preconceived ideas of class status in India, I was surprised to see Patidar women wearing saris and diamond earrings when receiving me at well-appointed homes in villages adjacent to Bhuj, and then with the same ease they donned shoes and socks, a man's shirt over their petticoats, a scarf over their head to protect their arms and head from the sun, when they went off to work in the fields.

2. Note the continuities of my discussion of everyday peace under militarization with the following description of the Kashmir valley which has been under Indian military occupation for decades: "military occupation of civilian areas is a prominent and almost permanent feature of the Valley; the military occupies civil buildings, migrant houses, office buildings, hotels, cinemas, industrial areas, college hostels, university guest houses, orchards, agricultural land, private buildings and so on" (Kazi 2009, 97). I draw attention to this to point out that the militarization of the everyday is as much a designator of "peacetime" as of "wartime" or "occupation."

3. Nosheen Ali (2019, 87) argues that employment in the military produces loyal subjects in Pakistan's Gilgit-Baltistan. These subjects are deeply enmeshed in the "status, opportunities, and privileges generated by army service," which in turn constitutes a source of military hegemony in the region.

4. The two shortest overland routes into Sindh would be through the famous black hills of Kutch—the Karo Dungar area of Khawda (from where it is about 15 miles to

Chad Bet, which was ceded to Pakistan after the 1971 war)—or through Lakhpat, about 22 miles from Pillar #1175 that marks the boundary.

5. A recent addition to the tourist circuit in Kutch is the "rakshak van," inaugurated in July 2018. Situated on the main driving route to the section of the Rann of Kutch that is packaged and marketed to tourists as the "White Rann": the rakshak van makes a double reference to the idea of both ecological (*van* is a forest) and military (*rakshak* is protector) protection, for it connotes both the idea of a protected forest (*van*) and a landscaped garden that is none other than a museum dedicated to the idea of an unequivocal Indian military victory in 1971.

6. In February 2016, police entered the campus of Jawaharlal Nehru University in New Delhi and arrested students on charges of sedition and "antinational" activities. In the months that followed, the government seemed bent on destroying a university that they saw as a bastion of "left" and "liberal" views (Khan 2015; Shankar 2017).

7. The year 1971 is an interesting coincidence for a memorial to the *virangana* as one cannot help but draw parallels to Bangladesh's appellation of *birangona* to Bengali women raped by West Pakistan's army during the liberation war of 1971 (see Mookherjee 2015).

8. In 2020, the HRD Ministry was renamed the Ministry of Education.

9. *Kutch Mitra*, Bhuj, August 28, 2015, 1.

10. "IAF Deals Heavy Blow to W. Pak Industry," *The Times of India*, December 9, 1971, 9; "Bhuj, Okha Port Bombed," *The Times of India*, December 6, 1971, 1.

11. "How 200 'Jhansi ki Ranian' Tamed Chengiz Khan," *The Times of India*, December 8, 2012, go.galegroup.com/ps/i.do?p=STND&sw=w&u=lom_umichanna&v=2 .1&id=GALE%7CA311299815&it=r&asid=b9a1749ff4b0a0d00a1179ef03fb90f9.

12. Vijay Karnik, commanding officer of Bhuj Airbase in 1971, quoted in "How 200 'Jhansi ki Ranian' Tamed Chengiz Khan."

13. Vijay Karnik, commanding officer of Bhuj Airbase in 1971, quoted in "How 200 'Jhansi ki Ranian' Tamed Chengiz Khan."

14. Vijay Karnik, commanding officer of Bhuj Airbase in 1971, quoted in "How 200 'Jhansi ki Ranian' Tamed Chengiz Khan."

15. Vijay Karnik, commanding officer of Bhuj Airbase in 1971, quoted in "How 200 'Jhansi ki Ranian' Tamed Chengiz Khan."

16. "Air Force Honours Brave Kutch Women for 1971 War," *The Times of India*, October 9, 2014, go.galegroup.com/ps/i.do?p=STND&sw=w&u=lom_umichanna&v=2 .1&id=GALE%7CA384940586&it=r&asid=8e4c91d032a98aa3f4bcead420495b29.

17. "How 200 'Jhansi ki Ranian' Tamed Chengiz Khan."

18. This temple is a ritual hub for Patidars that has benefited enormously from its devotees' overseas remittances.

19. Saraswati is the Hindu goddess of learning.

20. Women's recruitment into war, militant, and resistance movements is one strand of the argument that there is no "war front" that is separate and sealed off from a "home front" (Lutz 2001; Yuval-Davis 2013). This pertains, on the one hand, to the changing nature of the military that enables more women to participate directly in war as "feeding, clothing, nursing, clerical and communication services, ammunition production and sexual services have all needed, at least to an extent, to establish formal relationships with

the military" (Yuval-Davis 2013, 99). In other work, Sandya Hewamanne (2013) examines the classed and gendered aspects of civil-military blurring when women factory workers function as caregivers and nurturers to soldiers in the Sri Lankan civil war. In many of these cases, the domestic, affective, and the familial segues into the public or the domain of war, thereby rendering the two spaces inseparable in any definitive sense. The domestic and the familial domains are also central to women's mobilization into war and militancy where women's roles are not restricted only to performing supportive roles to primarily male actors even when they do not necessarily subvert their constitution as gendered, domestic, or maternal subjects. The domestic and the familial domains are also central to women's mobilization into war and militancy, and women do not only play a supporting role to male actors. Julie Peteet (1991) underscores the centrality of the family in women's mobilization into the Palestinian resistance movement where brothers and fathers were central figures in either the facilitation or hindrance to their ability to join the movement. However, even as their participation in the resistance required their politicization, she argues that their participation did not necessarily alter the sexual division of labor as "they were called upon to make available to the national struggle their domestic services" (Peteet 1991, 104). Similarly, symbols of motherhood and nurture intertwined with those of struggle and militancy were an important conduit for the politicization and mobilization of women in this movement as well as others, such as the resistance in Northern Ireland (Aretxaga 1997). In the Palestinian intifada, Peteet argues that women were able to reconstitute the meaning of motherhood, even when it provided the contours of political activism for some women. Thus, regardless of the fact that mothering was not constructed as opposed to militancy, the idiom of motherhood as the premise on which women participated in militant activity remained firm even if, as she argues, "reproductive and caring labor have acquired new public and militant meanings" (Peteet 1997, 107). Tarini Bedi (2009) suggests that women are as central to mobilizing other women as their natal or affinal male kin are; her discussion attempts to use the optic of "adjustment" to conjure a female subject whose emancipatory prowess does not necessarily lie in any consistent or overt subversion of the "domestic." As she points out in her study of Shiv Sena women in Mumbai city, the domains of kinship and politics are mutually intertwined, the one not necessarily in contradiction of the other. Kalyani Menon's (2012) ethnography of Hindu nationalist women in Delhi, on the other hand, highlights multiple nonfamilial ways in which women are recruited into the movement such as friendship or curiosity, oftentimes quite removed from any firm ideological commitment to the cause (see also Iqtidar 2011, chap. 3). Recruitment into Hindu nationalist organizations, she found, was as often through overt forms of what we would recognize as "indoctrination" as through forms of play, pleasure, and entertainment (Menon 2012, 142–145). Hewamanne (2013) examines the class and gendered dimension of women factory workers who function as caregivers and nurturers to soldiers in the Sri Lankan civil war. In many of these cases, the domestic, affective, and the familial segues into the public or the domain of war, thereby rendering the two spaces inseparable in any definitive sense. In Cabeiri deBergh Robinson's (2013) ethnography of the production of jihad in Kashmir, conjugality and domesticity are once again not constructed in any mutual opposition to each other. Sexual and familial duties are central to the evaluation of a *mujahid*'s duties, and his recruitment into jihad is seen as a function of the family rather than the mosque or religious school. Robinson writes of how militant organizations would not admit young men who were known to be only sons precisely because of their deemed duty toward the family. The militant and the family man were not constructed in opposition; women as wives bore witness to the violation of their husbands' bodies, straddling the revelation of intimate knowledge in the public domain. In contrast to this continuum between the family and the militant organization is the case described by Sharika Thiranagama (2013) in the Sri Lankan civil war where the spaces of home and militancy were seen as distinct. The latter celebrated the power of youth, promising horizontal forms of kinship that promised forms of sociality that could emancipate militant recruits from the older, gerontocratic forms of caste society that were embodied in the family. Thus, "ideas about the household, caste, and marriage, rather than being the preexistent and stable foundation of nonpolitical 'cultural life,' were in fact the very subject of potential political transformation" (Thiranagama 2013, 184). In the context of women's empowerment through militant recruitment, she argues, however, that militant femininity ended up not challenging the domestic code enough, remaining "parasitic on the sexualized kinship of the household, which continued to be reproduced as the appropriate mode for sexual relations" (Thiranagama 2013, 217).

21. "Air Force Honours Brave Kutch Women for 1971 War."

22. "Hail the Soldier! Hail the Farmer!" was a popular patriotic slogan of the 1960s that gave equal emphasis to the farmer (food security) and the soldier (national security). In Hiru's outburst, she refers to the fact that the military has been recognized through the slogan but not the women who actually built the runway.

3. Policing Muslim Marriage

1. Kolkata (formerly Calcutta), a city in the Indian state of West Bengal.

2. I return to this theme in more detail in chapter 4.

3. Even though families may have started out by choosing migrant brides to marry men who were considered "unmarriageable" in the local context—due to advanced age, multiple marriages, mental disability, lack of employment, and so on, as will be seen in Zain's case discussed in this chapter—over time, the migrant bride has also come to be a preferred choice for reasons that are discussed in chapter 4.

4. See Citizenship Amendment Bill (2016) for a copy of the bill introduced in Parliament.

5. In this respect, I suggest a departure from the South Asian literature on law and the family that argues for a congruence or alliance between the state and the family, the sexual contract as a particular iteration of the social contract (see, e.g., Das 2007).

6. For an ethnography of reconstruction discourse, see Simpson 2013.

7. The relationship between the *adivasi* and the Muslim in contemporary Gujarat is a fraught one. Although similar to each other in terms of their common distinction from Hindus (represented primarily through their meat eating as against the normative vegetarianism of Hindus in Gujarat), they were also recruited by Hindu right-wing organizations and mobilized against Muslims in the 2002 pogrom.

8. Another reminder of the "less than perfect" habits that foreclosed his identifying as a "true Muslim" in his view.

4. Blood and Water

1. Here, Bano's statement can be read in line with John Borneman's (1997) critique of the anthropology of kinship, where he suggests a shift in the object of anthropological research from marriage, kinship, and gender to the more inclusive notion of care. Transnational marriage migration has also been linked to the primary role of women as caregivers, recasting the perceived understanding of women's migration as wives to be somehow passive (Gardner 2006). Bano's emphasis on care for an older husband was something I found in a number of narratives from "Bengali" wives.

2. See Charsley 2013 on the *rishta* as a bridge between emotion and strategy in the arranging of transnational marriages among British Pakistanis.

3. For example, the Meos follow *gotra* and clan exogamy like Hindu groups and have only taken to matrilateral cross-cousin marriage relatively recently (Chauhan 2003). Matrilineal Muslim communities are negotiating dominant trends toward patriliny in coastal Kerala (Osella 2012), thus rendering it extremely problematic to think of "Muslim" marriage practices in the singular.

4. There are a large number of Muslim communities in Kutch spread across both Shi'a and Sunni denominations. In my work, I have focused exclusively on Sunni Muslims. Although there are different customs and traditions followed by each endogamous Muslim "caste," there are certain broad similarities in marriage practices, and it is these that I refer to in this chapter when I refer to *Muslims*.

5. Anthropologists of marriage have remarked on the fluidity between "love" and "arranged" marriage in practice, especially in middle-class marriage (Fuller and Narasimhan 2008; Mody 2008) even when the two genres are discursively projected as being poles apart (e.g., Donner 2016). The genre of the "self-chosen" marriage may not be desired solely in pursuit of individualism or notions of romantic love but equally to achieve a series of other goals such as the desire for social or economic prosperity (Davin 2005), security, companionship, or other practical considerations as demonstrated below in the example of Sonal arranging for her fiancé to be vetted through her own social networks rather than relying on her parents. On the other hand, a normatively arranged marriage does not preclude aspects of "love" and self-choice, rendering the two types of marriage on a continuum.

6. English words that are italicized indicate that they were used originally by speakers.

7. Spicy snacks that are popular street foods across Kutch.

5. The Work of Belonging

1. I refer to the district of TharParkar as it was administratively reconstituted in 1990. Historically, it was a part of Rajputana, and Hindus constitute almost 50 percent of the population of the district (Mahmood 2014, 13). Dominant non-Muslim groups in TharParkar are Rajputs, Bheels, Kolis, and Meghwars.

2. See Citizenship Amendment Bill 2016 for the full text of the act.

3. Italicized English words are reproduced as they were originally used.

4. Except in the case of Ram Singh, who has established contact directly with the central government, both other interviewees describe their interactions with the district collector when they make a formal plea for Indian citizenship, which would then have been forwarded to the central government. The Citizenship Amendment Act in 2004 empowered district collectors to directly adjudicate in citizenship matters of Hindus coming from Pakistan especially in Rajasthan and Gujarat (Jayal 2013, 67).

5. Interview with P. H. Bhatti, Bhuj, November 16, 2015.

6. Gluckman (1956) argues that the paradox at the heart of the family lies in the fact that the connection between men and their heirs is dependent on women who are potentially "outsiders" to the group. Variegated bonds of love and loyalty thus cut across the family, rendering it an unstable unit of analysis without reference to a larger social terrain that takes into account relationships at multiple levels.

Conclusion

1. See Sidharthan Maunaguru (2020) for a lucid analysis of "vulnerable sovereignty" where the Tamil militant organization LTTE was forced to accommodate its aspiration for a totalizing sovereign power with Hindu deities in Sri Lanka who engaged their own forms of sovereign power that were by definition relational—to the extent that they existed within a pantheon of several deities.

References

Abraham, Janaki. 2010. "Wedding Videos in North Kerala: Technologies, Rituals, and Ideas about Love and Conjugality." *Visual Anthropology Review* 26 (2): 116–127.

Agamben, Giorgio. 1998. *Homo Sacer: Sovereign Power and Bare Life*. Stanford, CA: Stanford University Press.

Ahmad, Imtiaz. 1972. "For a Sociology of India." *Contributions to Indian Sociology* 6:172–178.

Ali, Nosheen. 2013. "Grounding Militarism: Structures of Feeling and Force in Gilgit-Baltistan." In *Everyday Occupations: Experiencing Militarism in South Asia and the Middle East*, edited by Kamala Visweswaran, 85–114. Philadelphia: University of Pennsylvania Press.

Ali, Nosheen. 2019. *Delusional States: Feeling Rule and Development in Pakistan's Northern Frontier*. New Delhi: Cambridge University Press.

Andrejevic, Mark. 2005. "The Work of Watching One Another: Lateral Surveillance, Risk, and Governance." *Surveillance and Society* 2 (4): 479–497.

Andrijasevic, Rutvica. 2010. "The Cross-Border Migration." In *Migration, Agency and Citizenship in Sex Trafficking*, 26–56. London: Palgrave Macmillan.

Aretxaga, Begoña. 1997. *Shattering Silence: Women, Nationalism, and Political Subjectivity in Northern Ireland*. Princeton, NJ: Princeton University Press.

Arnold, David. 1976. "The Police and Colonial Control in South India." *Social Scientist* 14 (2): 3–16.

Basu, Srimati. 2015. *The Trouble with Marriage: Feminists Confront Law and Violence in India*. New Delhi: Orient Blackswan.

Baxi, Pratiksha. 2000. "Rape, Retribution, State: On Whose Bodies?" *Economic and Political Weekly* 35 (14): 1196–1200.

Baxi, Pratiksha. 2006. "Habeas Corpus in the Realm of Love: Litigating Marriages of Choice in India." *Australian Feminist Law Journal* 25 (1): 59–78.

Baxi, Pratiksha. 2014. *Public Secrets of Law: Rape Trials in India*. New Delhi: Oxford University Press.

Bedi, Tarini. 2009. *Shiv Sena Women and the Gendered Politics of Performance in Maharashtra, India*. Urbana: University of Illinois Press.

Berenschot, Ward. 2011. "Political Fixers and the Rise of Hindu Nationalism in Gujarat, India: Lubricating a Patronage Democracy." *South Asia: Journal of South Asian Studies* 34 (3): 382–401.

Berlant, Lauren. 1997. *The Queen of America Goes to Washington City: Essays on Sex and Citizenship*. Durham, NC: Duke University Press.

Bhan, Mona. 2013. *Counterinsurgency, Democracy, and the Politics of Identity in India: From Warfare to Welfare?* London: Routledge.

Bhattacharya, D. P. 2012. "Bengali-Speaking Girls Being Trafficked to Kutch District of Gujarat." *India Today*, August 16. https://www.indiatoday.in/mail-today/story/bengali-speaking-girls-human-trafficking-kutch-flesh-trade-113435-2012-08-16.

Bishara, Amahl. 2015. "Driving while Palestinian in Israel and the West Bank: The Politics of Disorientation and the Routes of a Subaltern Knowledge." *American Ethnologist* 42 (1): 33–54.

Borker, Hem. 2018. *Madrasas and the Making of Islamic Womanhood*. New Delhi: Oxford University Press.

Borneman, John. 1997. "Caring and Being Cared For: Displacing Marriage, Kinship, Gender and Sexuality." *International Social Science Journal* 49 (154): 573–584.

Bourdieu, Pierre. 1994. "Rethinking the State: Genesis and Structure of the Bureaucratic Field." *Sociological Theory* 12 (1): 1–18.

Brass, Paul R. 2011. *The Production of Hindu-Muslim Violence in Contemporary India*. Seattle: University of Washington Press.

Brenner, Suzanne 1998. *The Domestication of Desire: Women, Wealth, and Modernity in Java*. Princeton, NJ: Princeton University Press.

Burke, Jason. 2015. "Indian Writers Return Awards in Protest against 'Climate of Intolerance.'" *The Guardian*, October 14. https://www.theguardian.com/books/2015/oct/14/indian-writers-return-awards-in-protest-against-climate-of-intolerance.

Caldeira, Teresa. 2013. "The Paradox of Police Violence in Democratic Brazil." In *Policing and Contemporary Governance: The Anthropology of Police in Practice*, edited by William Garriott, 97–124. New York: Palgrave Macmillan.

Carsten, Janet. 1997. *The Heat of the Hearth: The Process of Kinship in a Malay Fishing Community*. New York: Oxford University Press.

Chakravarti, Uma. 1996. "Wifehood, Widowhood and Adultery: Female Sexuality, Surveillance and the State in 18th C. Maharashtra." In *Social Reform, Sexuality and the State*, edited by Patricia Uberoi, 3–21. New Delhi: Sage.

Chandavarkar, Rajnarayan. 1998. *Imperial Power and Popular Politics: Class, Resistance and the State in India, c. 1850–1950*. Cambridge: Cambridge University Press.

Charsley, Katharine. 2013. *Transnational Pakistani Connections: Marrying "Back Home."* London: Routledge.

Chatterjee, Anasua. 2017. *Margins of Citizenship: Muslim Experiences in Urban India*. New Delhi: Routledge.

Chatterji, Joya. 2007. *The Spoils of Partition: Bengal and India, 1947–1967*. Cambridge: Cambridge University Press.

Chauhan, Abha. 2003. "Kinship Principles and the Pattern of Marriage Alliance: The Meos of Mewat." *Sociological Bulletin* 52 (1): 71–90.

Chowdhry, Prem. 1997. "Enforcing Cultural Codes: Gender and Violence in Northern India." *Economic and Political Weekly* 32 (19): 1019–1028.

Chowdhry, Prem. 2004. "Caste Panchayats and the Policing of Marriage in Haryana: Enforcing Kinship and Territorial Exogamy." *Contributions to Indian Sociology* 38 (1–2): 1–42.

Citizenship Amendment Bill. 2016. As Introduced in the Lok Sabha. Bill No. 176 of 2016. Accessed September 20, 2020. https://www.prsindia.org/uploads/media/Citizenship/Citizenship%20(A)%20bill,%202016.pdf.

Clark-Decès, Isabelle. 2014. *The Right Spouse: Preferential Marriages in Tamil Nadu*. Stanford, CA: Stanford University Press.

Comaroff, Jean, and John L. Comaroff. 2016. *The Truth about Crime: Sovereignty, Knowledge, Social Order*. Chicago: University of Chicago Press.

Cons, Jason. 2013. "Narrating Boundaries: Framing and Contesting Suffering, Community, and Belonging in Enclaves along the India-Bangladesh Border." *Political Geography* 35:37–46.

Cons, Jason. 2016. *Sensitive Space: Fragmented Territory at the India-Bangladesh Border*. Seattle: University of Washington Press.

Das, Veena. 1995. "National Honour and Practical Kinship: Of Unwanted Women and Children." In *Critical Events: An Anthropological Perspective on Contemporary India*, 55–83. New Delhi: Oxford University Press.

Das, Veena. 2004. "The Signature of the State: The Paradox of Illegibility." In *Anthropology in the Margins of the State*, edited by Veena Das and Deborah Poole, 225–252. New Delhi: Oxford University Press.

Das, Veena. 2007. *Life and Words: Violence and the Descent into the Ordinary*. New Delhi: Oxford University Press.

Das, Veena, J. M. Ellen, and I. Leonard. 2008. "On the Modalities of the Domestic." *Home Cultures* 5 (3): 349–371.

Das, Veena, and Deborah Poole. 2004. "The State and Its Margins." In *Anthropology in the Margins of the State*, edited by Veena Das and Deborah Poole, 3–33. New Delhi: Oxford University Press.

Davin, Delia. 2005. "Marriage Migration in China: The Enlargement of Marriage Markets in the Era of Market Reforms." *Indian Journal of Gender Studies* 12 (2–3): 173–188.

de Genova, Nicholas. 2013. "Spectacles of Migrant 'Illegality': The Scene of Exclusion, the Obscene of Inclusion." *Ethnic and Racial Studies* 36 (7): 1180–1198.

Desh Gujarat. 2015a. "After Two Pakistani Intruders, Kutch Police Nabs Bangladeshi Woman." *Desh Gujarat*, July 25. https://www.deshgujarat.com/2015/07/25/after-two -pakistani-intruders-kutch-police-nabs-bangladeshi-woman/.

Desh Gujarat. 2015b. "'Mentally Unstable' Man from Pakistan Held by BSF in Gujarat." *Desh Gujarat*, August 5. https://www.deshgujarat.com/2015/08/05/mentally -unstable-man-from-pakistan-held-by-bsf-in-gujarat/.

Donner, Henrike. 2016. "Doing It Our Way: Love and Marriage in Kolkata Middle-Class Families." *Modern Asian Studies* 50 (4): 1147–1189.

Donzelot, Jacques. 1979. *The Policing of Families*. New York: Random House.

Dreze, Jean. 2017. "Dissent and Aadhaar." *The Indian Express*, May 8. http://indianexpress .com/article/opinion/columns/dissent-and-aadhaar-4645231/.

Durkheim, Emile. 2013. *The Division of Labour in Society*. Basingstoke, UK: Palgrave Macmillan.

Evans-Pritchard, Edward E., and Meyer Fortes. 1950. *African Political Systems*. Oxford: Oxford University Press.

Fassin, Didier. 2011. "Policing Borders, Producing Boundaries: The Governmentality of Immigration in Dark Times." *Annual Review of Anthropology* 40:213–226.

Fassin, Didier. 2013. *Enforcing Order: An Ethnography of Urban Policing*. Cambridge, UK: Polity.

Feldman, Ilana. 2015. *Police Encounters: Security and Surveillance in Gaza under Egyptian Rule*. Stanford, CA: Stanford University Press.

Felman, Shoshana. 2002. *The Juridical Unconscious: Trials and Traumas in the Twentieth Century*. Cambridge, MA: Harvard University Press.

Foucault, Michel. 2001. "Governmentality." In *Power: The Essential Works of Foucault 1954–1984*. Vol. 3, edited by James D. Faubion, 201–222. New York: New Press.

Fuller, Chris J., and Haripriya Narasimhan. 2008. "Companionate Marriage in India: The Changing Marriage System in a Middle-Class Brahman Subcaste." *Journal of the Royal Anthropological Institute* 14 (4): 736–754.

Gardner, Katy. 2006. "The Transnational Work of Kinship and Caring: Bengali-British Marriages in Historical Perspective." *Global Networks* 6 (4): 373–387.

Garriott, William. 2011. *Policing Methamphetamine: Narcopolitics in Rural America*. New York: New York University Press.

Garriott, William. 2013. "Introduction. Police in Practice: Policing and the Project of Contemporary Governance." In *Policing and Contemporary Governance: The Anthropology of Police in Practice*, 1–28. New York: Palgrave Macmillan.

Gayer, Laurent, and Christophe Jaffrelot, eds. 2012. *Muslims in Indian Cities: Trajectories of Marginalisation*. New Delhi: HarperCollins.

Ghassem-Fachandi, Parvis. 2012. *Pogrom in Gujarat: Hindu Nationalism and Anti-Muslim Violence in India*. Princeton, NJ: Princeton University Press.

Ghosh, Sahana. 2017. "Relative Intimacies: Belonging and Difference in Transnational Families." *Economic and Political Weekly* 52 (15): 45–52.

Glaeser, Andreas. 2011. *Political Epistemics: The Secret Police, The Opposition, and the End of East German Socialism*. Chicago: University of Chicago Press.

Gluckman, Max. 1956. *Custom and Conflict in Africa*. Oxford: Basil Blackwell.

Gold, Ann Grodzins, Bhoju Ram Gujar, Madhu Gujar, and Chinu Gujar. 2014. "Shared Knowledges: Family, Fusion, Friction, Fabric." *Ethnography* 15 (3): 331–354.

Goldstein, Daniel M. 2010. "Toward a Critical Anthropology of Security." *Current Anthropology* 51 (4): 487–517.

Grover, Shalini. 2011. "'Purani aur nai shaadi': Separation, Divorce, and Remarriage in the Lives of the Urban Poor in New Delhi." *Asian Journal of Women's Studies* 17 (1): 67–99.

Gupta, Charu. 2001. *Sexuality, Obscenity, Community: Women, Muslims, and the Hindu Public in Colonial India*. New Delhi: Permanent Black.

Gupta, Radhika. 2013. "Allegiance and Alienation: Border Dynamics in Kargil." In *Borderland Lives in Northern South Asia*, edited by David Gellner, 47–71. Durham, NC: Duke University Press.

Hansen, Kathryn. 1988. "The Virangana in North Indian History: Myth and Popular Culture." *Economic and Political Weekly* 23 (18): WS25–WS33.

Hansen, Thomas Blom. 2005. "Sovereigns beyond the State: On Legality and Authority in Urban India." In *Sovereign Bodies: Citizens, Migrants, and States in the Postcolonial World*, edited by Thomas Blom Hansen and Finn Stepputat, 169–191. Princeton, NJ: Princeton University Press.

Hansen, Thomas Blom, and Finn Stepputat. 2005. Introduction to *Sovereign Bodies: Citizens, Migrants, and States in the Postcolonial World*, 1–36. Edited by Thomas Blom Hansen and Finn Stepputat. Princeton, NJ: Princeton University Press.

Hansen, Thomas Blom, and Finn Stepputat. 2006. "Sovereignty Revisited." *Annual Review of Anthropology* 35:295–315.

Harcourt, Bernard E. 2009. *Illusion of Order: The False Promise of Broken Windows Policing*. Cambridge, MA: Harvard University Press.

Harlan, Lindsey. 1992. *Religion and Rajput Women: The Ethic of Protection in Contemporary Narratives*. Berkeley: University of California Press.

Harms, Erik, Shafqat Hussain, Sasha Newell, Charles Piot, Louisa Schein, Sara Shneiderman, Terence Turner, and Juan Zhang. 2014. "Remote and Edgy: New Takes on Old Anthropological Themes." *HAU: Journal of Ethnographic Theory* 4 (1): 361–381.

Heitmeyer, Carolyn. 2016. "Intimate Transgressions and Communalist Narratives: Inter-Religious Romance in a Divided Gujarat." *Modern Asian Studies* 50 (4): 1277–1297.

Hewamanne, Sandya. 2013. "The War Zone in My Heart: The Occupation of Southern Sri Lanka." In *Everyday Occupations: Experiencing Militarism in South Asia and the Middle East*, edited by Kamala Visweswaran, 60–84. Philadelphia: University of Pennsylvania Press.

Hornberger, Julia. 2017. "The Belly of the Police." In *Police in Africa: The Street Level View*, edited by Jan Beek, Mirco Göpfert, Olly Owen, and Johnny Steinberg, 199–212. New York: Oxford University Press.

Ibrahim, Farhana. 2009. *Settlers, Saints, and Sovereigns: An Ethnography of State Formation in Western India*. New Delhi: Routledge.

Ibrahim, Farhana. 2019. "Policing in Practice: Security, Surveillance, and Everyday Peacekeeping on a South Asian Border." *Comparative Studies in South Asia, Africa, and the Middle East* 39 (3): 425–438.

Iqtidar, Humeira. 2011. *Secularizing Islamists? Jama 'at e Islami and Jama 'at ud Dawa in Urban Pakistan*. New Delhi: Permanent Black.

Jauregui, Beatrice. 2013. "Beatings, Beacons, and Big Men: Police Disempowerment and Delegitimation in India." *Law and Social Inquiry* 38 (3): 643–669.

Jauregui, Beatrice. 2016. *Provisional Authority: Police, Order, and Security in India*. Chicago: University of Chicago Press.

Jayal, Niraja Gopal. 2013. *Citizenship and Its Discontents: An Indian History*. New Delhi: Permanent Black.

Jeffery, Patricia, Roger Jeffery, and Craig Jeffrey. 2004. "Islamization, Gentrification and Domestication: 'A Girls' Islamic Course' and Rural Muslims in Western Uttar Pradesh." *Modern Asian Studies* 38 (1): 1–53.

Jeganathan, Pradeep. 2004. "Checkpoint: Anthropology, Identity, and the State." In *Anthropology in the Margins of the State*, edited by Veena Das and Deborah Poole, 67–80. New Delhi: Oxford University Press.

Jensen, Steffen. 2005. "Above the Law: Practices of Sovereignty in Surrey Estate, Cape Town." In *Sovereign Bodies: Citizens, Migrants, and States in the Postcolonial World*, edited by Thomas Blom Hansen and Finn Stepputat, 218–238. Princeton, NJ: Princeton University Press.

Jha, Satish. 2015. "DGP Conference: Modi's New Mantra, from 'Smart' to 'Sensitive' Policing." *Indian Express*, December 21. http://indianexpress.com/article/explained/dgp-conference-modis-new-mantra-from-smart-to-senstive-policing/.

Jusionyte, Ieva. 2015. *Savage Frontier: Making News and Security on the Argentine Border*. Berkeley: University of California Press.

Kalpagam, U. 2005. "'America Varan' Marriages among Tamil Brahmans: Preferences, Strategies and Outcomes." *Indian Journal of Gender Studies* 12 (2–3): 189–215.

Kapur, Ratna. 2010. *Makeshift Migrants and Law: Gender, Belonging, and Postcolonial Anxieties*. New Delhi: Routledge.

Kapur, Ratna, and Brenda Cossman. 1996. *Subversive Sites: Feminist Engagements with Law in India*. New Delhi: Sage.

Karpiak, Kevin G. 2013. "Adjusting *la police*: The Use of Distance in the Calibration of Legitimate Violence among the Police Nationale." In *Policing and Contemporary Governance: The Anthropology of Police in Practice*, edited by William Garriott, 79–95. New York: Palgrave Macmillan.

Kaur, Ravinder. 2012. "Marriage and Migration: Citizenship and Marital Experience in Cross-Border Marriages between Uttar Pradesh, West Bengal and Bangladesh." *Economic and Political Weekly* 47 (43): 78–89.

Kazi, Seema. 2009. *Between Democracy and Nation: Gender and Militarisation in Kashmir*. New Delhi: Women Unlimited.

Kempadoo, Kamala. 2005. "Introduction: Abolitionism, Criminal Justice, and Transnational Feminism: Twenty-First-Century Perspectives on Human Trafficking." In *Trafficking and Prostitution Reconsidered: New Perspectives on Migration, Sex Work, and Human Rights*, edited by Kamala Kempadoo, Jyoti Sanghera, and Bandana Pattanaik, vii–xxxv. Boulder, CO: Paradigm.

Khan, Shahrukh. 2015. "'I Am Not Going to Leave. So Shut Up': SRK to BJP Litany 'Go to Pakistan.'" *The Citizen*, November 5. https://www.thecitizen.in/index.php/en

/NewsDetail/index/2/5720/I-Am-Not-Going-to-Leave-So-Shut-Up-SRK-To-BJP-Litany-Go-to-Pakistan.

Khanikar, Santana. 2018. *State, Violence, and Legitimacy in India.* New Delhi: Oxford University Press.

Krishna, Sankaran. 1994. "Cartographic Anxiety: Mapping the Body Politic in India." *Alternatives* 19 (4): 507–521.

Kumar, Abhimanyu. 2017. "The Lynching that Changed India." *Al Jazeera*, October 5. https://www.aljazeera.com/indepth/features/2017/09/lynching-changed-india-170927084018325.html.

Luibhéid, Eithne. 2002. *Entry Denied: Controlling Sexuality at the Border.* Minneapolis: University of Minnesota Press.

Lutz, Catherine. 2001. *Homefront: A Military City and the American Twentieth Century.* Boston: Beacon.

Mahmood, Sadia. 2014. "Minoritization of Pakistani Hindus (1947–1971)." PhD diss., Arizona State University.

Malinowski, Bronislaw. 2002. *Argonauts of the Western Pacific: An Account of Native Enterprise and Adventure in the Archipelagoes of Melanesian New Guinea.* London: Routledge.

Marsden, Magnus. 2012. "Fatal Embrace: Trading in Hospitality on the Frontiers of South and Central Asia." *Journal of the Royal Anthropological Institute* 18 (1): S117–S130.

Martin, Jeffrey T. 2013. "Police as Linking Principle." In *Policing and Contemporary Governance*, edited by William Garriott, 157–180. New York: Palgrave Macmillan.

Maunaguru, Sidharthan. 2014. "Transnational Marriages: Documents, Wedding Photos, Photographers and Jaffna Tamil Marriages." In *Marrying in South Asia*, edited by Ravinder Kaur and Rajni Palriwala, 253–270. New Delhi: Orient Blackswan.

Maunaguru, Sidharthan. 2020. "Vulnerable Sovereignty: Sovereign Deities and Tigers' Politics in Sri Lanka." *Current Anthropology* 61 (6): 686-712.

McGranahan, Carole. 2016. "States, Anthropological Complicity, and Theorizing the Political." *HAU: Journal of Ethnographic Theory* 6 (2): 441–446.

Menon, Kalyani. 2012. *Everyday Nationalism: Women of the Hindu Right in India.* New Delhi: Social Science Press.

Mishra, Paro. 2013. "Sex Ratios, Cross-Region Marriages and the Challenge to Caste Endogamy in Haryana." *Economic and Political Weekly* 48 (35): 70–78.

Mody, Perveez. 2008. *The Intimate State: Love-Marriage and Law in India.* New Delhi: Routledge.

Mookherjee, Nayanika. 2015. *The Spectral Wound: Sexual Violence, Public Memories, and the Bangladesh War of 1971.* Durham, NC: Duke University Press.

Mulla, Sameena. 2014. *The Violence of Care: Rape Victims, Forensic Nurses, and Sexual Assault Intervention.* New York: New York University Press.

Mulla, Sameena. 2015. "Sexual Violence, Law, and Qualities of Affiliation." In *Wording the World: Veena Das and Scenes of Inheritance*, edited by Roma Chatterji, 172–190. New Delhi: Orient Blackswan.

Nair, Anil. 2007. "Exfiltration: The New Threat to Border Security." *Rediff.com*, February 21. https://www.rediff.com/news/report/exfil/20070221.htm.

Nair, Avinash. 2016. "Tourism: On Lines of Wagah, 'Border Viewing Point' Now Opened in India." *Indian Express*, December 24. https://indianexpress.com/article

/india/tourism-on-lines-of-wagah-border-viewing-point-now-opened-in-gujarat -4443665/.

Navaro-Yashin, Yael. 2012. *The Make-Believe Space: Affective Geography in a Postwar Polity*. Durham, NC: Duke University Press.

Newsclick. 2019. "Why We Need to Talk about Gujarat Model." *Newsclick*, May 14. https:// www.newsclick.in/Gujarat-Model-Hate-Politics-BJP-RSS-Modi-Shah-Communalism.

Nigam, Sanjay. 1990. "Disciplining and Policing the 'Criminals by Birth', Part 1: The Making of a Colonial Stereotype—The Criminal Tribes and Castes of North India." *Indian Economic and Social History Review* 27 (2): 131–164.

Nugent, David. 2010. "States, Secrecy, Subversives: APRA and Political Fantasy in Mid-20th-Century Peru." *American Ethnologist* 37 (4): 681–702.

Osella, Caroline. 2012. "Desires under Reform: Contemporary Reconfigurations of Family, Marriage, Love and Gendering in a Transnational South Indian Matrilineal Muslim Community." *Culture and Religion* 13 (2): 241–264.

Osella, Caroline, and Filippo Osella. 2007. "Muslim Style in South India." *Fashion Theory* 11 (2–3): 233–252.

Osuri, Goldie. 2018. "Sovereignty, Vulnerability, and a Gendered Resistance in Indian-Occupied Kashmir." *Third World Thematics: A TWQ Journal* 3 (2): 228–243.

Peteet, Julie. 1991. *Gender in Crisis: Women and the Palestinian Resistance Movement*. New York: Columbia University Press.

Peteet, Julie. 1997. "Icons and Militants: Mothering in the Danger Zone." *Signs: Journal of Women in Culture and Society* 23 (1): 103–129.

Piliavsky, Anastasia. 2013. "Borders without Borderlands: On the Social Reproduction of State Demarcation in Rajasthan." In *Borderland Lives in Northern South Asia*, edited by David Gellner, 24–46. Durham, NC: Duke University Press.

Plunkett, Frances Taft. 1973. "Royal Marriages in Rajasthan." *Contributions to Indian Sociology* 7 (1): 64–80.

Pocock, David Francis. 1972. *Kanbi and Patidar: A Study of the Patidar Community of Gujarat*. Oxford: Clarendon.

Poole, Deborah. 2004. "Between Threat and Guarantee: Justice and Community in the Margins of the Peruvian State." In *Anthropology in the Margins of the State*, edited by Veena Das and Deborah Poole, 35–65. New Delhi: Oxford University Press.

Postans, Marianna. 1839. *Cutch: Or, Random Sketches, Taken during a Residence in One of the Northern Provinces of Western India*. London: Smith, Elder.

Raikes, Stanley Napier. 1859. *Memoir on the Thurr and Parkur Districts of Sind: Selections from the Records of the Bombay Government*. Bombay: Education Society's Press.

Rao, Anupama. 2010. *The Caste Question: Dalits and the Politics of Modern India*. New Delhi: Permanent Black.

Reeves, Madeleine. 2014. *Border Work: Spatial Lives of the State in Rural Central Asia*. Ithaca, NY: Cornell University Press.

Reiner, Robert. 2010. *The Politics of the Police*. Oxford: Oxford University Press.

Robinson, Cabeiri de Bergh. 2013. *Body of Victim, Body of Warrior: Refugee Families and the Making of Kashmiri Jihadists*. Berkeley: University of California Press.

Roy, Anupama. 2010. *Mapping Citizenship in India*. New Delhi: Oxford University Press.

Samimian-Darash, Limor, and Meg Stalcup. 2017. "Anthropology of Security and Security in Anthropology: Cases of Counterterrorism in the United States." *Anthropological Theory* 17 (1): 60–87.

Sarkar, Tanika. 2001. *Hindu Wife, Hindu Nation: Community, Religion and Cultural Nationalism*. New Delhi: Permanent Black.

Satyogi, Pooja 2019. "Law, Police and 'Domestic Cruelty': Assembling Written Complaints from Oral Narratives." *Contributions to Indian Sociology* 53 (1): 46–71.

Scroll.in. 2020. "Folk Dances, Yoga and a Walk in the Desert: Pictures of PM Modi's Travels in Kutch." *Scroll.in*. https://scroll.in/article/776979/folk-dances-yoga-and-a-walk-in-the-desert-pictures-of-pm-modis-travels-in-kutch.

Sethi, Manisha. 2014. *Kafkaland: Prejudice, Law, and Counterterrorism in India*. New Delhi: Three Essays Collective.

Shah, Archana. 2013. *Shifting Sands: Kutch, Textiles, Traditions, Transformation*. Ahmedabad, India: Bandhej Books.

Shankar, Aranya. 2017. "JNU's Nationalism Lectures Are Now a Book." *Indian Express*, January 1. https://indianexpress.com/article/lifestyle/books/jnu-nationalism-lectures-are-now-a-book-4454208/.

Simpson, Edward. 2008. "The Changing Perspectives of Three Muslim Men on the Question of Saint Worship over a 10-Year Period in Gujarat, Western India." *Modern Asian Studies* 42 (2–3): 377–403.

Simpson, Edward. 2013. *The Political Biography of an Earthquake: Aftermath and Amnesia in Gujarat, India*. London: Hurst.

Singh, Bhrigupati. 2015. *Poverty and the Quest for life: Spiritual and Material Striving in Rural India*. New Delhi: Oxford University Press.

Spodek, Howard. 2010. "In the Hindutva Laboratory: Pogroms and Politics in Gujarat, 2002." *Modern Asian Studies* 44 (2): 349–399.

Sreenivasan, Ramya. 2004. "Honoring the Family: Narratives and Politics of Kinship in Pre-Colonial Rajasthan." In *Unfamiliar Relations: Family and History in South Asia*, edited by Indrani Chatterjee, 46–72. New Delhi: Permanent Black.

Strathern, Marilyn. 2005. *Kinship, Law and the Unexpected: Relatives Are Always a Surprise*. Cambridge: Cambridge University Press.

Taussig, Michael T. 1999. *Defacement: Public Secrecy and the Labor of the Negative*. Stanford, CA: Stanford University Press.

Thiranagama, Sharika. 2013. *In My Mother's House: Civil War in Sri Lanka*. New Delhi: Zubaan.

van Schendel, Willem. 2001. "Working through Partition: Making a Living in the Bengal Borderlands." *International Review of Social History* 46 (3): 393–421.

van Schendel, Willem. 2004. *The Bengal Borderland*. London: Anthem.

Vatuk, Sylvia. 1975. "Gifts and Affines in North India." *Contributions to Indian Sociology* 9 (2): 155–196.

Verdery, Katherine. 2014. *Secrets and Truth: Ethnography in the Archive of Romania's Secret Police*. Budapest: Central European University Press.

Wacquant, Loïc. 2009. *Punishing the Poor: The Neoliberal Government of Social Insecurity*. Durham, NC: Duke University Press.

Wahl, Rachel. 2017. *Just Violence: Torture and Human Rights in the Eyes of the Police*. Stanford, CA: Stanford University Press.

Warner, Michael. 2002. "Public and Private." In *Publics and Counterpublics*, 21–63. Cambridge, MA: MIT Press.

Williams, Raymond Brady. 1984. *A New Face of Hinduism: The Swaminarayan Religion*. Cambridge: Cambridge University Press.

Yusuf, Kulsum. 2011. "Bangladeshi Held from Kutch." *Times of India*, May 2. https://timesofindia.indiatimes.com/city/rajkot/Bangladeshi-held-from-Kutch/articleshow/8146604.cms?referral=PM.

Yuval-Davis, Nira. 2013. *Gender and Nation*. London: Sage.

Index

CPSIA information can be obtained
at www.ICGtesting.com
Printed in the USA
LVHW111626231021
701313LV00003B/143